Phish

The Baker's Dozen
Madison Square Garden
21 July – 6 August 2017

Brent Waltz

SONICBOND

sonicbondpublishing.com

Sonicbond Publishing Limited
www.sonicbondpublishing.co.uk
Email: info@sonicbondpublishing.co.uk

First Published in the United Kingdom 2025
First Published in the United States 2025

British Library Cataloguing in Publication Data:
A Catalogue record for this book is available from the British Library

ISBN 978-1-78952-361-4

Typeset in ITC Garamond Std & ITC Avant Garde Gothic
Printed and bound in England

Graphic design and typesetting: Full Moon Media

Acknowledgements

I am indebted to Stephen Lambe. His professionalism has made writing my first book easier than I could have hoped for and he should be commended for the team he has assembled at Sonicbond Publishing. A special thanks as well to Dominic Sanderson – his comments and suggestions greatly improved this manuscript.

A comparable debt is owed to Trey Anastasio, Jon Fishman, Mike Gordon and Page McConnell, along with Chris Kuroda, Paul Languedoc and Tom Marshall, plus everyone who has ever contributed to www.phish.net. What these people have created, curated and disseminated has improved innumerable lives … my own included.

No debt settlement would be complete without mentioning Scott and Blake. Your opinions on music are second to none, and I have enjoyed every conversation we have had. The rare times we have disagreed have made me a better listener and more thoughtful in my responses. When it comes to recommendations, you are the only algorithm I will ever need. Along the same lines, I would be remiss if I did not also mention Allen and Ski. Your interest in music is passing, but your friendship is not.

Although it does not have to be this way, loving music leads to reading about music. I have been lucky enough to have read innumerable books by people more insightful than me. Whatever I've brought to this book was made possible by the writings of Hanif Abdurraqib, Marc D. Allen, Michael Azerrad, Rob Bowman, Dean Budnick, Davide Byrne, Aaron Carnes, Kyle Chayka, Elvis Costello, Roger Ebert, Stephen Thomas Erlewine, Jeff Gomez, Walter Holland, Barney Hoskyns, Steven Hyden, Jesse Jarnow, David Lemieux, Jenny Odell, Ed Johnson-Ott, Kim Mack, Griel Marcus, Whitney Matheson, Alec Palao, Parke Puterbaugh, Rob Sheffield, Hank Shteamer, David Steinberg, Shawn Taylor, Ahmir Thompson and Richie Unterberger.

I mentioned when we started that this book is for people who are not heavily invested in Phish. That would include my parents, Terry, Diane and Rick, and my sisters, Erica and Jill. Even if this book does not convince them to soundtrack our next gathering with some Phish, my feelings for you all will remain unchanged. Also, a special shout-out to my niece, Rowan, who has at least feigned an interest in Phish.

I've distinct musical memories for each of my kids, but because they are my kids, I will spare them the embarrassment of sharing them here. Regardless, Vanessa, Zach, Gabby and Cassidy are the finest kids a father could ask for. I hope they continue to illuminate my blind spots with all the things they're passionate about.

And finally, this book is for my wife, Helena. If it were socially acceptable and if she were more tolerant of public displays of affection, this book would include 37 pages of content related to how unworthy I am of her grace and companionship. I hope I have convinced her that, although she does not share my affinity for Phish, that's okay. The two of us are alike in all the ways that I want – and different in all the ways that I need.

Foreword

People used to make records
As in a record of an event
The event of people playing music in a room
Ani DiFranco, 'Fuel', *Little Plastic Castle*

When Phish took the stage at Madison Square Garden those 13 nights during the summer of 2017, they also intended to make a record of an event. Since their beginning, Phish's concerts have been recorded (either for the band's benefit, their audience's benefit or both). With the advent of the internet and Phish's expanding online presence, their tours have become asynchronous experiences for many of their fans.

Obviously, those in attendance are likely to have a stronger connection to these songs than someone who is listening after the fact. Those in the room are likely to associate certain musical moments with Madison Square Garden's vibe, Chris Kuroda's lighting or their partner's awkward dance moves. With that being said, another individual's connection to a piece of music is no less valid because they were not in the room when it was recorded. If watching *The Last Waltz*, you do not have to have a belly full of Bill Graham's Thanksgiving turkey dinner to respond to Garth Hudson's concluding saxophone solo in 'It Makes No Difference'.

Certain classic albums were only possible because of in-studio trickery. Can's *Tago Mago* and Miles Davis's *Bitches Brew* were spliced together from individual, non-related moments. Their composition was as indebted to their editors as it was to the performers. For *The Baker's Dozen*, Phish went beyond executing their songs; they improvised elements in real-time, each song a non-repeatable performance where every decision was instinctual and, arguably, perfect. Listening to these concerts after the fact, knowing where the band will end up 20 minutes later, does not diminish the experience any more than knowing how 'Miles Runs The Voodoo Down' ends.

There is no 'gatekeeping' involved with the Phish community. From the beginning, fans have proselytized the band because of how much they love the music and how far they want that music to spread. The Phish community, with their online presence and the concert recordings they freely shared, were 'gatebreaking' before the term was even coined.

My family and I attend Faith United Church of Christ, 'an open and inclusive congregation that welcomes you no matter where you are on life's journey. Whether you are liberal or conservative, gay or straight, new to church, or have been part of the church for a long time, you are welcome here.' This book has a comparable creed – it was written for people who love Phish, who have a tough time loving Phish or who just want to better understand someone who loves Phish. It is for anyone who is aware that the band exist, has started to dive a little deeper or is looking for something Phish-related to read. I hope this book provides a foundational understanding of Phish, their influences and their discography. More importantly, it is meant as an appreciation of the band and what they accomplished during one of their 40+ summers.

on stage ...

Phish

The Baker's Dozen

Contents

Band History

Phish formed in the progressive college town of Burlington, Vermont, in 1983. The band initially came together when guitarist Ernest 'Trey' Anastasio III (born in 1964), drummer Jon Fishman (born in 1965), bassist Mike Gordon (born in 1965) and guitarist Jeff Holdsworth (born in 1963) began playing together. Keyboardist Page McConnell (born 1963) joined in 1985, and Holdsworth left the band the following year. Since then, the lineup has remained stable, with all four members contributing songs and vocals (but Anastasio being the primary songwriter and vocalist).

The band's music blends an eclectic mix of rock, funk, jazz, bluegrass, reggae, psychedelic, folk, blues, country, barbershop, ambient, classical, electronic music and more. Although their sound defies easy classification (one can easily hear the influence of artists such as The Beatles, Genesis and Frank Zappa), they are typically (and rightfully) grouped under the 'jam band' umbrella. This is because that catch-all term more easily encapsulates their scene's approach to music (rather than how the bands within that label reflect a specific genre).

The band's time is divided into three eras. I have sketched out each of those below. I will point out that there is some debate about whether the post-pandemic era of the band should be referred to as 4.0. Since this occurs after *The Baker's Dozen*, an opinion is not required here.

Phish 1.0 (1980s – 7 October 2000)

Phish's regional popularity steadily increased during the 1980s. Critics have noted Phish's 'bar band' feel during these initial years. Their national popularity began in earnest during the 1990s. Starting around 1993, the band's jams became more exploratory and international popularity followed. The band adopted a more groove-based approach to their jams around 1997. The band's four-date *Island Tour* from April 1998 is a great representation of this change. Dubbed 'cow funk', a phrase we will refer to often, this musical era lasted until the band began their first hiatus in 2000. In the summer of 2000, the band announced that they would take an 'extended time-out' following their upcoming fall tour. The goal of the hiatus was to allow the band to spend more time with their friends and expanding families while also preventing the band from making the same mistakes the Grateful Dead previously made (diminishing results on stage and increasingly cumbersome organization off the stage). After closing their 7 October 2000 show with 'You Enjoy Myself', the band went their separate ways. During this two-year window, the frequency with which they released archival titles increased.

Phish 2.0 (31 December 2002 – 15 August 2004)

The band regrouped in December 2002. They performed on *Saturday Night Live* (with Al Gore as the host) and then on *The Late Show With David Letterman* (with the *Catch Me If You Can*-promoting Tom Hanks as the night's main guest). Their first full concert was on New Year's Eve at Madison Square Garden. The final concert of 2.0 occurred at their own Coventry Festival (held in Coventry, Vermont, on 14 and 15 August 2004). This concert is infamous for things out of the band's hands (heavy rain and highway traffic) as well as things the band should have had better control over (the ability to play songs they had played innumerable times before and their on-stage composure). Unlike the original hiatus, this was announced ahead of time as an official disbanding of the group. Not announced at the time, but later admitted, was that Trey's substance abuse contributed to the band's breakup. During this on-stage estrangement (they remained in each other's lives), the band continued their habit of releasing archival concerts 'from the vaults'.

Phish 3.0 (6 March 2009 – ???)

Almost five years later, Phish reunited for a series of concerts. In this latest era, they have all found ways to tour and release music outside of Phish. These albums and tours allow the band to workshop songs they can then bring to the group, or to explore songs they have previously played together with musicians who have different skill sets. Considering the strength of every tour they have mounted in the 3.0 era, they have finally found a way to thrive amidst the pressure of being Phish.

In a 2007 *Relix* interview, prior to the band's 6 March 2009 reformation at the Hampton Coliseum (in Hampton, Virginia), Page McConnell recalled a few whimsical tour ideas Phish had once kicked around but ultimately shelved for financial reasons. One concept involved playing only in the seven US states they'd never visited. Another imagined a 'baker's dozen' of shows – 13 nights at a single venue like Madison Square Garden or, with a wink to Phish's offbeat humor, the Providence Civic Center, then branded the Dunkin' Donuts Center. The band even envisioned giving away donuts and tailoring each show's theme to that night's flavor – say, a 'Boston Crème' night featuring covers of Boston and Cream. 'Even if creatively it made sense to the four of us,' McConnell admitted to *Relix*, 'the management – I don't want to say they wouldn't let us do it, but really, they just wouldn't let us do it.'

Years later, after reuniting and playing hundreds of shows, Phish finally brought the idea to life with *The Baker's Dozen* – a 13-night residency at Madison Square Garden to conclude their summer 2017 tour. Across the run, the band played 237 unique songs without a single repeat, entertaining roughly 227,385 fans and turning a long-shelved dream into a landmark moment in their storied career. Each of the 13 nights had an overarching, donut-based theme ('Red Velvet', 'Boston Cream', 'Jam-Filled', etc.). The setlists were designed to amuse and challenge the audience – people expected to hear The Beatles' 'Strawberry Fields Forever' on 22 July ('Strawberry Donut Night'), but nobody anticipated an a cappella version of Tay Zonday's 'Chocolate Rain' on 28 July ('Double Chocolate Donut Night'). The band, as is their custom, released digital versions of the shows via their LivePhish app. Professionally produced videos of select performances from each of the 13 concerts are available on the band's official YouTube page. In addition, physical copies were made available. A limited edition 36-disc boxset was available for purchase through their Dry Goods webshop, and an abridged, 13-track version (three CDs or six LPs) was made available to traditional retailers and streaming services. In Dean Budnick's contribution to *This Is Your Song Too: Phish And Contemporary Jewish Identity*, there is a quote from Trey that says the back cover of the three-CD set contains his 'favorite picture of our crowd right now.' Fishman responds, 'It's a lot of happy-looking people. That feels good.' Trey then clarifies that he likes it because 'there's not one cell phone in the air.'

Note

Although this is not a biography of the band, a bit of background information is appropriate. Readers looking for a detailed history of the band should obtain a copy of *Phish: The Biography*. This semi-official narrative, written by Parke Puterbaugh and published in 2009, was based on interviews with the entire band, their friends and associates. Another excellent resource is Walter Holland's contribution to Bloomsbury Academic's 33⅓ book series. His monograph on Phish's 1995 compilation, *A Live One*, is an in-depth look at what makes Phish, and that live album, so appealing. Finally, the *Long May They Run* musical documentary is available wherever you listen to podcasts. This ten-part series provides an excellent summation of the band and their impact on our culture.

Terminology

Most terms encountered within this text are spelled out as they appear. However, there are a few items important enough to warrant a special introduction.

Two different notations appear within the *Baker's Dozen* setlists. A right arrow ('>') indicates two songs were played back-to-back without clear demarcation between them – the preceding song simply stops and the following song immediately begins. A dash and right arrow (' >') illustrates a musical segway between two songs – the players gradually modify the preceding song so that the melody morphs into a new song.

There are two distinct types of jamming referenced within this narrative. The first, simply called 'Type I' jamming, features fixed chord progressions with variations on notes and tempos. The second, for obvious reasons called 'Type II' jamming, deconstructs the song structure through improvised chord progressions and/or alternate rhythms. To pull a quote from David Steinberg's *This Has All Been Wonderful*: 'The easiest way to describe the distinction between the two types is to have someone play you a mid-jam snippet that you've never heard before. If you can immediately identify the song, then it's

Type 1.' Both types occurred during the summer of 1994 tour he expertly documented and both types also appear frequently during *The Baker's Dozen*.

Prologue (Chicago, Dayton And Pittsburgh)

The summer 2017 tour started in Chicago on Friday 14 July, and over the course of three nights at the Huntington Bank Pavilion, Phish performed 57 songs, six of which were debuts that would later reappear during *The Baker's Dozen*. The Friday night show featured a cover of 'In The Good Old Summer Time' and Phish's debut performance of 'Everything's Right' (a song Trey had already performed a dozen times during the spring of 2017). In addition, that opening night also featured debut performances of two new compositions, 'Leaves' and 'Love Is What We Are'. On Saturday, Phish debuted their version of 'Corona'. Trey had included this original composition on his 2012 solo album *Traveler*, and he has been performing it occasionally since then. The final night of the opening run included one final debut, 'Thread'.

The next stop on the summer 2017 tour was Wright State University's Ervin J. Nutter Center near Dayton, Ohio. Phish opened this Tuesday show with a new-to-them song, (the appropriately named) 'Tuesday'. Like 'Corona', this was another track from a Trey solo project, but unlike the comparatively rarer 'Corona', 'Tuesday' had been frequently included in Trey's setlists. The second song that debuted at Guided By Voices frontman Robert Pollard's alma mater was Mike's 'Crazy Sometimes'.

The final stop of the Summer 2017 opening salvo was the Petersen Events Center in Pittsburgh, Pennsylvania. Two more songs debuted, 'Marissa' and 'Rise/Come Together'. In addition, 'Mr. Completely' was performed for the first time in over 14 years.

Going 'backwards down the number line', the band performed 93 songs, including 11 debuts/bust-outs, over six days (during five concerts in three cities) before they would start *The Baker's Dozen* in just two days. In Phish parlance, a bust-out refers to a song that hasn't been played in a long time, often years. These rarities are beloved by fans, who eagerly track the gaps between performances, and a well-timed bust-out can spark a frenzy of excitement in the crowd. By working a few of these into their pre-*Dozen* shows, Phish seemed to be loosening up the catalog, dusting off deep cuts and dropping hints that anything might be on the table.

Night 1: Friday 21 July ('Coconut')

Phish started *The Baker's Dozen* on Friday 21 July, after having taken 20 July off. Six of the 16 songs the band played on the opening night had been part of the band's repertoire since the 1980s.

Set 1

'Shake Your Coconuts' (Laursen/Mortensen/Troelsen)
Any band beginning an extended residency could be forgiven for easing into the gig. Playing something mellow or something that slowly builds to a climax would remind the audience that it is a marathon, not a sprint. Phish, as is their nature, do the opposite. Not only do they start the runoff with as much energy as they can, but they also start it off with a song they had never previously played. They trusted their audience to go along for the ride and, with lyrics like 'Just keep on dancing now/Just keep on getting down/Just keep on having fun/The party's just begun', they were not subtle about it. Junior Senior's 'Shake Your Coconuts' was originally released by the Danish group in 2002 and was made popular stateside by its inclusion in the film *Looney Tunes: Back In Action*. While the original recording sounds like the midpoint between LCD Soundsystem and the Apples In Stereo, Phish's version is slightly harder but no less fun because of it.

'Martian Monster' (Anastasio/Fishman/Gordon/McConnell)
The band then move on to the first fan-favorite of the run. Originally performed by the band as part of their 2014 Halloween concert, 'Martian Monster' was released as the closing track to Disney's 1964 album *Chilling, Thrilling Sounds Of The Haunted House*. Of the songs debuted as part of that 2014 'musical costume', 'Martian Monster' is the one they have returned to most frequently. Its 'Your trip is short' vocal sample is well-deployed by Page and this mid-summer audience's response to a Halloween-themed song hammers home the point made by 'Shake Your Coconuts': this audience is on board with whatever the band want to throw at them.

'Timber (Jerry The Mule)' (Gary/White) **> '555'** (Gordon/Murawski)
The first of many songs the band originally debuted in the 1980s, 'Timber (Jerry The Mule)' is a cover of a 1930s work song that had faded from popularity until it was revived by Harry Belafonte in the 1950s. Coincidently, Mr. Belafonte's version was released as the B-side to his 1952 RCA Victor single 'Man Smart (Woman Smarter)'. That A-side would enter the Grateful Dead's setlists on 2 July 1981 (roughly six years before Phish added 'Timber (Jerry The Mule)' to theirs). Phish played the song regularly during the 1.0 era, and the last version played before their first hiatus is available on the *Live In Vegas* DVD. Interestingly, 'Timber (Jerry The Mule)' might seem like a tune Trey Anastasio could pull out in other settings, but he plays it almost

exclusively with Phish. Aside from a lone solo acoustic version in 2011, he's steered clear of performing it outside of the band. That may be because the song thrives on the full band's dynamic tension – its eerie, galloping rhythm, atmospheric jamming and the interplay between Mike's brooding basslines and Page's spectral keys. Originally written in the late 1930s, 'Timber' has become less of a cover and more of a Phish séance, something that only fully conjures itself when all four are locked in.

'Timber (Jerry The Mule)' transitions into '555' – Mike's first lead vocal (and songwriting contribution) of the run. Pronounced 'five fifty-five', this track debuted as part of the band's Halloween 2013 'musical costume'. Unlike previous Halloweens, where another band's album was performed, this year, the band debuted a yet-to-be-recorded album, which, at the time, was to be titled *Wingsuit*. When it was released the following year, the album was renamed *Fuego,* and '555' was the second-most-played song from that album. No spoilers for what the most frequently played *Fuego* track is. Mike's introductory bass and Fishman's thundercrack drumming start things off. Soon, the full band are bringing musical and vocal funk to the party.

Although not a song that has ever been jammed to its full potential, it would (after *The Baker's Dozen*) finally get a workout as part of a noteworthy run in Las Vegas. The 28 October 2021 show featured a six-song first set of 'Also Sprach Zarathustra' > '1999' > '555' > '46 Days' and then 'Strawberry Letter 23' > 'Twenty Years Later'. All six of these songs would also be played at *The Baker's Dozen*, and they (again) reinforce a great point about Phish: they are not compared album-to-album; they are compared night-to-night.

'Pigtail' (Anastasio/Marshall)

The band allow the audience to take a breather after '555' (with Trey, just over 20 minutes into the show, considerately asking if they are tired yet). After a false start lovingly attributed to Fishman, the band start up Trey's midtempo 'Pigtail'. A song Trey routinely performs outside of Phish, this is one of few occasions in which the band have tackled it. It is a clear sign they're gearing up for the long haul – 13 nights, no repeats – and when it comes to song selection, it's all hands on deck. Deep cuts, crowd favorites, forgotten oddities – everything's in play. *The Baker's Dozen* isn't just a tour; it's a full excavation of Phish's musical archives. Regardless, this is my favorite song on Trey's *Traveler* album, and I enjoy hearing it played, either by this band, The Trey Anastasio Band or Trey and The Roots. As part of a charity set that Trey and the Roots performed on 7 September 2012, 'Pigtail' was performed (with additional vocals provided on 'Pigtail' and a few other songs by Grace Potter). Coincidentally, this performance (like *The Baker's Dozen* version) also starts off with a miscommunication between Trey and the drummer. But, because Questlove is second to none when it comes to professionalism, the song quickly takes shape.

'Halfway To The Moon' (McConnell)

The second *Fuego* track to be played during *The Baker's Dozen*, 'Halfway To The Moon' is a Page effort and he gives this performance his all. His piano fills are beautifully complimented by some of Fishman's best drum fills. When Trey's solo is factored in, 'Halfway To The Moon' becomes a stand-out Night 1 performance. Phish.net historian 'Doctor_Smarty' perceptively wrote that 'Musically, 'Halfway To The Moon' sounds like what may have been the result if Thom Yorke of Radiohead had originally composed the Allman Brothers' 'Melissa'.' Nobody will ever describe the song better.

Originally performed by the band back in 2010, 'Halfway To The Moon' was included in the second set for those initial performances. It was then quickly moved to the opening set (where it has, almost exclusively, stayed). Along with its consistent set placement, most versions of 'Halfway To The Moon' are interchangeable, but there are exceptions. The 31 December 2013 version (that leads into the set-closing 'Fluffhead') is a standout.

'Reba' (Anastasio)

Another song from the band's 1980s output, 'Reba' is a fan favorite and the strong jam that ends this version does not disappoint. Reviewing 'Reba' for *AllMusic*, Jim Smith praised 'Reba' for its 'absurd lyrics, intricate design and renegade momentum.' He continued his praise with the claim that 'Reba' is 'one of their best moments, neatly summarizing the band's philosophy in 12 minutes.' The second half of that quote refers to the fact that 'Reba', like many Phish compositions, features both composed sections and opportunities for the band to improvise. The audience response helps confirm that 'Reba' is always a welcome addition to the setlist, even if the composed versions are not perfectly played in this instance. This Night 1 'Reba' is perfectly placed within the flow of the show and the jammed portions are fun (and Trey's portion in the section leading into the nine-minute mark is especially beautiful). For another fun version of 'Reba', visit YouTube and check out the version performed at 'Amy's Farm' in Auburn, Maine, on 3 August 1991. This free concert was videotaped by several Phans, and it is hard to determine who is enjoying this version of 'Reba' more – the band or the audience. As a bonus, the 1991 version still contained the whistled section that started to be omitted in 1992.

'Moonage Daydream' (Bowie)

Once the response to 'Reba' dies down, the band launch into David Bowie's 'Moonage Daydream'. This was only the band's second performance (the first being the previous year's Halloween show in Las Vegas when they covered the *Ziggy Stardust* album in its entirety). Of the Bowie songs that debuted that night, 'Moonage Daydream' is the one they have started returning to on an almost annual basis. Considering how well Trey manages it every single time, I would not be surprised if it continues to make sporadic appearances in their setlists for years to come. This Night 1 version featured some of his best playing of the run (and if that original 31 October 2016 version did not exist, this version would be his definitive performance). As is, this 'Moonage Daydream' will have to be content with being in contention for 'Best Cover Performed During *The Baker's Dozen*.'

'Walls Of The Cave' (Anastasio/Marshall)
The band close their first set of this run with one of the strongest songs from one of their most underrated albums, *Round Room*. Recorded during rehearsals for their first 2.0 era shows, *Round Room* was (in my mind) not as well-received as it should have been. On *AllMusic*, it earned 2.5 stars and is tied for their lowest-rated album. (That it is tied with *The Story Of The Ghost* gives us more to unpack than we have time for right now.) In his review of *Round Room*, Stephen Thomas Erlewine (whose reviews are frequently faultless) describes the album as 'ramshackle, laid-back and haphazard.' Considering Phish's studio albums are occasionally overproduced, I consider these to be features, not bugs.

Premiering at MSG on NYE, 2002, the initial performance of 'Walls Of The Cave' was extended to almost 19 minutes due to the excellent Type II jamming it included. In fact, the band had so much faith in that debut performance that they slotted it as the final song in their third and final set of the night. The version played at *The Baker's Dozen* is not as long, but it is a strong finish to their opening set.

Set 2

'Tweezer' (Anastasio/Fishman/Gordon/McConnell) **> 'Seven Below'** (Anastasio/Marshall) **> 'Billy Breathes'** (Anastasio) **> 'Sparkle'** (Anastasio/Marshall)
Beginning with 'Tweezer', the first of two songs from 1992's *A Picture Of Nectar*, the second set starts off with an almost 40-minute run. Although a highlight of the night (and, for some, the entire run), this 'Tweezer' has too much competition to be considered one of the band's 'all-time best'. Phish have been playing this song consistently since the spring of 1990, and because of all the great versions they have managed throughout their various eras, it is hard for a recent version to gain traction. (Full disclosure: I am guilty of this myself. I have a tough time not comparing any version of 'Tweezer' to the version I fell in love with on *Live Phish Volume 18, 5.7.94* or to the 14 June 1995 version released from the archives onto the LivePhish app or to the Friday the 13th performance from Chicago in October 2023. Other phans might compare every new 'Tweezer' to a celebrated 'Tweezer' from a different show (for example, the 'Dayton 'Tweezer'' or the 'Tahoe 'Tweezer'' (30 November 1995 and 31 July 2013, respectively)). The point is that it's a warhorse of a tune and one that always finds a way to invigorate an audience. As of this writing, the most recent Herculean 'Tweezer' was a 40-minute

monster delivered on 30 July 2024 in St. Louis, Missouri. With Fishman being especially on point and the energy never lagging, the band took a moment afterwards to bask in the applause. Delivered as a standalone song (nothing leading into or out of it), this 'Tweezer' demonstrates how good its compositional bones are. With all that being said, the opening night of *The Baker's Dozen* also provides an excellent version of 'Tweezer' (and one that more than one phan has complimented for its more ambient portions).

Once they step out of 'Tweezer', the band roll into 'Seven Below' (aka, '-7'), a fan-favorite from 2002's post-hiatus release, Round Room. The original Rolling Stone review for Round Room complimented how the four band members worked together to give 'Seven Below' 'a sublime, impossibly fluid rhythm.' This version of '-7' pairs well with 'Tweezer'; those two songs are the main reason for the second set starting so strongly (and, to date, this is the only time the band have paired 'Tweezer' and '-7'). The Night 1 'Seven Below' features a nice jam that goes dark fairly quickly. Although led by Trey's guitar and Page's synths, Mike makes his presence known before Trey shifts the whole thing into a major key. The jam ends on a synth bed, leading into 'Billy Breathes'.

After '-7' takes Page's synth-playing to some interesting places and the band decide it has run its course, they move on to the title track of their 1996 release, *Billy Breathes*. The original studio version was considered a highlight of what Stephen Thomas Erlewine called 'the definitive Phish album', and this live version of 'Billy Breathes' is faithfully played (with the final minute being some of Trey's best playing of the night). One of Phish's best ballads, 'Billy Breathes' is a song that Trey has said on multiple occasions has special meaning to him (and, given the number of ballads the band wrote in its wake, it is assumed the warm reception gave the band the confidence needed to start writing more ballads). The band had been playing 'Billy Breathes' in concert for over 20 years by this point, but this was the first time they performed it at Madison Square Garden (MSG). Coincidently, they would not play it again until they were back at MSG almost a year and a half later for their 2018 NYE run.

Finally, the band conclude 'Billy Breathes' and then pick up the pace with 'Sparkle', a favorite of mine since the one-two punch of *Live Phish Volume 7, 8.14.93* and *Live Phish Volume 8, 7.10.99*. I purchased both albums upon their release in the spring of 2002, and they soundtracked my work commute for months afterwards. The frantic delivery makes it a fun one to sing along with while driving (especially when they hit the first 'You laugh and laughing, fall apart' – it sounds like they are channeling their inner Oak Ridge Boys). The studio version, included on their 1993 release, *Rift*, features better coordination among the vocalists, but this version (and most live versions) is infinitely more fun. Part of 'Sparkle's' charm is the constant sense that it's on the verge of total collapse – like a runaway cart barreling downhill with a wonky wheel. You can't help but wonder: is this the time the wheels finally fly off the wagon? They never do, of course, but the band teeter on that edge with such reckless precision; it always feels like disaster is just one beat away.

'Everything's Right' (Anastasio/Marshall) **> 'Slave To The Traffic Light'** (Abrahams/Anastasio/Pollak) **> 'Suzy Greenberg'** (Pollak)
The second half of the second set starts off with Phish's second-ever performance of 'Everything's Right'. Debuted by the band exactly one week earlier in Chicago, this soon-to-be concert staple features a jam that even contemporary reviews pointed out as being a high point. The band agreed and would include this song as the representative song for Night 1 when they released *The Baker's Dozen* sampler in 2018. Speaking of 2018, that is when live versions of 'Everything's Right' really began to take off (with the concert-opening performance on 28 October 2018 being especially fun). A studio version that is slightly longer than *The Baker's Dozen* performance would be included on the band's 2020 album *Sigma Oasis*. Sam Sodomsky, in a *Pitchfork* review that reads slightly better than its 6.5 score implies, writes:

> Something interesting happens halfway through 'Everything's Right', a 12-minute track on Sigma Oasis. For a while, it's everything you might expect from a Phish record nearly 40 years into their career: an intentionally mind-numbing chorus ('Everything's right/So just hold tight') set to a melody that cycles between sunny major chords like a beach ball infinitely bobbing through a crowd of outstretched arms. It's light and goofy – sorta funky. But then it shifts. Around the five-minute mark, after Trey Anastasio finishes a polite vamp on the word 'alright', he kicks off a guitar solo. Page McConnell follows on the organ. Soon, the whole band are in on it, listening intently to one another and changing shape, one note at a time. Suddenly, Phish are jamming, and you're right there with them.

After 'Everything's Right', the band move into 'Slave To The Traffic Light' (with some commenters feeling the segway is smooth enough to justify a ' >' marking instead of '>'). Regardless, 'Slave' is well-played and well-received. Lasting (only?) six minutes when originally played on 1 December 1984, 'Slave' would, within a decade, run twice as long. Introduced to most through *A Live One* and retroactively added to *The White Tape* in 1998, 'Slave To The Traffic Light' is a song that's as musically sophisticated as it is lyrically jejune. Only Phish can pair the self-evident lyrics 'See the city, see the zoo, traffic light won't let me through' with a guitar solo that better explains the sentiment behind them. Versions from 14 December 1995 and 9 October 1999 are also worth checking out, but admittedly, they are not as soulful as *The Baker's Dozen* version. This version, lasting 9:23 on the LivePhish app, was the perfect length to both maintain the energy from 'Everything's Right' into the sequence-closing 'Suzy Greenberg' without overtaxing the audience.

Another song the band had been playing since the 1980s, 'Suzy Greenberg' is one of the most zestful songs in the band's repertoire and another of their many 'fan-favorites'. When the band released the first wave of *LivePhish* CDs in 2001, 'Suzy' was on four of the six concerts. As popular as it is, a studio recording is still (as of this writing) unreleased. The question was posed by Parke Puterbaugh (in *Phish: The Biography*): 'Are you guys ever going to get around to recording 'Suzy Greenberg'? That sounds like your great lost top 40 single.' Trey is quoted as responding, 'It's funny. I wouldn't do it for that reason. We've had ample opportunity to record it because it was a good single, and we've chosen not to.' Thirty years after eschewing a hit single, the band performed a 13-night run at Madison Square Garden. This speaks to the diligence the band have applied to their career trajectory. To paraphrase another singer who was fond of New York, they did it their way. One of the best versions of 'Suzy Greenberg' was included on the *Vegas 96* live album. The band pulled out all the stops that night (6 December 1996) and the concert-closing 'Suzy' was no exception. *The Baker's Dozen* version is just as much fun, thanks in no small part to the extra mustard Fishman slathers on the word 'neurologist'. He stretches it out with theatrical, almost Monty Python-esque bravado – equal parts rock star and comic foil – turning a single word into a moment of pure, ridiculous joy.

'Coconut' (Liles/Nilsson)
The second set ends with one last debut: an a cappella cover of Harry Nilsson's 'Coconut'. As of this writing, this is the only time the band have tackled this signature 1971 *Nilsson Schmilsson* tune. Most commenters were on board with this song and the arrangement, but there were a few dissenters who would have preferred either an instrumental take or for it to have been paired with another song. Personally, I have never not enjoyed Phish's four-part harmonies, and I was on board the entire time (which, admittedly, was only slightly longer than two minutes).

Encore

'The Mango Song' (Anastasio) **> 'Good Times Bad Times'** (Bonham/Jones/Page/Plant)
The first night's encore contains two more songs the band had been playing since the 1980s (although they had never been previously paired together). 'The Mango Song' and 'Good Times Bad Times' ('GTBT') were both popular choices for the encore. Due to it being rarer than 'GTBT', 'The Mango Song' appears to have been a slightly more popular choice. 'The Mango Song' first debuted on 30 March 1989, and a studio version would later be included on *A Picture Of Nectar* in 1992. This was the third song of the night to be credited solely to Trey, and as mentioned, it is not played as often as other songs from that era. For an extra helping of 'The Mango Song', check out the second set from 26 July 2013. The entire second set is something special and the 'Mango' is one of several highlights it contains.

Immediately after 'The Mango Song', Led Zeppelin's 'Good Times Bad Times' closes out the night. First played in December 1986, this song is a reliable display of Trey's skills as a guitarist and is a consistent closing song. In fact, 'Good Times Bad Times' functioned as the encore for the opening night of the band's last Madison Square Garden run on 28 December 2016. Phish have covered over a dozen Led Zeppelin songs (and would include a second Zeppelin song, 'No Quarter', on Night 5). Fans of both artists should check out Phish's 2011 live album *Live Phish: 10/30/10, Boardwalk Hall, Atlantic City, NJ*. It features 'Whole Lotta Love' in the opening set and a second-set jam that incorporates 'Heartbreaker', 'Ramble On', 'Thank You' and 'Stairway To Heaven' (plus a set-closing 'Good Times Bad Times' that is more triumphant than *The Baker's Dozen* version).

Night 2: Saturday 22 July ('Strawberry')

Night 2 was comparable to Night 1 in that almost half of the previous night's played songs were originally performed in the 1980s. Going forward, the 1980s would still periodically be represented, but not to the degree they were on the first two nights.

Set 1

'Strawberry Fields Forever' (Lennon/McCartney)
Phish open their second night of *The Baker's Dozen* with an a cappella version of 1967's 'Strawberry Fields Forever', the first of three Beatles songs they performed during the run. Originally rush-released by The Beatles in the spring of 1967, it was originally intended for their *Revolver* follow-up, *Sgt. Pepper's Lonely Hearts Club Band*. Considered by *Rolling Stone* (in 2021) to be the seventh greatest song of all time, the hipper members of the audience seem to immediately recognize the song. The remainder of the audience start to cheer when the lyrics begin, but it is the cheers that erupt when the first verse ends that always make me smile. It is a happy moment and one that is beloved by all who have heard it. The band would only return to 'Strawberry Fields' once more, on 2 August 2022. But that still gives them two more in-concert performances of 'Strawberry Fields Forever' than The Beatles had.

'Halley's Comet' (Wright) **> 'The Moma Dance'** (Anastasio/Fishman/Gordon/Marshall/McConnell) **> 'Breath And Burning'** (Anastasio) **> 'Funky Bitch'** (Seals)
After disbursing from their shared microphones, the band pick up their instruments before beginning the extended vocal introduction to 'Haley's Comet'. Fishman's drums then kick in and the band start up a spirited version of this 1980s warhorse. Although not taken to the same length as other versions of the song – it has hit the 20-minute mark on several occasions – the Night 2 version is slightly longer than the version played three nights earlier in Pittsburgh. Of course, the biggest difference between this version and the Pittsburgh performance is the cheer that accompanied the line, 'How would you like to have your thick strawberry goo?' The song has yet to make an appearance on a studio album and, at this point, it remains unrecorded, such is also the case with the opening night's 'Reba'. If the band do decide to record it, they will have to decide if they are going to use original guest vocalist Richard 'Nancy' Wright or if Mike, Page and Trey will continue their lead vocal duties as they have done since the 14 March 1993 performance.

The band then move into one of their longest versions of 'The Moma Dance' (and their second longest song of Night 2). This iteration of the *Story Of The Ghost* classic features Type II jamming and some of Mike and Page's finest playing. Not to be outdone, Trey and Fishman contribute atmospheric vocals throughout the song's structured sections. The 16 October 2021 version from

San Francisco is worth checking out, as is the 29 September 2000 performance in Las Vegas (and you will be forgiven for bailing on the second set after 'Fluffhead' to ensure you don't get anywhere near Kid Rock's infamous on-stage appearance). In his three-and-a-half-star review for *Rolling Stone*, Greg Kot discusses almost every track on *Story Of The Ghost*, 'The Moma Dance' being one of the exceptions. We will just put 'The Moma Dance' under his complimentary remark about how Phish have 'got chops, but they also have a sense of humor.'

The band then move into 'Breath And Burning', a song they debuted in Noblesville, Indiana, the previous summer (and had most recently played at MSG during the third set of their 31 December 2016 performance). This rendition showcases excellent playing from everyone, including some sprightly fills by Page (which were especially appropriate considering the relish with which Trey delivered the line, 'We're gonna rage with Page at the dying of the light'). The only single from *Big Boat*, and the last single the band would release, 'Breath And Burning' is another of the band's trademark 'life-affirming' tracks. With lyrics like 'we'll be dancing here for days', the song always works as a motivator for the audience to groove, and for this one night only, it also works as a way for the band to transition into Son Seals' 'Funky Bitch'. Originally released on his 1978 album *Live And Burning*, Son Seals would release a studio version in 2000, produced by Conan O'Brien bandleader Jimmy Vivino, which featured Trey on guitar. By the time Phish launched into 'Funky Bitch' on 22 July, they'd already performed the song well over 200 times, and their comfort with it shows. Like most 3.0 renditions, this version is tight, energetic and deeply in the pocket, but what makes it stand out is the focused interplay between Page and Trey. Page's solo is a masterclass in blues phrasing – clean, confident and filled with just enough rhythmic push to keep the momentum building. It's arguably the highlight of the first set. Trey follows with a series of increasingly aggressive runs, each one more urgent than the last, layering tension with every bar. By the time he enters his final solo passage, just after the four-minute mark, the energy peaks so sharply that the audience's response sounds almost exhausted, shouting not out of surprise but out of shared catharsis. The crowd rally again around six minutes in, but the band offer only the briefest breather before diving straight into the next tune, maintaining the momentum with calculated precision.

'Mound' (Gordon)

Originally released on *Rift*, 'Mound' is one of Mike Gordon's more compositionally intricate contributions to the Phish catalog. Unlike many fan-favorites, it's not a jam vehicle, nor does it lend itself to the kind of danceable grooves that dominate much of the band's live repertoire. Its rhythmic complexity, abrupt changes and storytelling structure demand focused listening rather than physical movement. In that sense, affection for 'Mound' hinges almost entirely on one's appreciation for its craftsmanship. Personally, I think it's one of Mike's finest: a quirky, tightly wound narrative with a melody that worms its way in. Every time it makes an appearance, it feels like a little reward for paying attention. For an indisputably great version, check out the previously praised *Live Phish Volume 18, 5.7.94*. That show's second set tends to monopolize the conversation, but the opening set is equally great (and 'Mound' contributes to that). 'Mound' made its debut during an unusually fruitful weekend for Phish – 6-7 March 1992 – a stretch that also saw the first performances of several songs that would later resurface during *The Baker's Dozen*, including 'Maze', 'My Friend, My Friend', 'Silent In The Morning', 'The Horse', 'Weigh' and 'NICU'. It was a moment of serious creative output, and 'Mound' stood out then – as it does now – for its structural complexity and narrative quirk.

'Foam' (Anastasio)

After 'Mound', the band start up 'Foam'. This *Junta* song, heavily played in the late-80s/early-90s but now much rarer, does not reach the heights of the Page-centric version from November 1998 that was included on *Hampton Comes Alive*, but it is still a fun one to hear (especially with the addition of the closing riff from Scott Joplin's 'The Entertainer'). 'Foam' also appears in two underrated shows that are more than worthy of official release: 5 April 1994 (Montreal) and 10 June 2009 (Knoxville). In the Montreal show, 'Foam' is tucked into a tight, hour-long opening set that's full of precision and purpose – the kind of set where even the transitions feel rehearsed. The Knoxville version, meanwhile, is notable for being the first truly standout 'Foam' of the 3.0 era. What makes it memorable is how much it echoes the sharpness and intensity of a classic 1.0 take: Page and Trey trade solos with clarity and restraint, Fishman holds the rhythmic tension with pinpoint control and the dynamics breathe in a way that had been largely absent from the song in more recent years. It's not just a nostalgic callback; it's a sign that 'Foam' still had life left in it, even in a new era.

'Roggae' (Anastasio/Fishman/Gordon/Marshall/McConnell)

The band then slide into another of three songs they originally debuted in Denmark on 30 June 1998. 'Roggae', like 'The Moma Dance' (played earlier this evening) and 'Brian And Robert' (still to come), was originally performed during that European tour and was subsequently released on *The Story Of The Ghost*. Check out *Live Phish Volume 17, 7.15.98* to hear their American debuts. 'Roggae', written and sung by all four members, is one of their more contemplative numbers. The way the four of them trade vocals (and complementary sentiments) evokes some of The Band's best moments. It is not hard to imagine a version of this song appearing on side one of The Band's 1970 masterpiece *Stage Fright*. Although it is not always referenced when people praise Night 2, I think 'Roggae' is a key factor in what makes this night such a special part of the run. The band might agree; they included this 'Roggae' on *The Baker's Dozen* album.

'The Squirming Coil' (Anastasio/Herman/Marshall)

'The Squirming Coil' always reminds me of Roger Ebert's oft-cited rule: 'No good movie is too long. No bad movie is short enough.' This song (which is not merely good but great) is never, ever too long. Once the song runs its course, the spotlight is given to Page so that he can improvise a conclusion, and he never fails to stick the landing. Beyond the studio version, which opens *Lawn Boy*, and the version which concludes *A Live One*, a version worth seeking is the finale of Page and Trey's understated 2021 EP, *December*. Comprised of six stripped-back re-recordings of Phish songs, it underscores just how well the two of them are suited for one another. It is not just their expert musicianship or how their voices can blend, but it is the sensitivity they bring to their own playing when they recognize the other can better contribute to a moment. The version of 'The Squirming Coil' that closes out this opening set demonstrates the same idea, but writ large because of the inclusion of Mike and Fishman.

Set 2

'Down With Disease' (Anastasio/Marshall) **> 'Strawberry Letter 23'** (Otis) **> 'Birds Of A Feather'** (Anastasio/Fishman/Gordon/Marshall/McConnell)

The second set starts off with the longest song of the night, 'Down With Disease'. The lead single from the band's 1994 release *Hoist*, 'Down With Disease' was capable of being a legit hit single as well as a vehicle for some of the group's best jamming. Cracking the top 40 on the *Billboard* Mainstream Rock Tracks chart during the summer of 1994, the 4:13 length of 'Down With Disease' more than tripled in length by the time November rolled around (and crossed the 30-minute mark by the following December). The band played 'Down With Disease' four times in 2017 and would be a second-set opener each time. Of four appearances it made in 2017, the 22 July version is the only one that did not cross the 20-minute mark (falling just short at around 19 minutes). Although it is not bound for the record books, this 'Down With Disease' is made extra special by a rhythmic gallop that is not always present. It is a strong start to the second set and bonus points are awarded for teasing 'Pictures Of Matchstick Men' (the classic Status Quo song that was rejuvenated by another iconic band formed in 1983, Camper Van Beethoven).

The band move out of their Type II jam and into their debut performance of 'Strawberry Letter 23'. This was written by a 17-year-old Shuggie Otis for his 1971 release *Freedom Flight*, which also featured a suggestive co-write with his dad, Johnny Otis, on 'Sweet Thang' (a quasi-sequel to their 1969 release, *Snatch & The Poontangs*). 'Strawberry Letter 23' was later popularized by the Quincy Jones-produced version that the Los Angeles-based funk band The Brothers Johnson released in 1977. Phish's version is at once faithful, playful and ripe for Type II jams. Sadly, the band have only returned to 'Strawberry Letter 23' a handful of times since its debut. It has been played about twice per year since 2017 and I am hopeful it will continue to show up now and again. For a version that is just as fun (albeit a bit shorter), check out the band's 28 October 2021 performance at the MGM Grand Garden Arena in Las Vegas. Included as part of a setlist that consisted entirely of songs whose titles reference numbers, 'Strawberry Letter 23' is just one small part of a show that should not be slept on.

After hitting some quick noise that evokes the Type II jam that ended 'Down With Disease', the band return to 'Strawberry Letter 23' once more before moving into 'Birds Of A Feather'. The third and final song the band played from *The Story Of The Ghost* (for tonight at least), 'Birds Of A Feather' originally debuted as part of the band's 1998 *Island Tour*. Upon completing their 1997 NYE run at MSG, the band knew they were performing too well to take an extended break. They quickly scheduled two concerts in Rhode Island and two more on Long Island. Dubbed the *Island Tour*, these four shows (held on 2, 3, 4 and 5 April) demonstrated that the band intended to build on 1997's momentum. Over the course of these four nights (all of which are available to stream on the LivePhish app or on Spotify as part of the band's LivePhish series), the band debuted several new songs. 'Birds Of A Feather' is the strongest of those songs. The initial version on 2 April fell just short of the ten-minute mark, but its second performance on 5 April crossed the 15-minute mark. Later versions would exceed 20 minutes, but during this 22 July show, the audience would have to be satisfied with a concise, well-played, six-and-a-half-minute version that featured some excellent Type I jamming and the evergreen sentiment, 'It's not an experience if you can't bring someone along'.

'I Always Wanted It This Way' (McConnell) **> 'All Of These Dreams'** (Anastasio/Herman/Marshall)

The band then return to *Big Boat* for the second and final time of the night. Page had three songwriting credits on their album from the previous year, and 'I Always Wanted It This Way' was the one from the album that the band performed most frequently. In fact, the band played 'I Always Wanted It This Way' when they returned to MSG for their NYE run at the end of the year. For this 22 July performance, Trey (like he had on their two previous performances) utilizes a Marimba Lumina. Don Buchina (who, in the 1960s, developed modular synthesizers independently, yet concurrently, with Bob Moog) developed the Marimba Lumina in the 1990s. The device is a MIDI controller laid out like a marimba, and like that percussion instrument, it is played using mallets. Although Fishman added a Marimba Lumina to his on-stage arsenal in 2013, Trey did not begin playing one with any regularity until

2016. In fact, the 9 July 2016 version of 'You Enjoy Myself' from Hartford, Connecticut, is available on YouTube and features a great Trey jam on the Marimba Lumina.

After 'I Always Wanted It This Way' concludes, the band move into their only *Round Room* song of the night, 'All Of These Dreams'. This Trey-sung ballad, with beautiful harmony vocals from Mike and Page, was the band's re-introduction to the world after their initial hiatus. Although considered good enough to be performed on the 19 December 1992 episode of *The Late Show With David Letterman*, this song did not make the cut for their New Year's Eve reunion concert at MSG, nor for their following concert on 2 January at the Hampton Coliseum in Hampton, Virginia. The song made its 'official' live debut at their 3 January show (again, still at the Hampton Coliseum). The band played six of the 12 *Round Room* tracks during that two-night run at the Hampton Coliseum. *The Baker's Dozen* performance was only its tenth concert appearance, and if you enjoyed this Night 2 version, you should also check out the 5 September 2021 version. Although only two performances occurred between them, the 2021 version is especially strong because of how it comes out of the preceding 'Sigma Oasis' and acts as a breather before an extra-spicy 'Reba'.

'Split Open And Melt' (Anastasio) **> 'Down With Disease'** (Anastasio/Marshall) **> 'Shine A Light'** (Jagger/Richards)

The final sequence of the second set begins with the second *Lawn Boy* tune of the night: a particularly intense rendition of 'Split Open And Melt'. This version is especially dissonant, with Mike pushing the low end into deep, subterranean territory that gives the jam a claustrophobic weight. Fishman fractures the groove into off-kilter rhythms, creating a kind of rhythmic vertigo that keeps both the band and audience teetering on the edge of chaos. It's not the first time 'Split Open And Melt' has gone to such dark places. Back on 21 November 1997, the band debuted their cover of The Rolling Stones' 'Emotional Rescue' (with Mick proving, once again, that he's no Roy Orbison), then dove straight into a version of 'Split Open And Melt' that, while still shadowy, was a touch more restrained than its *Baker's Dozen* counterpart. Those two songs make up the opening 30 minutes of the *Hampton/Winston-Salem '97* box set and are well worth revisiting. And don't stop there: the rest of that second set includes a luminous 'Beauty Of My Dreams' and a late-show 'AC/DC Bag' > 'Slave To The Traffic Light' pairing that has lost none of its charm over time.

After the band take 'Split Open And Melt' as far as they can, they (quickly) reel it back in to ferociously return to the 'Down With Disease' jam they had moved on from roughly 37 minutes earlier. In the 'Best of Baker's Dozen?' thread on the r/phish Reddit forum, user 'ohpleasenotagain' wrote that this 'Down With Disease' 'turned me into a fan' and it is hard to feel that they are the only one. After spending a little over seven minutes triumphantly completing the 'Down With Disease' that started this second set, they move on to the set's final number: the Rolling Stones classic, 'Shine A Light'.

Originally introduced during Phish's full-album cover of *Exile On Main St* at their own *Festival 8* in 2009, 'Shine A Light' has since become a beloved rarity in the band's repertoire. It's made just 28 appearances, typically as a second-set closer or encore, where its gospel-tinged optimism and soaring chorus provide a cathartic release. A notable outlier occurred on 2 September 2011 when the band opened a show with it as part of a playful theme: every song that night started with the letter 'S'. The second set's 'Seven Below' > 'Suzy Greenberg' > 'Scents And Subtle Sounds' jam sequence is massive, and the show-closing bust-out of the Beastie Boys' 'Sabotage' is the kind of unhinged fun that only Phish pull off with a straight face. The *Baker's Dozen* performance of 'Shine A Light' closes the show with remarkable poignancy. After a 'Disease'-ridden second set, 'Shine A Light' arrives as a kind of benediction. Trey's vocals are clear and heartfelt, and Page's piano lifts the final chorus into something transcendent. The song's spiritual overtones and lyrical message – 'May the good Lord shine a light on you' – takes on new meaning in the context of *The Baker's Dozen*, where each night felt like both a celebration and a communion. It wasn't just a cover; it was a moment of emotional resolution and a gentle landing after one of the most daring sets of the run.

Encore

'Peaches En Regalia' (Zappa) **> 'Cities'** (Byrne)**, 'My Sweet One'** (Fishman)

Night 2 featured the first encore placement of Frank Zappa's 'Peaches En Regalia' since 1989 (and the only time the track transitions into the Talking Heads' 'Cities'). 'Peaches En Regalia', with its Shuggie Otis(!!) bassline, was the leadoff track from *Hot Rats*, Zappa's almost entirely instrumental 1969 classic. The band have often spoken of their appreciation for Frank Zappa, and many phans have commented about how their debt to Zappa is greater than the (mistakenly held) belief that they are version 2.0 of the Grateful Dead. When Rolling Stone published their October 2023 ranking of the 250 Greatest Guitarists of All Time, they included a Trey Anastasio quote from 2005: 'When I was learning how to play guitar, I was obsessed with that album (*Shut Up 'N' Play Yer Guitar*). Every boundary that was possible on the guitar was examined by him in ways that other people did not.' Fishman took his appreciation a step further in 2002 when Rhino asked if he would curate a mix CD of his favorite Zappa tracks. In the essay accompanying the compilation, Fishman wrote:

> The man put out so much great music in his lifetime that I could think of at least ten of his albums off the top of my head that I could just slap my name on and my job would be done. 'Jon Fishman of Phish presents the Frank

> Zappa albums *Hot Rats, Sheik Yerbouti, Roxy & Elsewhere, Apostrophe ('), Fillmore East – June '71, The Grand Wazoo, Joe's Garage, Freak Out!, Waka/Jawaka, One Size Fits All, Just Another Band From L.A.'* ... the list goes on for quite a while.

When Zappa did his final America tour in 1988, all four members of Phish went to the Burlington, Vermont, show on 12 March 1988. Afterwards, they performed a set of their own at their usual Saturday night gig at Nectar's. They did not perform 'Peaches En Regalia' that night, but they did perform their first-ever full run-through of their *Gamehendge* song cycle – but we are getting ahead of ourselves.

After concluding 'Peaches En Regalia', the band move immediately into David Byrne's Talking Heads classic, 'Cities'. A band that some might argue means more to Phish than Zappa, the Talking Heads are a definite touchstone for the group both before their formation and after they achieved some level of success. The band began performing 'Cities' in 1984 and would continue to do so throughout their career. For what I consider to be their definitive take, check out the version which opens their 1997 live classic *Slip Stitch And Pass*. After covering 'Cities' for over a decade, the band would debut eight more Talking Heads classics on 31 October 1996, when they covered *Remain In Light* in its entirety. But, again, we are getting ahead of ourselves.

Once the band conclude 'Cities', the audience are thanked, and you would be forgiven for thinking the night was over. But the band (upon the insistence of Fishman?) start up a blistering version of their bluegrass classic, 'My Sweet One'. Written by Fishman but sung by the other three, this *Lawn Boy* classic has been in heavy rotation since 1989. When performed as part of the *Festival 8* acoustic set (1 November 2009), 'My Sweet One' sounds like something the Beastie Boys could have included on their oft-bootlegged *Country Mike* EP. Of course, Phish followed their *Festival 8* 'My Sweet One' with a 'Let Me Lie' that is well outside the scope of what the Beasties can do, no disrespect intended. This Night 2 version of 'My Sweet One' concludes with an extended pause before the band hit their marks one last time and call it a night.

Night 3: Sunday 23 July ('Red Velvet')

While the parallels between Phish and the Grateful Dead are often overstated (usually boiling down to 'they jam' and 'the fans wear tie-dye'), there is one arena where the comparison lands: the concert experience. Both bands skip opening acts, structure shows around a two-set format and elevate the Sunday performance to near-mythic status. For Phish fans, 'Never miss a Sunday show' isn't just a meme but it is a guiding principle. That devotion was rewarded during the *Baker's Dozen* run, with the Sunday sets yielding four tracks for the official compilation: 'More', 'Twist', 'Waves' and 'Miss You'.

Set 1

'Sunday Morning' (Cale/Reed)

Predicting a Velvet Underground cover on 'Red Velvet' night would not have been difficult. Predicting the group would debut their cover of 'Sunday Morning' would have required a bit of cleverness. Predicting Fishman would make a dramatic entrance wearing both a cape and a mitre while tossing incense around the stage would require a level of prescience not known to modern Phandom. Once Page begins the opening melody of 'Sunday Morning', it becomes clear that the night is to begin with a Velvet Underground track.

Delivering the vocals in his characteristic style, Fishman opens the third night of the run in the funniest way imaginable. Written by Lou Reed for *The Velvet Underground & Nico*, 'Sunday Morning' is (per Velvet's guitarist Sterling Morrison) 'how you feel when you've been up all Saturday night and you're crawling home while people are going to church. The sun is up and you're like Dracula, hiding your eyes.' After semi-successfully wrapping up 'Sunday Morning' and its implied promise that (once again) anything was possible, Fishman replaces Trey on the drums and the night is underway.

'Axilla' (Anastasio/Herman/Marshall)

The energy level goes up 1,000% as the band rip into 'Axilla' (the Phish song most likely to do serious damage to my steering wheel as I drum along). Originally from 1992, 'Axilla' is another of Phish's unrecorded classics (although its 'sequel', 'Axilla (Part II)', was included on 1994's *Hoist*). The shortest song of the night, 'Axilla I' still packs the punch the band intended. For another great 'Axilla', as well as more of Phish's reverence for The Velvet Underground, check out *Live Phish Volume 16, 10.31.98*. The first set starts with a rocking 'Axila', and the second set features a front-to-back performance of the Velvet's last indisputable classic, *Loaded*. A classic version was played on 21 February 1993 (and included on the *Phish At The Roxy* box set) and an underrated version was played in Landover, Maryland on 28 December 1997.

'Your Pet Cat' (Anastasio/Fishman/Gordon/McConnell) **> 'Back On The Train'** (Anastasio/Marshall)

Next up is the band's second callback to *Chilling, Thrilling Sounds Of The Haunted House*. Night 1 featured the most-played track from their Halloween '14 'musical costume' ('Martian Monster') and now Night 3 brings the second-most-played track, 'Your Pet Cat'. Unlike 'Martian Monster', which ran past the 14-minute mark in its debut and continues to be occasionally jammed, 'Your Pet Cat' has always stayed close to its original parameters (approximately 5:37 the first time played and around 5:33 this time). One notable exception came during the opening night of the summer 2017 tour in Chicago. The 14 July version of 'Your Pet Cat' featured an unexpected interstitial moment – what might seem like a digression, but is actually a transitional jam that deepens the flow with 'Golden Age' – that added both depth and playfulness to the set. The full sequence – 'Your Pet Cat' > 'Golden Age' > 'Your Pet Cat' – unfolds over 15 inventive minutes and showcases the band's ability to thread thematic callbacks into a jam without losing momentum. It's more than just a detour; it's a musical sidebar with purpose. The version of 'Your Pet Cat' played on 23 July is improved upon by the 'Back On The Train' that immediately follows it. The band had been playing 'Back On The Train' for a year when the studio version dropped on *Farmhouse*. Although the initial versions were performed solo acoustic by Trey (including its debut performance at the Murat Theatre in Indianapolis, Indiana), 'Back On The Train' quickly entered the group's setlists and has been arriving at regular intervals ever since. An especially memorable version occurred in Japan and was included on *Live Phish Volume 4, 6.14.00*. Starting off the second set, 'Back On The Train' leads the group into a 'Twist' > 'Jam' > 'Walk Away' > 'Also Sprach Zarathustra' sequence that the band thought was special enough to be released with the first wave of *Live Phish* compilations 15 months later. For this Night 3 performance, the band work their way through the lyrics and then begin an underrated Type I jam that they ride well past the ten-minute mark. This 'Your Pet Cat' > 'Back On The Train' pairing is a high point of Night 3, and since it was so successful, the band could not be faulted for repeating it at subsequent shows. Alas, it has only been attempted once more (on 19 June 2019). Considering the diminished results, they knew that the first pairing was a 'lightning in a bottle' moment.

'How Many People Are You' (Gordon/Murawski)

The band then turn their attention to a Mike song they had been playing for over two years by that point, 'How Many People Are You'. Written by Mike and his then-current songwriting partner Scott Murawski, this one was originally performed during Mike's June 2015 tour and then by Phish in the July 2015 tour that followed. Despite being in regular rotation for nine months by the time the band entered the studio in March 2016, 'How Many People Are You' was not included on *Big Boat*. Mike would eventually record a version with Leo Kotke for their 2020 collaboration, *Noon*, but not including it on *Big Boat* still seems like a missed opportunity. I will not diminish any of the *Big Boat* songs by saying 'How Many People Are You' exceeds their quality, but it is their equal. An especially fun version occurs during the opening set of the underrated 29 August 2021 show. That night, the band spent half an hour running through a 'How Many People Are You' > 'Bathtub Gin' > 'Back On Train' sequence. Regardless, the playing on the 23 July version is tight during the composed sections and joyous during Trey's solo. This opening set has not even hit the halfway mark, and they have had yet another high point.

'Glide' (Anastasio/Fishman/Gordon/Marshall/McConnell)
After wrapping up Mike's first songwriting contribution of the night, the band give the audience a quick breather before delivering a song that demands little from them. In fact, all the band want the listener to know is that they are 'glad glad glad that you're alive'. Originally performed by the band on 27 September 1991 (but allegedly written about a decade earlier), 'Glide' was included on 1992's *A Picture Of Nectar* and, in terms of sequencing, provided a nice break between two of the album's more complex songs: 'The Landlady' and 'Tweezer'. Although the lyrical sentiment is positive (it's always nice to know people are 'glad that you're alive'), the track becomes ominous whenever the instruments don't quite rhythmically align. Luckily, the mood dissipates as the rhythms lock into place and the lyrics are sung and there is nothing to indicate the band are being lyrically insincere. Fans are encouraged to check out the especially fun 'Fee' > 'Split Open And Melt' > 'Glide' > 'Nellie Kane' > 'Divided Sky' sequence from 9 August 1993.

'Theme From The Bottom' (Anastasio/Fishman/Gordon/Marshall/McConnell) **> 'It's Ice'** (Anastasio/Marshall) **> 'More'** (Anastasio)
The opening set's second extended sequence begins with 'Theme From The Bottom' – a Phish original from *Billy Breathes*, not to be confused with the bass-thumping world of Florida DJ Techmaster P.E.B. Despite what the title might suggest, this 'Theme' is less about trunk-rattling subwoofers and more about introspection, tension and melodic layering – a slow-blooming piece that's become a fan-favorite for its emotional depth and atmospheric build. First performed in concert on 16 May 1995, 'Theme From The Bottom' was a barnburner from the very start. About a month after its debut, 'Theme From The Bottom' opened Phish's very first show at the legendary Deer Creek Music Center in Noblesville, Indiana. That 19 June performance set the tone for one of the most celebrated shows of one of their most celebrated tours. The crowd were electric, and fan sites are still filled with nostalgic reflections on both the music and the scene. Less than two weeks later, the Grateful Dead played their final Deer Creek show, an ending many saw coming. Phish's Deer Creek debut was filmed and later released as part of their

Dinner And A Movie series during the 2020 lockdown. The audio also lives on as an archival release in the LivePhish app. Although this Night 3 version is not as celebrated as their Deer Creek debut, or the version played a few weeks later during their Labor Day run at Dick's Sporting Goods Park, it is a solid version with a great Type I jam. Recently, the band have started returning to 'Theme From The Bottom' as an improvisational vehicle.

Once 'Theme From The Bottom' concludes, the band transition into the darkest (debatable) and longest (undeniable) version of 'It's Ice'. The band initiate this *Rift* classic, riding the track through until they are ready for some extended Type II jamming. They eventually work their way back to familiar ground before wrapping it up at around the 15-minute mark. Speaking of 'It's Ice', the band, collaborating with fellow Vermonters Ben & Jerry, previously developed the 'It's Ice ... Cream' with proceeds going to charity (much as they did with the ever-popular 'Phish Food' flavor). To bring it full circle and back to *The Baker's Dozen*, the band reteamed with Ben & Jerry for this run and developed another charitable concoction, 'Freezer Reprise' (which consisted of sweet cream ice cream, vanilla glaze, chocolate donut pieces, chocolate donut swirls and fish-shaped pieces of fudge). An excellent version of 'It's Ice' was performed by Phish at the Fox Theatre in St. Louis on 23 November 1994. The show-opening sequence – 'Wilson' > 'Sparkle' > 'Simple' > 'It's Ice' > 'Mind Left Body Jam' > 'It's Ice' > 'If I Could' – is both ambitious and fluid, and the second set's 'You Enjoy Myself' > 'The Vibration Of Life' > 'You Enjoy Myself' reinforces the night's exploratory spirit. It's a performance that proves the Grateful Dead weren't the only band capable of conjuring magic at the Fox. Much like the Dead's legendary early-1970s shows at the venue – check out the Dead's 20-disc box set, *Listen To The River: St. Louis '71 '72 '73* for numerous examples – Phish tapped into the room's energy and delivered a set that felt at once spontaneous and deliberate, playful and profound.

After 'It's Ice', the band head into another track from their then-most-recent album, *Big Boat*. 'More' is the song from *Big Boat* that most sounds like it could have come from their *Farmhouse* album over a decade-and-a-half earlier. Like 'Farmhouse' and 'Heavy Things', it utilizes direct, heartfelt lyrics instead of abstract wordplay. The refrain – 'There must be something more than this/There's got to be something more than this' – echoes the plainspoken folksiness of 'Farmhouse's 'I never ever saw the northern lights/I never really heard of cluster flies'. Like those *Farmhouse* tracks, 'More' leans into Trey's pop sensibilities by smoothing out his quirks and taking advantage of the polish that producer Bob Ezrin provided. The version of 'More' performed on Night 3 is only its seventh performance overall, and like the previous six versions, it was a set closer. With its Type I jams, opportunities for each member to shine and the sing-along lyrics that close it out, it almost seems custom-built for that slot, and I will never begrudge the band for returning to it. Since *The Baker's Dozen*, the band have experimented with alternate placements for 'More' (once, on 28 July 2023, they even opened a set with it). For the reasons previously mentioned, though, it works best as a closer or encore, and that is where it will (hopefully) spend most of its time.

Set 2

'AC/DC Bag' (Anastasio) **> 'Wolfman's Brother'** (Anastasio/Fishman/Gordon/Marshall/McConnell) **> 'Twist'** (Anastasio/Marshall) **> 'Waves'** (Anastasio/Herman/Marshall) **> 'Miss You'** (Anastasio)

After wrapping up the first set with a song from their latest project, the band begin the second set with a song from their earliest project: Trey's 1987 senior thesis at Goddard College, *The Man Who Stepped Into Yesterday* (*TMWSIY*).

'AC/DC Bag' is, in that *TMWSIY* context, the story of an accountant (Roger Palmer) who is executed for embezzlement. In Mr. Palmer's eyes, the crime is justified because his boss (Wilson) is the tyrannical leader of Gamehendge, and the funds are financing the anti-Wilson force's revolution. Outside the *TMWSIY* context, 'AC/DC Bag' is a kick-ass rock song that is fun to sing along with (especially when Trey wants to 'get down to the nitty-gritty'). The version performed on Night 3 is over twice as long as the version the band self-released through their online store, Dry Goods, but less than a third of the length of the longest versions. In its debut performance, on 1 April 1986, it was the third song in a set-opening run of 'Help On The Way' > 'Slipknot!' > 'AC/DC Bag'. The entire 18-minute section is fun, and it would be nice if the band revisited it someday (or at least found a way to work the Grateful Dead's 'Help On The Way' > 'Slipknot!' back into the rotation). Another great version is available on the archival release, *Live Phish 12.30.97*. Once again opening the second set, this version runs past the 25-minute mark before ending up (like it did in its original 1 April 1986 debut) in 'McGrupp And The Watchful Hosemasters'. Both the 'AC/DC Bag' and the 'McGrupp' performed on 30 December 1997 are highlights of an extremely strong show.

For Night 3, the band knew exactly how long to take the post-lyric jam on 'AC/DC Bag' before moving into 'Wolfman's Brother'. Included on *Hoist*, 'Wolfman's Brother' is one of their most celebrated songs. In August 2014, band biographer Richard Gehr contributed a listicle to *Spin* magazine entitled 'All 333 Phish Songs, Ranked' that ranked 'Wolfman's Brother' as their 13th-best Phish song. Although subsequent songs have made that list outdated, the sentiment Gehr attached to the song remains valid: "So with meaningless excitement/And smooth atonal sound/It's like a cross between a hurricane/And a ship that's run aground'. Phish never came closer to characterizing their peculiar allure than in these lines from a deeply funky account of Anastasio and Fishman's first encounter.' In an interview clip that occasionally airs on SiriusXM's Phish channel, co-writer Tom Marshall mentions the Dylan-esque nature of the lyrics and how adopting that writing style allowed the song to develop into something special. I do not disagree. The band performed a memorable version of 'Wolfman's Brother' on 1 August 2023 and (almost exactly 25 years earlier) performed another version that would be a high point on the *Star Lake 98* DVD.

After taking 'Wolfman's Brother' further than the audience anticipated, including into some deep Type II waters, the band transition into 'Twist'. Originally considered for 1998's *The Story Of The Ghost*, 'Twist' would not receive a studio release until the band revised it for 2000's *Farmhouse.* I already consider *The Story Of The Ghost* and *Farmhouse* to be perfect albums in their own right, but if there were ever a way to make perfection even better, it might be by moving 'Twist' from the latter to the former. It just feels like it would slot effortlessly into *Ghost*'s sonic palette. There is a darkness to 'Twist' that brings balance to the lighter moments on *Farmhouse*, but that same darkness would be right at home on *The Story Of The Ghost,* allowing the now-abridged *Farmhouse* to be even brighter. The version of 'Twist' included on *Live Phish Volume 5, 7.8.00* is admittedly workman-like, but that show is worth listening to for both the solid 'Wolfman's Brother' that appears in the first set and the 'Heavy Things' > 'Piper' > 'Rock And Roll', 'Tweezer' > 'Walk Away' sequence that immediately precedes 'Twist'. For a version that does hold its own, check out the 'Prince Caspian' > 'Twist' > 'Piper' section of the 5 July 1997 show in Como, Italy. It is a 25-minute representation of what Phish could deliver that summer. The 'Twist' performed on Night 3 of *The Baker's Dozen* provides Page with another opportunity to be the evening's 'most valuable player' before it becomes another four-way tie at the finish line.

The second set's extended sequence of opening songs continues with the third consecutive jam vehicle, 'Waves'. Another *Round Room* track that seems designed for Type II exploration, 'Waves' would be played at over a fourth of the 2.0 era shows and would provide numerous noteworthy jams during the 3.0 era. One of the all-time best is the version the band released on the second installment of their 'Live Phish On Long-Playing' vinyl series (*LP On LP*). That 'Waves', recorded during a technical rehearsal at the Bethel Woods Center for the Arts, was nearly 30 minutes long and was released (across two sides of vinyl) on *LP On LP 02 (Waves 5/26/2011)*. The Night 3 version is roughly a third of that length but, at its best, is just as blissful.

Moving out of 'Waves', the band begin the *Big Boat* ballad, 'Miss You'. Played with customary passion – and acting (like it usually does) as a cooldown track – 'Miss You' may not always be the song that the crowd are clamoring for, but it tends to be the one that quietly recalibrates the room. Those not fully on board with 'Miss You' should check out Phish's performance at the Ascend Amphitheater in Nashville, Tennessee, on 18 October 2016. The band bring the Grateful Dead's Bob Weir out on stage for almost an hour of music. Trading off between Phish and Grateful Dead tracks (plus Bob Dylan 's 'Quinn The Eskimo' as an encore), the band allow Weir to sing lead on 'Miss You'. To me, it illustrates how the song serves the same purpose as 'Looks Like Rain' did for the Grateful Dead – it allows the band a chance to lower the temperature in the room while also making the peaks feel that much higher. To paraphrase (the unfairly maligned) *Vanilla Sky*, 'without the bitter, the sweet ain't as sweet.'

'Boogie On Reggae Woman' (Wonder)
Once the band settle the audience down, they take a few moments for a quick breather before firing up Stevie Wonder's 'Boogie On Reggae Woman'. Originally included on Stevie's 1974 classic *Fulfillingness' First Finale* and first heard by most Phish fans on the six-disc *Hampton Comes Alive* box set in 1999, 'Boogie On Reggae Woman' gives Trey one last chance to sing lead for the night (and the band one last chance to bring the funk). Given their shared affection for optimism and groove, it is surprising that more Stevie Wonder songs are not covered by the band. 'Master Blaster (Jammin')' seems like a natural choice. Although 'I Wish' was covered during the 1980s, three other tracks from 1976's *Songs In The Key of Life* album – 'Sir Duke', 'Contusion' and 'Pastime Paradise' – seem like they would be in the band's wheelhouse.

Speaking of *Songs In The Key Of Life*, Zeth Lundy (in his excellent overview of that masterpiece) writes that:

> There's an unreasonable demand placed upon artists by their fair-weather audiences, one that insists that the temporary period of enlightenment be sustained for years, even decades. Such expectations are ridiculous for all-too-obvious reasons. Part of the appeal in witnessing a Rolling Stones concert in the 21st century seems to be the gamble of it, the dim hope that somehow a pack of elderly icons will miraculously deliver a performance that would rival one from 30 years earlier.

His argument is completely valid (and especially on point with the Rolling Stones being his example). With that being said, I'd like to think that Phish has moved on from having fair-weather fans and that everyone who listens to a 21st-century concert is going to get a moment that is comparable to a moment they loved in a 20th-century show.

'Wading In The Velvet Sea' (Anastasio/Marshall)
The final song of Night 3's set – 'Wading In The Velvet Sea' – is more than just a nod to the night's 'Velvet' theme. It is a moment of emotional stillness, a quiet exhale after the expansive stretch of music that precedes it. Written during the same fertile period as 'Twist', and ultimately making the cut for *The Story Of The Ghost*, 'Wading In The Velvet Sea' has always carried a gentle, bittersweet power, but the *Baker's Dozen* version adds new weight to its legacy.

Like all 3.0 performances of the song, this one resonates especially deeply for fans who remember its haunting appearance at the band's 'farewell' show on 15 August 2004. That night, following a nearly 20-minute 'Down With Disease', the band eased into 'Velvet Sea', only for Page to find himself overcome with emotion and unable to sing the opening verse. His repeated attempts, the band's quiet support and the audience's unwavering love transformed the moment into something unforgettable: a painful, beautiful reminder of the bond between band and audience.

At *The Baker's Dozen*, 'Wading In The Velvet Sea' carries that emotional history into Madison Square Garden, this time with Page's voice clear and steady. It is a subtle triumph, a performance that doesn't need to be flashy to be deeply felt. The song's simple, aching beauty is the perfect way to close the set and a reminder that in Phish's vast catalog, some of the quietest songs still speak the loudest.

Both 'Wading' and 'Twist' – and many other fan-favorites from this era – can be found in early, raw forms on Trey and Tom Marshall's absolutely essential 2000 release, *Trampled By Lambs And Pecked By The Dove*. A collection of rough drafts and demos from the late 1990s songwriting surge that would fuel *The Story Of The Ghost*, *Farmhouse* and countless live staples, the album is a look behind the curtain. With 25 sketches that would have been enough to build most artists' entire careers, it is an album that captures the strange, spontaneous alchemy that continues to define Phish's music to this day.

Encore

'Sweet Jane' (Reed)

The smart money would have been for Phish to wrap up 'Velvet' night with the familiar (and reliable) cover of the Velvet Underground's 'Rock & Roll'. But, true to form, the band take a less obvious route and end the set with another *Loaded* track: 'Sweet Jane'. Though most closely associated with their 1998 Halloween 'musical costume', 'Sweet Jane' actually made its Phish debut a few months earlier at the Merriweather Post Pavilion. This *Baker's Dozen* performance marked just the fourth time they'd played it. The band's affection for 'Sweet Jane' is clear in the way they deliver it here – faithful, warm, and full of heart – and the crowd's reaction reflects that same appreciation. As of now, they've performed 'Sweet Jane' just five times, making each appearance feel like a special treat.

Night 4: Tuesday 25 July ('Jam-Filled')

After having their first night off, a well-rested Phish returned to fulfill the promise of a 'Jam-Filled' show. By now, the application of each night's theme was clear: the theme would not be its sole component, but it would be sprinkled throughout the night. For the 'Jam Filled' sets, options included the band playing extended versions of traditionally shorter songs, the band playing multiple songs that they had historically jammed out and the band playing a seamless sequence of songs for the duration of a set. The band opted to do all three.

Set 1

'Sample In A Jar' (Anastasio/Marshall)

The band start the night off with a powerful performance of their *Hoist* classic, 'Sample In A Jar'. For a song that had originally debuted almost 25 years earlier, 'Sample In A Jar' never received a proper workout until Night 4. Clocking in at over ten minutes (almost double the typical five-to-six-minute length), 'Sample In A Jar' went so far past its comfort zone that, around the eight-minute mark, it *almost* sounds like the band are going to lose control. But before that blasphemous thought can be fully formed, they snap back into focus and Trey starts the chorus anew, 'I wheeled around because I didn't hear what you had said...'

In his essay, 'Phish: The Undefeated Season', for *Relix*, Benjy Eisen wrote:

> As of this writing, Phish have officially performed 'Sample In A Jar' live exactly 287 times. And all of them are – nearly – identical. It's a song, not a vehicle. It's another 'Rift', another 'Cavern'. There's an altered inflection here; there's a spontaneous fill there. It's a great song that, when placed right, fulfills a certain function for setlist construction – but it is nobody's highlight of the night. And yet, during *The Baker's Dozen*, when they opened with it on 'Jam Filled' night, it took the band all but two and a half minutes before they went off script. And the crowd went wild. It is worth noting that the crowd went wild *before* the jam got started. The crowd went wild at the mere indication that there would, indeed, be a jam. Trey plays a note that is significantly different to whatever has come before, stating his intention, and it seems everyone in the audience notices it instantaneously. That was us and the band, looking up at the sky, being reminded of endless possibilities. LOOK UP!! LOOK UP!! It only took them 287 times to find the 'Sample In A Jam'. But they found it.

Since *The Baker's Dozen*, Phish have jammed out 'Sample In A Jar' a few more times. For about a year, the 22 July 2022 version had the record for being the longest played. The band took the stage at Bethel Woods Center for the Arts and delivered a 'Golgi Apparatus' > 'Sample In A Jar' that needs to be heard to be believed. Although it lost that title when the band were back at MSG on 1

August 2023, it is still worth mentioning when discussing the best opening one-two punch of the 3.0 era.

'Lawn Boy' (Anastasio/Marshall) **> 'My Friend, My Friend'** (Anastasio/Marshall) **> 'Stash'** (Anastasio/Marshall)

After taking a moment to bask in the (well-deserved) applause, the band begin their faux-lounge classic, 'Lawn Boy'. To set a baseline, the band played 'Lawn Boy' seven times in 2016, and its average length was 3:27 (in fact, no single version ever crossed the four-minute mark, and the shortest version barely crossed the three-minute mark). The version played on 'Jam Filled' night clocked in at 29:59. Not to be hyperbolic, but that is practically a 1,000% increase. Comparing previous versions of 'Lawn Boy' to this version is like comparing Hemingway's shortest story with Tolstoy's longest novel. Putting the numbers aside, 'Lawn Boy' is typically played in a manner faithful to its original recording. However, if you think that this night's version is a chance for Page to process his inner Tormé and for the audience to catch their breath, think again. After starting the song off in its traditional fashion, the band take it to outer space on a keytar-fueled rocket. The entire performance is available on their YouTube page and it is highly recommended (especially if keytars are your thing). It is remarkable whenever a band can drive a three-minute song past the 30-minute mark and never once take a side quest into tedium. If suggestions are ever sought for a Live *Phish On Long Play* release, this 'Lawn Boy' is likely to be in contention.

Once they bring 'Lawn Boy' back to earth, the band transition into 'My Friend, My Friend'. Unlike 'Sample In A Jar' and 'Lawn Boy', this *Rift* track had been previously jammed, but never to such an extent. 'My Friend, My Friend' is another of those 'best of both worlds' Phish songs. It has structure and a built-in groove, as well as opportunities for the band to extend the more chaotic moments as far as they feel that night's audience needs to go. Apparently, the Night 4 audience needed to go further than previous audiences because this version of that 1992 classic would hold the record for the longest version for almost six years (until 14 July 2023). One of the all-time great versions occurred at Deer Creek on 25 July 1999. Early in the first set, the band found themselves taking 'My Friend, My Friend' to the 'Whipping Post' (by way of 'My Left Toe') for the first time in over 200 shows. Whenever the band play this Allman Brothers classic, the show is worth checking out. More recently, during the second night of the band's Mondegreen Festival in 2024, a great version of 'My Friend, My Friend' started off the second set. This version hit all the usual points, plus found a way to tease Led Zeppelin's 'Moby Dick'.

After getting through 'My Friend, My Friend', the band move into 'Stash'. Although it was originally released on 1992's *A Picture Of Nectar*, 'Stash' was first heard by a substantial percentage on 1995's *A Live One*. As the second song (after the typically 'brief' (4:08) 'Bouncing Around The Room'), the

12-and-a-half minute 'Stash' was the first Phish jam many phans heard ... in fact, it is likely the first ever jam many of them ever heard. Considering it is the track that first introduced a sizable percentage of listeners to Phish's talents, it went unremarked at the time. Robert Christgau, *Rolling Stone* and Stephen Thomas Erlewine all reviewed *A Live One* (their scores were C-, three stars and five stars, respectively), but none of the three felt 'Stash' was a song worth mentioning. As a song that has been played approximately 450 times (admittedly not as often as it used to be), it's a cornerstone of their discography and a great representation of what they were up to (musically) in the early-to-mid-1990s. With its jazz-inspired chord progression and shifting time signatures, 'Stash' is Phish at their most Zappa-esque. In fact, if stripped of its lyrics and placed on an unmarked mixtape, 'Stash' could be passed off as a *Waka/Jawaka*-era outtake. Phans looking to hear more should just pick any 'Stash' from either 1994 or 1995 ... there is not a bad version in the bunch.

'Bathtub Gin' (Anastasio/Goodman)
'Stash' concludes just after the opening set passes the one-hour mark. The band then fire up 'Bathtub Gin' (and Trey finally delivers the 'huh' that was missing from the opening verse of 'Sweet Jane' two nights earlier). Another track from *Lawn Boy*, and another whose composed sections are indebted to songwriters several generations prior, 'Bathtub Gin' is played with an energy more associated with the 29 July 1998 version that smuggled itself in as filler on *Live Phish Volume 17, 7.15.98*. The band's 29 December 1995 show in Worcester, Massachusetts, featured a fantastic 'Bathtub Gin' that included a nine-minute detour through The Who's *Quadrophenia* classic, 'The Real Me'. 'Bathtub Gin', like its Night 4 predecessor 'Stash', features a bit of audience participation. In the former, the audience insert rhythmic handclaps (in lieu of Fishman's previously provided drum fills), and in the latter, the audience take over the vocal duties from Trey to announce, 'We love to take a bath'. The crowd-pleasing 'Bathtub Gin' also acts as the closing number of the opening set. The band leave the stage, having already delivered five spot-on performances.

Set 2

'Fuego' (Anastasio/Fishman/Gordon/McConnell) **> 'Thread'** (Anastasio/Marshall) **> 'Crosseyed And Painless'** (Byrne/Eno/Frantz/Harrison/Weymouth) **> 'Makisupa Policeman'** (Anastasio/Marshall) **> 'End Of Session'** (Anastasio/Fishman/Gordon/Marshall/McConnell) **> 'Tuesday'** (Anastasio/O'Brien) **> 'Cavern'** (Anastasio/Herman/Marshall)
The second set of their 'Jam Filled' show is one long 80-minute sequence of songs. Starting off with *Fuego*'s title track, which GQ described as 'a madcap prog shape-shifter that's a perfectly silly showcase for their childlike curiosity and endless musical aplomb', and then moving into the recently debuted

'Thread', the opening 26-plus-minutes demonstrate the band's mastery of form and groove but also of formless, ambient textures not typically associated with the bands that sell out Madison Square Garden. 'Fuego' especially runs the gamut between structure and seemingly ad hoc playing. Although the groove-based moments will always be my favorites (I need a rhythm to latch on to at all times), the sounds generated by the four of them during 'Fuego' are grounded enough that even I can stay tethered to them. Although a strong song from its Halloween 2013 debut, 'Fuego' took things to the next level in 2016. The 2 July performance in Saratoga Springs, New York, is a notable example of what the band were doing with the song around that time. Post-*The Baker's Dozen*, the 30 July 2022 version is worth hearing (especially since it is one of only a dozen or so instances where the band take a song into a performance of 'Sigma Oasis').

Once the band work their way out of the 'Fuego', it's time for 'Thread'. Channeling a muscular midpoint between *Foxtrot*-era Genesis and *Drama*-era Yes, 'Thread' would only make two more appearances before it was released in studio form on 2020's *Sigma Oasis,* and after that album's release, it only made a few more appearances before being (seemingly) shelved. It is a shame because it is a fantastic song and one that deserves more chances to develop. Fortunately, the band did dust off 'Thread' during their Summer 2024 tour. As part of a first set on 21 July that also included an amazing 'Bathtub Gin' and the first 'Connection' in almost five years, 'Thread' held its own.

The audience response to 'Thread's conclusion is muted, but they make themselves heard when the band rip into Talking Heads' 'Crosseyed And Painless'. With its high success rate, this groove-based bop always gets people moving, and as online reviewer 'Petestick' wrote on phish.net, 'A Talking Heads song in NYC just always feels perfect, especially that one.' Originally played during their Halloween 1996 *Remain In Light* 'musical costume', 'Crosseyed And Painless' received numerous opportunities to shine in the subsequent 20+ years. Although fan-favorite performances, including a not-to-be-missed version from North Charleston, South Carolina, on 16 October 2010, tend to hover around the 15-minute mark, a handful of 'Crosseyed And Painless' jams have crossed the 20-minute mark – tonight's version exceeds 33 minutes. The fact that a 33-minute 'Crosseyed And Painless' was not the unanimous choice, being a split decision between that and a mammoth 'Lawn Boy', is illustrative of just how unpredictable this band can be. After working through 'Crosseyed And Painless' and exploring all the Type I and Type II jams the audience's tailfeathers could handle, the band slink into their reggae homage, 'Makisupa Policeman'.

Sounding like an authentic, old-school reggae song (that might have been learned via a Madness cover), 'Makisupa Policeman' is a Phish original that has been in their setlists since their earliest days. In fact, one of my favorite versions is from the band's 29 August 1987 show at The Ranch in South Burlington, Vermont. The way the band can play 'Makisupa Policeman' one moment and the completely disparate 'Big Black Furry Creature From Mars' the next is always impressive. But the first version I ever heard was from a decade later. The band's Binghamton, New York, show features a traditional 'Makisupa Policeman' paired with a great Type I 'Split Open And Melt'. I was able to hear this show when the band released it as *Live Phish Volume 1, 12.14.95*. Musically, not much improvisation happens in this *Baker's Dozen* version; the differences lie in the lyrics. In the Night 4 version, Trey sticks with the standard chorus whenever it comes around, but during the verses, he improvises lines about waking up, stumbling onto the stage and only showing up to listen to Page. Obviously, a skanky keyboard part follows. After running through the chorus once again, Trey performs a bit of Bob Marley's 1977 single 'Jamming' and sings about how it is the music he likes (especially when jammed by Mike), which then leads into Mike's bass solo. The band do not end 'Makisupa Policeman', but instead, they subtly reshape the melody to get themselves into their almost 20-year-old, never-before-played 'End Of Session'.

Originally released as the concluding track on *The Story Of The Ghost*, 'End Of Session' is a subtle gem that many listeners initially overlooked. Experienced in the live setting, the song's delicate melody and introspective lyrics evoke a clear homage to the gentler, more exploratory passages found in the Grateful Dead's "Dark Star," especially during their performances in the spring of 1969. The band have only returned to 'End Of Session' once more after *The Baker's Dozen*. On 20 October 2021, the band inserted it near the end of a 20-minute, set-closing 'Split Open And Melt' > 'End Of Session' > 'Split Open And Melt' sequence.

After making their way through 'End Of Session', Phish move on to their second-ever performance of Trey's oft-played solo tune 'Tuesday'. Like the debut performance in Dayton exactly one week earlier, this Tuesday performance of 'Tuesday' is firing on all cylinders. A workhouse within Trey's solo band shows, 'Tuesday' has (so far) only made these two appearances with the Phish format. Originally recorded and released in 2005 for Trey's solo album, *Shine*, 'Tuesday' sounds like it could have been written a decade earlier by Jeff Tweedy for one of those first two Wilco albums. *Shine* was Trey's debut album with Columbia Records (and the only studio album he released with that historic label). Working with Bruce Springsteen's then-producer Brendan O'Brien (in the window between *The Rising* and *Devils & Dust*), Trey launched his post-2.0 solo career with one of his strongest solo albums. *Rolling Stone*'s three-star review observes that the album 'rocks efficiently' and is complimentary towards the 'hooky dance rock of 'Tuesday'.'

After that 'Crosseyed And Painless', the band restrain themselves for a few songs in order to have plenty of gas in the tank for both 'Tuesday' and the set-closing 'Cavern'. Another *Picture Of Nectar* song and a workhorse since its debut in 1990, 'Cavern' is always a reliable number to end a night on. With its unabashed rawk and nonsensical lyrics that demand to be sung along with,

'Cavern' is the Phish equivalent to a Guided By Voices song (although played for the duration of half a dozen of Robert Pollard's mini-masterpieces). The band's 21 July 1991 concert at Arrowhead Ranch in Parksville, New York, features a great introductory 'Cavern' that leads into an equally great 'Divided Sky'. During this period, 'Cavern' and 'Divided Sky' would often be paired together, but they tended to flip positions in the sequence. Starting later in 1991, 'Divided Sky' would almost exclusively appear before 'Cavern'. Personally, I prefer 'Cavern' > 'Divided Sky', but there are too many excellent examples of 'Divided Sky' > 'Cavern' to mount a successful argument.

Encore

'Julius' (Anastasio/Marshall) **> 'Lawn Boy'** (Anastasio/Marshall)
After having spent the evening cramming a week's worth of highlights into just over two-and-a-half hours, including eight songs they had been playing since the 1980s/1990s, the band begin their encore on 'Julius'. Played heavily during the mid-to-late-1990s, 'Julius' to this day still makes a couple of appearances each year. The Patterson, New York, performance on 13 July 1994 and the Lakewood Amphitheatre show on 23 July 1997 are both worth checking out. The band give this Night 4 version of the *Hoist* classic all they have in the form of some excellent Type I jamming and one last surprise. Once the final notes are played out, and the band do some end-of-night vamping, they segway once again into 'Lawn Boy' and its concluding lyrics. Delivered with a cheesiness that only a Vermonter could offer, 'Lawn Boy' perfectly ends a splendid night.

Night 5: Wednesday 26 July ('Powdered')

In a 'state of the union' type piece summarizing the first five nights of *The Baker's Dozen* for *Rolling Stone*, Jesse Jarnow wrote: 'Traditional powdered donuts on night five brought a bit of everything: big jams, but also a sense that some music had been left on the table.'

Set 1

'White Winter Hymnal' (Pecknold)

For the opening number of Night 5, Phish return to their Night 2 playbook and debut an a cappella cover. Unlike 'Strawberry Fields Forever', the Fleet Foxes' 'White Winter Hymnal' originated as a vocal showcase. Since that initial version was already scaled back, musically, Phish's version did not have to work too hard to peel back the instrumentation that songwriter Robin Pecknold had originally applied. When asked about the cover on Instagram, the Grammy-nominated Mr. Pecknold responded with 'cool' and 'So wild!' The night following Phish's version, Fleet Foxes returned the favor by playing a bit of 'Bouncing Around The Room' (before reclaiming 'White Winter Hymnal' as their own). In what should be the final word on Phish's version of 'White Winter Hymnal', Steven Hyden wrote in his *Baker's Dozen* summary for *Uproxx*: 'I realize that the prospect of listening to Phish do an a cappella cover of Fleet Foxes' 'White Winter Hymnal' or a mind-blowing 24-minute version of the 1990s chestnut 'Chalk Dust Torture' might seem like actual torture to many. But take Phish out of the equation: don't you wish your favorite artist behaved this way?'

'Cars Trucks Buses' (McConnell)

After demonstrating their vocal prowess, the band move on to Page's instrumental classic, 'Cars Trucks Buses'. Included on *Billy Breathes*, this relatively short (6:11 on the night under discussion) number allows the band (and the audience) to warm up a bit. Although not included on too many of the band's physical releases, great versions of 'Cars Trucks Buses' occur frequently. Concert-opening versions occurred on 18 June 2011, 2 September 2012 and 29 October 2013 (North Carolina, Colorado and Pennsylvania, respectively).

'My Soul' (Chenier)

The band follow the jazzy 'Cars Trucks Buses' with 'My Soul' (which, ironically, has even more drive than 'Cars Trucks Buses'). Originally performed by Phish in 1997 and performed as the opening song exactly one week earlier in Pittsburgh, 'My Soul' was written and recorded by Clifton Chenier and was included on his essential 1993 compilation, *Zydeco Dynamite*. Since Phish's rendition leans heavily into blues-rock territory – with gritty guitar riffs, a driving groove and tonal flavors more reminiscent of ZZ Top than traditional zydeco – it is possible the band learned the song through Texas blues legend Johnny Winter's 1984 Alligator Records debut, *Guitar Slinger*. Phish included an extra tight version of 'My Soul' on their under-rated (only two-and-a-half stars by *AllMusic*) 2001 archival release, *Live Phish Volume 5, 7.8.00*.

'Roses Are Free' (Freeman/Melchiondo) **> 'The Very Long Fuse'** (Anastasio/Fishman/Gordon/McConnell)

There is excitement within the audience when the band begin their version of Ween's 'Roses Are Free'. Like Clifton Chenier, Ween are a band that few other bands cover. In fact, Phish are likely the only band that routinely cover songs from both. 'Roses Are Free' was one of the many cover songs first heard by Phish's record-buying phans on 1999's *Hampton Comes Alive*. In fact, almost half of the songs on that six-disc set (20 of 44) had not previously been released on a Phish album. Phish initially covered Ween's Prince-indebted track on 11 December 1997. Footage of the band learning the song was included in Todd Haynes' 2000 documentary *Bittersweet Motel*. Although not initially a concert staple for Ween, they included it in more of their sets because of its Phish-powered popularity. In fact, in his book on Ween's *Chocolate And Cheese*, writer Hank Shteamer states that Phish's cover of 'Roses Are Free' led to 'an influx of jam-band fans at shows, a development that coincided with Ween coming into their own as an improvisational force onstage.'

No disrespect to *Hampton Comes Alive*, the definitive archival release of Phish's version of 'Roses Are Free' was included on the digital-only *Island Tour* collection. On the second night of this spring 1998 tour, Phish closed the opening set with 'My Soul' and then delivered an epic second set that was initiated by 'Roses Are Free'. The band spent just over an hour working their way through 'Roses Are Free' > 'Piper' > 'Loving Cup' > 'Run Like An Antelope'. Although all four songs make excellent appearances in *The Baker's Dozen*, these versions played on 3 April 1998 are hard to top.

For the *Baker's Dozen*, the band take the outro of 'Roses Are Free' into the sampled vocals that light 'The Very Long Fuse'. Another Halloween 2014 number from *Chilling, Thrilling Sounds Of The Haunted House*, 'The Very Long Fuse' has a groove that could potentially lead to some interesting places. In fact, Phish.net contributor 'sausagemahoney' provides an incredibly apt description of that groove, writing that it's a 'half-rolling, half-bouncing jazz fusion groove that sounds like the Allman Brothers doing Weather Report and is tailor-made for the treadmill; the slightly ominous melodic theme evokes a 1970s network sitcom that was too oddball to make it big.' Like the imaginary sitcom referenced by 'sausagemahoney', 'The Very Long Fuse' was canceled too soon; it is a shame the band (seemingly) retired it after Night 5.

'Gumbo' (Anastasio/Fishman)

Once the dust settles from the 'The Very Long Fuse's song-closing explosion, the band play 'Gumbo'. This sixth song of the night is the first to feature original vocals by the band (the preceding five songs consisted of an original instrumental and four covers). 'Gumbo' is, like 'Stash', another song introduced to a generation of Phish vans via *A Live One*. In its earlier performances, 'Gumbo' was likely to be extended (and even more likely to be extended if the band had a horn section sitting in with them). The version on Night 5 is, like most 3.0 versions, relatively contained – but that doesn't make it any less potent. Page's playing on the back half of this version is not hailed often enough. Although he is occasionally referred to as the 'Chairman of the Boards', performances like this prove it's not just an honorific. Another notable version was performed at an all-around excellent Deer Creek show on 22 July 2003. Beyond 'Gumbo', the night featured excellent versions of 'Split Open And Melt' and 'Walls Of The Cave'. Although not performed adjacent to one another, those three songs could be sequenced together in an hour-long sampler of what Phish were bringing in 2003.

'Yarmouth Road' (Gordon/Murawski)
Mike then leads the band down 'Yarmouth Road' from one of his then-recent(ish) solo albums, *Overstep*. With a reggae drive, story-song lyrics and quirky vocal delivery, 'Yarmouth Road' is a fun contribution to the Phish oeuvre. Alas, the majority of the band's performances were in the rearview mirror when the song was played at *The Baker's Dozen*. Performed over two dozen times before Night 5 and only a handful of times since, 'Yarmouth Road' might have to be content with making appearances during Mike's fun solo shows (such as the encore performance on 28 January 2020 and the opening number of the second set on 27 June 2023).

'Pebbles And Marbles' (Anastasio/Marshall)
As the opening track on 2002's *Round Room*, 'Pebbles And Marbles' helped set that album's tone and almost acted as a representative for what would follow. The version the band bust out on Night 5 (after an absence of 106 shows) could also act as a representative for this opening set. It is melodic when it needs to be, aggressive in places and indicative of how the band could shelve a song for almost three years and then pick it up and play it again as if it were their latest single. Although it is now generally placed mid-set, I think 'Pebbles And Marbles' works well as a closer. For the three appearances in February 2003 (16 February in Las Vegas, 20 February in Rosemont and 25 February in Philadelphia), the band closed a set with 'Pebbles And Marbles'. All three versions are worth hearing, but the appearance on 20 February in Illinois is the best of that bunch.

'Farmhouse' (Anastasio/Marshall)
After *Round Room*'s opening track, the band play the opening track to its predecessor, 2000's *Farmhouse*. Concluding with Trey's best playing of the night (so far), this 'Farmhouse' is notable for being one of the last versions to

keep its 'No Woman No Cry' influences on the down low. Although the lyrics have always informed the listener that things will 'be alright', future versions would also include musical teases to Bob Marley's classic song. Robert Christgau closed his B- review of the *Farmhouse* album by quoting the title track's lyrics and comparing them unfavorably with lyrics from the Grateful Dead's 'St. Stephen': "Each betrayal begins with trust/Every man returns to dust'. 'One man gathers what another man spills' was taken.' It is a snarky, undeserved comment, but it's funny. Although the band almost always deliver an excellent 'Farmhouse' (7 November 1998, 2 December 1999, 23 June 2000, and most (in)famously, 31 August 2012), the solo acoustic versions that Trey delivers are also worth checking out. Both his 19 May 1999 and 24 April 2018 concerts are worth listening to in their entirety, in part because of 'Farmhouse' and its placement in the show. For the best of both worlds, the phenomenal 'Farmhouse' the band played at the Las Vegas Sphere on 18 April 2024 features Trey starting and ending the song on an acoustic guitar.

'Tube' (Anastasio/Fishman)

The opening set's tenth (and final) song is the expertly delivered 'Tube'. All four members turn its 14-and-a-half minutes into a promise for what the second set holds. After having delivered more songs during the first set than any prior night of the run, 'Tube's extended jam nicely foreshadows the second set's musical adventures.

Originally performed by the band back in the 1990s and never included on a studio album, 'Tube' works well as an opener, a mid-set song or a closer. A great opening version is available on the *Alpine Valley* DVD, a great mid-set version is available on 7 December 1997's *Live Phish* archival release and a great closing version is available on 31 December 2003 (which, admittedly, was made special as a set-closer because it actually started off as a set-opener the previous night). 'Tube', along with 'First Tube' and 'Last Tube', forms the 'Tube Trilogy'. Although the band have never performed the songs back-to-back, Trey did perform a first set 'Tube', a second set 'Last Tube' and an encore of 'First Tube' on 20 May 2022 in Salt Lake City, Utah. The whole show is enjoyable, but it is the inclusion of all three 'Tube'-related songs that makes it memorable.

Set 2

'Carini' (Anastasio/Fishman/Gordon/McConnell) **> 'Mr. Completely'** (Anastasio) **> '1999'** (Nelson) **> 'Steam'** (Anastasio/Marshall) **> 'No Quarter'** (Jones/Page/Plant)

The second set of the night starts off with a ferocious 'Carini'. This earth-shaker's debut (17 February 1997) was later immortalized on 2015's *Amsterdam* box set. Originally sandwiched between 'Down With Disease' and 'Taste' as part of a larger 70+ minute jam, 'Carini' wasted no time in making its presence known to Phans. Exceptional versions exist throughout its existence, but versions from 2013 (18 October and 29 December, for example) and 2018 (30 July and 28 August, for example) are freakishly strong. This Night 5 version starts off strong and then when the Type I riffing has run its course, a Type II jam takes the band into their third-ever performance of a song Trey had been performing on his own since 2001.

'Mr. Completely' was originally included on Trey's *McCartney*-esque 1998 album *One Man's Trash* and was later reworked for his self-titled 2002 album (which is the album that has been a consistent cornerstone for the Trey Anastasio Band's setlists ever since). In a joint concert with Carlos Santana on 31 May 2003, the Trey Anastasio Band had Carlos sit in for the second set and their opening collaboration on 'Mr. Completely' is a must-hear. With the first half sounding like all seven songs from side two of *Revolver* played at once, and the back half sounding like a lost performance from Santana's classic lineup, this 'Mr. Completely' is a trip. Stick around past that and besides a 'John The Revelator' that foreshadows some of Trey's later shows with Derek Trucks, you'll get the Beastie Boys' 'Root Down' performed by a band three times larger. Phish debuted their version of 'Mr. Completely' on 15 July 2003, and they proceeded to spend the next 53 minutes moving in and out of it. This sequence of 'Mr. Completely' > 'Low Rider' > 'Big Black Furry Creature From Mars' > 'Buried Alive' > 'Big Black Furry Creature From Mars' > 'Ha Ha Ha' > 'Big Black Furry Creature From Mars' > 'Mr. Completely' > 'Spread It 'Round' would be a highlight of the *Live Phish 07.15.03* CD but, unfortunately, that is where it would remain. The band seemingly retired 'Mr. Completely' after that performance, but two days before starting *The Baker's Dozen* (and a week before this show), Phish brought back 'Mr. Completely' (but not, unfortunately, the unfairly forgotten 'Spread It 'Round'). Although this 21-minute 2017 performance in Pennsylvania is shorter than the Utah performance from 2003, it is still a monster of a song and the perfect vehicle between the Zeppelin-esque 'Carini' and the band's version of Prince's '1999'.

As any third-rate wedding DJ can tell you, getting people to dance to '1999' is not difficult. But even though the song has already done the heavy lifting, the band still put in the effort, and they work for every ounce of sweat they get out of the crowd. In fact, the jam out of '1999' is so melodic and full of inspired playing by all four members that the Live Phish app considers it its own song (titled 'MSG Jam' in the songwriting credits). The band take their improvised composition past the nine-minute mark before they cool things down for about 30 seconds and move straight into 'Steam'.

Originally debuting in the summer of 2011 but not being released in a studio form until 2020, 'Steam' is a Phish original that allows them to utilize sound effects that would not be out of place on a *Chilling, Thrilling Sounds Of The Haunted House* track. By the time 'Steam' starts up, the band have been playing continuously for around 45 minutes and 'Steam' gives no indication that they are stopping anytime soon. In fact, at around the six-and-a-half-minute mark, they start noodling on the Rolling Stones' *Sticky Fingers* classic 'Can't You Hear Me Knocking', and they take that riff further in 50 seconds than Keef has in 50 years. When the band returned to Madison Square Garden for their New Year's Run, they would perform an equally strong 'Steam' on 30 December. This version was part of an hour-long sequence of 'Down With Disease' > 'Steam' > 'Light' > 'Farmhouse'; that initial 42-minute section of 'Down With Disease' > 'Steam' was a highlight of that run. For *The Baker's Dozen*, the band eventually work their way back to 'Steam' and then onto another bit of early-1970s British rock: Led Zeppelin's 'No Quarter'.

The band started playing this *Houses Of The Holy* classic on 1 June 2011, three days before they debuted 'Steam'. Although it is played with roughly a third of the frequency of 'Steam', it is always a solid offering and yet another chance for Page to prove he's the 'most valuable player' of whatever night they're playing it. Examples of when he used this song to take home the title would include 17 August 2011, 28 October 2018 and 14 August 2021.

'Character Zero' (Anastasio/Marshall)

After a relatively short 'No Quarter', the band take their first pause of the set before starting up one of their longer versions of the *Billy Breathes* classic, 'Character Zero'. Debuting as a one-off during the summer of 1996 before gaining traction during the subsequent fall tour, it took 'Character Zero' until the fall of 1997 to come into its own. Fantastic versions abound, but oddly, the band have commercially released comparatively subdued versions. Both the encore performance included on *Live Phish Volume 11, 11.17.97* and the first set-closing version from 23 November 1997 that was included on the *Hampton/Winston-Salem '97* box set suffer when compared to other versions played around the same time. Nobody could consider *The Baker's Dozen* version subdued, though. All four band members give 100% of themselves to this version. Their playing on 'Character Zero' sounds like they have still got a full tank of gas and can go for another three hours. Alas, after Trey and Mike are through with the friendliest duel imaginable, the band come together to ensure 'Character Zero' is the best possible ending to one of their best sets ever.

Encore

'Powderfinger' (Young)

The band could have skipped their customary encore and nobody would be able to say they were cheated. But the band love their phans too much to do that to them, so they come back out and deliver one of the best encores of *The Baker's Dozen*. 'Powderfinger' is both a debut for the band and the first of two Neil Young songs they will play during *The Baker's Dozen*. First commercially released by Neil in 1979 (on *Rust Never Sleeps*), 'Powderfinger' is one of his most celebrated songs. It is surprising the band had not previously played it. Of course, they had never before had a night devoted to 'Powdered' songs.

In a mid-run recap for *Rolling Stone*, Jesse Jarnow (discussing the conclusion of the first five nights) wrote, 'The band have yet to repeat a single song. The non-formula strikes a balance between well-laid surprises, long passages of relaxed, conversational interplay and the goofball, groove-oriented exuberance that makes Phish repugnant to civilians and beloved to Phishheads.' It is both accurate of what had already transpired and prescient about what was still to come.

Night 6: Friday 28 July ('Double Chocolate')

The band's second Friday night show had a 'Double Chocolate' theme – and the band used every opportunity to have some fun with it.

Set 1

'Chocolate Rain' (Bahner)
Much like they did on Night 1 (with 'Shake Your Coconuts'), Phish open with a cover that never completely devolves into novelty (although I would not mount too strong of an argument if your opinion differed). Tay Zonday's 'Chocolate Rain' is the opening number for Night 6, and even though it has been a decade since the song originally went viral, the audience are on board as soon as they realize what is going down. Starting off with a dramatic lead-in from Page and then him launching the backing track via his MIDI keyboard, Phish deliver an a cappella (and bass-heavy) performance of 'Chocolate Rain'. There's a great fan-shot video of the performance on YouTube. If you seek it out, don't miss their perfectly timed Tay Zonday-indebted 'move away from the mic to breathe in' choreography and the shit-eating grins that make it even more delightful.

'Ass Handed' (Fishman)
The band do not pivot too hard with their second song: Fishman's recently adopted mantra, 'Ass Handed'. With a structure that would not be out of place on The Beatles' self-titled 'White Album', 'Ass Handed' features just two lines (a la 'Why Don't We Do It In The Road') and a gnarly guitar solo (a la 'Helter Skelter'). About a year earlier, on 23 July 2016, the band actually did 'Ass Handed' twice during the opening set. Although those earlier performances might better match Night 6's 'Double Chocolate' theme, this performance demonstrates Fishman's quiddity and allows the band to continue to ease into the night.

'Free' (Anastasio/Marshall)
After a two-song preamble, the band rips into their top-ten hit from 1996, 'Free'. Peaking at number seven on *Billboard*'s Adult Alternative Airplay chart (for the week of 23 November 1996), 'Free' is a fan favorite song and, quite possibly, the radio 'hit' that first exposed many Phans to Phish. Although the Night 6 version is not as strong as the performance a week earlier in Dayton or as massive as the version performed on 17 June 2004, documented on the *Live In Brooklyn* DVD, it is still an excellent way to get fully into the opening set.

'Weigh' (Gordon) **> 'Undermind'** (Anastasio/Herman/Marshall) **> 'The Oh Kee Pa Ceremony'** (Anastasio)
The first extended sequence of the night starts off with Mike's 'Weigh'. Originally included on *Rift* but made famous by its inclusion on the classic *Slip Stitch And Pass*, 'Weigh' exists as the muddled-mind midpoint between

The Beatles' 'Maxwell's Silver Hammer' and The Ramones' 'Chainsaw'. In addition to the Slip Stitch and Pass version, a great 'Weigh' > 'Rift' > 'Guelah Papyrus' sequence was included on the *Live Phish* archival release of the 7 November 1996 show in Lexington, Kentucky. Another great version, although not yet officially released, is the 2 August 1998 version of 'Weigh' > 'Birds Of A Feather' from Deer Creek.

The second song in the sequence, 'Undermind', was the title track of the band's second (and final) 2.0 album. In their review of *Undermind*, *AllMusic* damned it with faint praise while pointing out that 'shades of the band's winter could be subtly interpreted by various song lyrics.' They used 'Undermind' as Exhibit A of that argument. Although periodically played by the Trey Anastasio Band during the 2.0 years, Phish did not debut the song until they launched their 3.0 era in 2009. Although a great version was played at *Festival 8* on 1 November 2009, the (arguably) best version appeared at the Gorge Amphitheater on 27 July 2013. That second night in George, Washington, the band played a massive 'Down With Disease' > 'Undermind' pairing that was roughly the first third of a tremendous 90-minute second set. The Night 6 version is solid (as, admittedly, most versions are), but 'Undermind' is a song that is almost always elevated when horns are present. For a stellar example of this, check out the version that the Trey Anastasio Band released on their 2020 tour compilation *Burn It Down*.

After wrapping up 'Undermind', the band conclude the night's first sequence with 'The Oh Kee Pa Ceremony'. A studio version of this instrumental classic was included on *Lawn Boy*, and most live versions are followed by 'Suzy Greenberg'. For an example of this pairing, keep watching the aforementioned *Live In Brooklyn* DVD and it'll occur roughly 45 minutes after 'Free' ends. But, since the band had committed to the 'no repeats' bit (and 'Suzy Greenberg' was played on Night 1), the band use 'The Oh Kee Pa Ceremony' as a way to conclude the first extended sequence of Night 6.

'The Dogs' (Anastasio/Fishman/Gordon/McConnell) **> 'Destiny Unbound'** (Gordon)

After a very brief pause, the band launch the fourth (of five) *Chilling, Thrilling Sounds Of The Haunted House* songs they would play during *The Baker's Dozen*, 'The Dogs'. Making periodic appearances since its 31 October 2014 debut, 'The Dogs' is a high-energy track that works especially well in the opening set (which the band seem to realize since they have placed it exclusively there for almost a decade). Two additional versions to seek out occurred on 28 July 2015 and 30 October 2021. In the former, the band gave 'The Dogs' its final second set appearance when they ripped through it as part of a 13-minute '46 Days' > 'The Dogs' > '46 Days' jam. In the latter, the band opened their animal-themed show with 'The Dogs' and then proceeded to spend the rest of the evening playing songs about turtles, antelopes, camels, etc.

With its customary vigor, 'The Dogs' is a nice transition into 'Destiny Unbound'. Almost a distant cousin to the Grateful Dead-popularized 'Me And My Uncle', 'Destiny Unbound' is an up-tempo story song that wasn't regularly played prior to *The Baker's Dozen*. In a pre-concert write-up for Relix, Raffaela Kenny-Cincotta listed 'Destiny Unbound' first in a listicle of songs the band had never performed at MSG. Since its MSG debut, the song's frequency has increased – but it is still not included often enough to be considered a 'regular'. After 16 consecutive performances where it went 'Landlady' > 'Destiny Unbound', the band originally shelved the song on 15 November 1991 and would not bring it back until 28 February 2003. This Nassau Veterans Memorial Coliseum performance is currently the oldest commercially released version of 'Destiny Unbound' the band have released (including it on the *Live Phish 02.28.03* CD). It is likely that the Live Phish Archives will officially release a show from the autumn of 1991 (hopefully the Gothic Theatre show from 1 November) and a prime 'Destiny Unbound' will be more widely available.

'Divided Sky' (Anastasio)

Next up is a song that is almost incapable of not being a set's centerpiece: *Junta*'s 'Divided Sky'. Although fans seem predisposed to loving 'Divided Sky', the version performed on Night 6 earned its adulation. Starting off a little rougher than usual – with some loose phrasing and exploratory timing – this 'Divided Sky' takes its time finding its footing, stretching beyond its typical length and leaning into the spaciousness of the moment. Once the song is fully underway and the more rhythmic sections kick in, the band are in sync and they deliver one of the most memorable versions of the 3.0 era. For distinctive versions from earlier eras, the *Chicago '94* version of 'Divided Sky' does 1.0 proud and the 10 July 2003 version shows that the song was just as strong in 2.0.

'Divided Sky' also shares its name with Trey's residential recovery facility in Vermont. The Divided Sky Foundation was established, in his words, to provide 'a safe environment for men and women to build the foundation necessary to live a productive, healthy and sober life.' Trey's path to sobriety began in 2006 when he was arrested in upstate New York for drug possession and driving under the influence. He pleaded guilty to a reduced charge and entered a rigorous 14-month drug court program that included daily meetings, frequent drug testing and community service. After completing the program in 2008, his conviction was reduced to a misdemeanor. Trey has credited that experience – and the arrest itself – with helping turn his life around. Years later, long after fulfilling his legal obligations and maintaining sobriety since early 2007, he became an outspoken advocate for drug court programs, even sharing his story on Capitol Hill. The Divided Sky Foundation represents the next chapter in that journey: a commitment to giving others the same chance at recovery that he was once given.

'Things People Do' (McConnell)
Included on *Big Boat*, Page's Pinterest-promoting 'Things People Do' is another Night 6 song that recalls The Beatles. With a country-adjacent melody that would not be out of place on *Rubber Soul* or *Help*, 'Things People Do' is a song of acceptance (and likely about the acceptance of the still unbelievable 2016 Presidential election results). Almost a week-and-a-half before *The Baker's Dozen*, they played a fun 'Things People Do' (along with 'Bug' > 'Rocky Top') as the encore for their Pittsburgh show (although hearing Page fumble with the lyrics makes this Night 6 version more fun).

'Sand' (Anastasio/Lawton/Markellis/Marshall)
Because they have only just made it past the one-hour mark, the band have time for one more extended number before taking their set break. Due to time constraints, the band do not take 'Sand' as far as they have done in the past (or have since), but they still use it as an excuse to get into a groove with the audience. A notable 'Sand' that opened a set is the 2 September 2012 version. The band started their second set with a nearly 50-minute 'Sand' > 'Ghost' > 'Piper' sequence. The whole concert is worth hearing (including, for an indescribable reason, the first set's 'Ride Captain Ride'), but that second set 'Sand' is especially brilliant. Of course, other excellent versions exist within the Phish cannon and in Trey's solo catalog. In his 2003 review of Trey's recently released concert compilation, *Plasma*, Stephen Thomas Erlewine specifically mentions the 16-minute 'Sand' when writing: 'These are jams that go places, often very interesting places, and they suggest numerous possibilities for Anastasio to go in the future.' The same sentiment applies to this *Baker's Dozen* version. Although this *Farmhouse* classic is more likely to open a set than close it, the performance laid out on Night 6 is a potent promise for what the second set holds.

Set 2

'Have Mercy' (Ferguson/Shaw/Simpson)
Recorded by The Mighty Diamonds for their Virgin Records debut, *Right Time*, 'Have Mercy' is another cover song that Phish selectively deploy. Although their follow-up album *Ice On Fire* did not match the highs of *Right Time*, it did include production work from Allen Toussant (and a cover of his 'Sneakin' Sally Through The Alley', which Phish covered on Night 10). Two especially great versions of 'Have Mercy' were previously released by the band. The band's 12 November 1994 show at Kent State was added as an archival release to the Live Phish app (largely because of the 'Down With Disease' > 'Have Mercy' > 'Down With Disease', but I would like to think the fun bluegrass-y version of Boston's 'Foreplay/Long Time' helped). The greatest inclusion of 'Have Mercy', however, was likely the 14 August 1993 version from the World Music Theatre that the band released as (the continually praised) *Live Phish Volume 7, 8.14.93*. During a stint with *AllMusic*, the

inestimable Jesse Jarnow wrote that 'The improvisations – such as the long second-set sequence that connects the band's own 'Run Like An Antelope' with The Who's 'Sparks', The James Gang's 'Walk Away' and The Mighty Diamonds' 'Have Mercy' – are schizophrenic and hyper, but also absolutely enthralling if one is willing to surrender to their momentum.' He's not wrong; that 35-minute sequence of 'Also Sprach Zarathustra' > 'Run Like an Antelope' > 'Sparks' > 'Walk Away' > 'Run Like An Antelope' > 'Have Mercy' > 'Run Like An Antelope' anchors this legendary show, and the 'Have Mercy' is neck-and-neck with the 'Sparks' > 'Walk Away' segue for best moment within the sequence.

'Chalk Dust Torture' (Anastasio/Marshall)

The first extended moment from the set occurs during the band's early 1990s workhorse, 'Chalk Dust Torture'. Originally included on *A Picture Of Nectar* and improved upon with *A Live One*, 'Chalk Dust Torture' (or 'Choc-dust Torture', in honor of the night's theme) is medicinal-grade Phish. With the kind of language that implies the singer earned an 800 on the readin' and writin' portion of the SAT, Trey rips through a song of teenage angst while shouting out about 'flagons of rice' and 'vasoconstrictors' coming 'slowly undone'. With an appearance approximately every three shows, 'Chalk Dust Torture' rarely stays out of the setlist for too many nights in a row. Beyond the aforementioned version on *A Live One*, listeners are also encouraged to check out 10 July 1999 (aka, *Live Phish Volume 8, 7.10.99)*, 3 August 2003 (aka 'the last night of the *IT Festival*') and 30 October 2010 (aka 'the one with Zeppelin's 'Whole Lotta Love' sandwiched into the middle') versions. Those looking to complete their post-graduate work on 'Chalk Dust Torture' should seek out jam-band blogger Ryan Storm's 12 October 2021 post: 'Jam Breakdown – 7/28/17 Chalk Dust Torture'. He provides a play-by-play recap of this epic moment (and a link to an hour-long podcast where he discusses why this version is the greatest of the 500+ versions the band have played).

At a high level, this version of 'Chalk Dust Torture' features multiple magical moments in each of its sections. With both Type I and Type II jamming, the Night 6 'Chalk Dust Torture' runs well past the 20-minute mark and earned its place on the *Baker's Dozen* compilation. After the band (and the audience response) peak around the 23-minute mark, they take that as their cue to start winding it down. They only give the audience a few moments of downtime before launching the set's main sequence.

'You Sexy Thing' (Ainsworth/Brown) **> 'Mercury'** (Anastasio/Marshall) **> 'You Sexy Thing'** (Ainsworth/Brown) **> 'Backwards Down The Number Line'** (Anastasio/Marshall) **> 'Rock And Roll'** (Reed)

Originally included on the British soul band's self-titled second album, *Hot Chocolate*, 'You Sexy Thing' gives Phish (and especially Mike) a chance to have some fun with the night's theme. Rather than play it for cheap laughs, they dig in by stretching the groove, teasing the melody and warping the song's silky disco-soul veneer into something far stranger and more compelling. What begins as a playful homage soon evolves into a full-blown jam, with Mike laying down the kind of bass work that feels both reverent and ridiculous in the best possible way. There's a moment when it seems like they've wrung all they can out of this funky detour, but instead of wrapping it up with a bow, they pivot – seamlessly, almost sneakily – into the intricate time signatures and layered textures of 'Mercury', their sprawling prog-rock odyssey.

In mentioning 'Mercury' in their *Sigma Oasis* reviews, Greg M. Schwartz and Sam Sodomsky (writing for *PopMatters* and *Pitchfork*, respectively) both state the studio version falls short of the versions the band have played on stage. Both could have used *The Baker's Dozen* version as Exhibit A in their arguments. Although more than double the length of the studio cut, the version played on Night 6 is relatively brief compared to others. But it still manages to work as a song and as a side quest. Having come out of the people-pleasing 'You Sexy Thing', 'Mercury' gives the band a chance to discuss weightier topics ('The days that are met with onlyness/Aid and abet this loneliness) before working their way back into that Hot Chocolate classic. Once they have (finally) finished with 'You Sexy Thing' completely, the band play the first song that Tom Marshall and Trey Anastasio wrote after Trey started rehab and began his sober lifestyle, 'Backwards Down The Number Line'. Included on *Joy* and memorably performed by Trey during his January 2015 Tiny Desk Concert for *NPR*, 'Backwards Down The Number Line' provides an extra dose of upbeat energy to the set. Although the song kicks into an even higher gear at the two-thirds mark, it does not quite reach the heights of the version played a week earlier in Pittsburgh. The audience do not seem to mind, however, and the band take the energy they obtain from 'Backwards Down The Number Line' and use it to power their way into the Velvet Underground's classic 'Rock And Roll'. Although not the jam vehicle it was during earlier eras, 'Rock And Roll' does not need to be. It is high-octane music delivered by four guys who have spent the preceding hour demonstrating their mastery of reggae, soul, prog and pop and who want to end the set with a reminder to the audience that they can also rock.

'You Sexy Thing' would make a few additional appearances in setlists since *The Baker's Dozen*. The most noteworthy was its follow-up appearance on 5 August 2018. The band opened the first set with it and then returned to it again at the conclusion of the second set. During the unforgettable show-closer, '2001', the band returned to 'You Sexy Thing', the also-played-that-night 'Petrichor' and 'Tweezer Reprise', plus a bit of George Gershwin's 'Rhapsody In Blue'. The song that has been musically developed the most post-*Baker's Dozen* is 'Mercury'. Numerous strong versions were performed in 2018 and 2019, but the opening night of the 2019 Labor Day run (30 August) featured an 'Everything's Right' > 'Mercury' > 'Shade' > 'Light' > 'Party Time' sequence worth hearing in its entirety. A much later version, from 12 July 2023, went in a different direction and ended up as the only 'Mercury > Free' pairing performed by the band.

Always a fun song, 'Backwards Down The Number Line' has been played countless times, but a few performances stand out. Two lesser-known gems include 11 August 2009 – featuring a great jam sequence into 'Carini' and 'Gotta Jibboo' – and 18 October 2014, where it anchors a huge mid-set run alongside 'Down With Disease', 'Golden Age' and others. A particularly creative version came on 28 October 2021 during a show where Phish built their setlists around descending numbers. That night included songs like '2001', '1999', '555', '46 Days' and so on, all the way down to 'Backwards Down The Number Line' in the encore (fittingly). They ended with 'Grind', customized to recap all the night's songs and reveal that the numbers added up to 4,680 – a number that would resurface when the band debuted their futuristic alter ego, Sci-Fi Soldier, just days later. That one-off project has since produced several live staples and the studio album *Get More Down*.

Rightly or wrongly, Phish's most legendary version of 'Rock And Roll' will likely never see an official release. Performed during their epic nine-hour overnight set at Big Cypress on 31 December 1999, it sits near the end of an astonishing hour-long stretch from 'Heavy Things' through 'Twist' > 'Prince Caspian' > 'Rock And Roll'. That 30-minute jam may only account for about 5% of the show, but it casts a long shadow in Phish lore. Big Cypress wasn't just a concert, but it was a once-in-a-lifetime event that helped define the band and its community. Portions of the performance were broadcast live as part of ABC's 2000 Today millennium coverage, giving Phish their largest television audience to date. And while the full magic was reserved for the 85,000 phans who made the trek to the Florida Everglades, high-quality audience recordings still circulate, preserving a night that remains the stuff of legend.

Encore

'Fee' (Anastasio)

The first song of the encore, 'Fee' features Trey singing his verses through a megaphone (as he has tended to do since 1992). Another story song, albeit much sillier than 'Destiny Unbound', 'Fee' is a *Junta* classic that has never strayed too far from the band's setlists (but this is the only version to conclude with the lyrics, 'so have a chocolate donut and catch your breath.') Two great versions of 'Fee' from two great shows include 14 August 1996 and 1 July 2012. The former (which, as of this writing, has not been officially released) opens with a 'Wilson' > 'Down With Disease' that then rolls into a 'Fee' > 'Poor Heart' (featuring an all-time great transition). The latter show, which is available via the Live Phish site, features a standalone 'Fee' in the opening set and then a nearly-90-minute monster of a second set that never disappoints (especially the opening hour of 'Crosseyed And Painless' > 'No Quarter' > 'Light' > 'Ghost' > 'Back On The Train' > 'Farmhouse').

'Space Oddity' (Bowie)
The night's closing number is another a cappella gem: Phish's barbershop-style rendition of David Bowie's 'Space Oddity'. First debuted during the band's 2016 summer tour – not long after Bowie's death in January of that year – the arrangement is both surprising and striking. It strips away the original's lush instrumentation and replaces it with layered vocal harmonies that highlight the song's haunting sense of isolation and wonder. Some fans have compared it to Phish's long-standing a cappella cover of Lynyrd Skynyrd's 'Freebird', since both are reimagined in a vocal-only format that plays with audience expectations. But where 'Freebird' is delivered with a wink – as the band's preemptive response to a cliched request – 'Space Oddity' feels more reverent. There's a tenderness to the performance, a quiet acknowledgment of Bowie's artistry and influence, particularly the way his music fused theatrical flair with musical sophistication. Singing 'Space Oddity' a cappella draws attention to the complex chord changes and emotional nuances that often get lost beneath the glam-rock mystique. The only time Phish have played 'Space Oddity' as an opener came on 19 July 2022, a choice that raised a few eyebrows. They followed it with 'Martian Monster', which may have been a subtle joke or cosmic pun, but the moment quickly gave way to serious musical business with a standout 'Halley's Comet' > 'Stash' pairing that anchored the set. Whether as a heartfelt tribute or left-field curveball, 'Space Oddity' remains one of Phish's most unexpected and affecting covers.

Night 7: Saturday 29 July ('Cinnamon')

Before the start of the opening song – in fact, well before the lights went down – a Woodstock homage played over the PA when the audience were advised against eating the brown donuts (a la the brown acid that caused trouble in 1969). The band included this dialogue at the start of their officially released recording of Night 7. As of this writing, the entire night is currently available on the band's official YouTube Channel.

Set 1

'Llama' (Anastasio)

The run's midpoint started off with one of the band's more popular opening numbers, 'Llama'. A belated contribution to *Gamehendge* and included on *A Picture Of Nectar*, 'Llama' tells the tale of a rebel's sacrifice (although different performances place his martyrdom at different points in the story). As of this writing, the most recent full performance of *Gamehendge* happened on NYE 2023 and is available on the band's YouTube channel – it is highly recommended. For additional versions of 'Llama', start with the archival release of the 13 August 1993 Murat Theatre show in Indianapolis. The band opened the first set with 'Lengthwise' > 'Llama' and later (after a memorable first set and fairly concise second set) encored with 'Amazing Grace' and 'Highway To Hell'. On 26 October 2010, a standalone (yet interesting) 'Llama' was included in a great first set, and to end the second set, the band performed a fantastic 'Ghost' > 'The Mango Song' > 'Weekapaug Groove' > 'Llama Reprise'.

'Wilson' (Anastasio/Marshall/Woolf) **> 'Stealing Time From The Faulty Plan'** (Anastasio/Herman/Marshall) **> 'Ya Mar'** (Ferguson)

Another *Gamehendge* song, albeit one that was included from the very beginning, 'Wilson' is an early fan-favorite (due largely to the audience participation that is sought whenever the opening chords play). With their chants of 'Wilson', the audience are on board for what will be the longest version since the original 1.0 era. Speaking of 1.0, the most famous 'Wilson' is obviously the version which opened the 30 December 1994 performance (and that was later included on *A Live One*). Another great 1.0 performance was also included on the *Vegas 96* release. This 6 December concert opened with 'Wilson' > 'Peaches En Regalia' > 'Poor Heart' > 'Also Sprach Zarathustra' > 'Llama' and, to date, this is the last time the band played the fun 'Wilson' > 'Peaches En Regalia' combo.

After 'Wilson', the band move into another song they would take further than they typically do, 'Stealing Time From The Faulty Plan'. Another upbeat track off *Joy*, 'Stealing Time From The Faulty Plan' is almost a spiritual sequel to 'Chalk Dust Torture' (one in which the protagonist, through no fault of his own, has graduated into middle-management). *Rolling Stone* referred to it as an 'I-will-survive rocker' and singled out the couplet, 'Got a blank space where my mind should be/Got a Clif Bar and some cold green tea'. Originally performed by Phish on 2 June 2009 (the same night they debuted 'Kill Devil Falls'), 'Stealing Time From The Faulty Plan' is a comparable vibe to The Gorillaz's classic song 'Clint Eastwood', which Trey started performing during his solo concerts in 2011. Another great version (albeit with less effervescence than the *Baker's Dozen* version) is from the San Francisco show on 2 August 2013. Coming out of Harry Hood, the band deliver a delightful 'Stealing Time From The Faulty Plan' before wrapping up that second set with a 'Squirming Coil'.

The band close up Night 7's first extended sequence with their oft-performed cover of 'Ya Mar' – a fantastic addition to *The Baker's Dozen*. This Caribbean island classic (learned by Mike from a version performed by The Mustangs) has been played by the band hundreds of times, and, in fact, they delivered an especially memorable version on 13 August 1993 (the Murat Theatre show referenced in the write-up of the set-opening 'Llama'). For an even better version of 'Ya Mar', the fourth disc of the *Gorge '98* box set should be played. For the 17 July 1998 show included on *Gorge '98*, the band opened the first set with a double dose of fun by playing 'Makisupa Policeman' > 'Ya Mar'. To add to the fun, the 'Ya Mar' featured a tease of the Yes classic 'Close To The Edge' (which must have still been on Trey's mind after having teased it during three different songs during three different concerts in 1997). The *Gorge '98* box set is also worth hearing for the 'Gumbo' that follows 'Ya Mar' as well as the four-song second set featured on the fifth disc. This hour-long jam of 'Also Sprach Zarathustra' > 'Mike's Song' > 'Weekapaug Groove' > 'Character Zero' is still discussed over 25 years later (and for reasons beyond the monumental 24-minute 'Also Sprach Zarathustra' that opened the sequence).

'Tela' (Anastasio)

After giving the audience a respectful amount of time to catch their breath from that 'Ya Mar', the band then make their third visit of the night to *Gamehendge* with 'Tela'. This Page-sung ballad features excellent guitar work from Trey (especially during the section that leads into the outro). Although not a vessel for jams, 'Tela' is a terrific addition to any setlist. The 28 June 2012 show at Deer Creek featured a great set-closing 'Tela' > 'Stealing Time From The Faulty Plan', but this was not the venue's best-ever 'Tela'. That title belongs to the version included on *Live Phish Volume 12, 8.13.96*. After opening with a Page-powered 'Divided Sky' and a rocking 'Tube', the band brought 'Tela' > 'Maze' to central Indiana. Night 7 was the band's first-ever performance of 'Tela' at MSG, and they performed it for the second time at MSG during the 2022 New Year's run. During their 31 December 2023 performance at MSG, the band would perform their third (and possibly greatest) version of 'Tela' during their complete run-through of *Gamehendge*.

'The Birds' (Anastasio/Fishman/Gordon/McConnell) **> 'The Line'** (Anastasio/Fishman/Gordon/McConnell)

The next mini sequence includes a pairing of two songs about overcoming adversity (one external and the other internal). 'The Birds' is a groove-based tale (that features well-deployed samples of Laura Olsher's original *Chilling, Thrilling Sounds Of The Haunted House* recording) about overcoming seemingly ceaseless bird attacks. 'The Line' is a *Fuego* original about overcoming self-doubt before an act and moving on after the fact (regardless of the outcome).

To date, 'The Birds' has only taken flight a handful of times. It always gets the job done. This pairing with 'The Line' is especially nice since it allows the band to work through a few different grooves in a relatively short amount of time. Although played comparatively more than 'The Birds', 'The Line' has only been drawn in the setlists around 30 times. For previously played versions of both: 'The Birds' had a great airing when it opened the 29 October 2016 concert in Las Vegas, and for 'The Line', go back almost three years earlier to hear its 31 October 2013 debut in Atlantic City.

'Water In The Sky' (Anastasio/Marshall)

The band then deliver a sprightlier-than-usual take on 'Water In The Sky'. This version – upbeat, crisp and confidently played – compares favorably to the studio version included on *The Story Of The Ghost*. Once again, Page takes the spotlight, sprinkling just the right amount of honky-tonk shimmer across the top. For contrast, check out the slower, more wistful rendition on the *Walnut Creek* DVD, which leans into a Gram Parsons vibe and serves as a gentle comedown after the fiery 'Runaway Jim' > 'My Soul' that precedes it and the heady 'Stash' that follows. Or, for a performance with approximately 37% more Buck Owens, find the 2 July 1997 version from the *Amsterdam* box set. That one kicks off in full country mode before executing a whip-fast pivot into 'Weekapaug Groove', a seamless shift from twang to funk that only Phish could pull off. And let's not forget the *Bittersweet Motel* documentary. The segment featuring 'Water In The Sky' during the soundcheck portion is brief but brilliant, a quiet highlight that captures the band's offstage chemistry and charm.

'Vultures' (Anastasio/Herman/Marshall) **> 'Train Song'** (Gordon/Linitz) **> 'Horn'** (Anastasio/Marshall)

The third and final mini set within this overarching opening set starts off with a proggy 'Vultures' that provokes cheers from the audience at all the right moments. Another song featured on both the *Walnut Creek* DVD and the *Amsterdam* box set, 'Vultures' includes a rapid-fire vocal bridge that always grabs my attention. Lately, the rhythm and delivery of that section – 'Timing is everything, that much I know/Sometimes I'm faster and sometimes I'm slow' – have started to remind me of the lyrical style used by Lin-Manuel Miranda, the composer and performer best known for *Hamilton*. It's that tightly packed, rhythmic spoken-word flow that feels more like dialogue set to music than traditional singing. That's not a complaint about either the song or Miranda; it is just an unexpected but oddly fitting association my brain makes whenever that 'patter' section kicks in.

The band then move into Mike's mellow *Billy Breathes* classic, 'Train Song'. This is one of Mike's best ballads (and it features some of Trey's most sympathetic contributions to a Mike song). Two great shows that feature 'Train Song' are 5 August 1996 and 31 December 2014. The 1996 show from Red Rocks features a second set that is dominated by the band playing acoustic instruments and, in the case of Fishman, a smaller drum set. For the NYE show in Miami, the band expertly sequenced 'Train Song' between standalone versions of 'Kill Devil Falls' and 'Waiting All Night'. The playing is not perfect, but the whole thing just works somehow. More worth seeing from that night, however, is the opening of the 'countdown to midnight' third set. Phish debut a version of 'Dem Bones', and when technical difficulties seem to derail Fishman's vacuum cleaner solo, guitar techs attempt to fix the issue by changing the settings from 'suck' to 'blow', causing a giant inflatable Fishman to emerge from the stage and float over the audience.

After using 'Train Song' to cool things down, the band keep the introspective mood alive, this time shifting from locomotives ('The train whistle melody wove through the trees') to something a bit less romantic: a date's car horn ('I'll pick you up at eight as usual, listen for my horn'). This arrangement of 'Horn' is close to the version included on *Rift* (much like how the preceding 'Train Song' is comparable to the version recorded for the *Billy Breathes* album). 'Horn' is almost always a tightly delivered composition, and for Night 7, the band don't deviate from the pattern. In under four minutes, Trey delivers a pointed farewell to someone he just can't let go of and doesn't linger. But it's worth remembering the one time they did break form: the 15 July 1998 performance (captured on *Live Phish Volume 17*) where 'Horn' unexpectedly segued into a jam, then into 'Chalk Dust Torture'. It's a must-hear, not just for how wild the jam gets, but for how rare such a departure is. A moment like that should echo in every fan's mind the next time someone writes off a song as 'standard' in the forums.

'I Am The Walrus' (Lennon/McCartney)

The second of their three Beatles covers wraps up the first set of Night 7. With excellent playing by all four (and some fun scatting by Trey), 'I Am The Walrus' is everything an audience member could want in a closing number. While The Beatles' original version mixed in a BBC recording of King Lear, Phish were more self-referential during the 'freak out' portions of their version, which teased five *Chilling, Thrilling Sounds Of The Haunted House* recordings ('Your Pet Cat', 'Shipwreck', 'The Unsafe Bridge', 'The Birds' and 'Martian Monster'), plus Van Halen's hair metal classic, 'Runnin' With The

Devil'. Of course, the band could have included 'I Am The Walrus' in a 'Custard' night-themed show ('...yellow matter custard...'), but then they would need to explain to some less enlightened Phans why Led Zeppelin's 'Custard Pie' was not also covered on this 14th night. The band had only attempted 'I Am The Walrus' a few times prior to *The Baker's Dozen* and they would only return to it a few more times afterwards. The most successful attempt might be the most recent version: on 11 October 2023 in Dayton, Ohio. The second set of the night started with a massive 'Down With Disease' > 'Ruby Waves' that is worth hearing before it concluded with a magnificent 'I Am The Walrus'.

Set 2

'Blaze On' (Anastasio/Marshall) **> 'Twenty Years Later'** (Anastasio/Marshall) **> 'Alumni Blues'** (Anastasio) **> 'Letter To Jimmy Page'** (Anastasio) **> 'Alumni Blues'** (Anastasio) **> 'Meatstick'** (Anastasio/Fishman/Gordon/Herman/Marshall/McConnell) **> 'Dirt'** (Anastasio/Herman/Marshall) **> 'Harry Hood'** (Anastasio/Fishman/Gordon/Long/McConnell)

After squeezing a full 12 songs into their 80-minute opening set, Phish take a break before returning to deliver a seven-song sequence for their second set. Starting with *Big Boat*'s magnificent 'Blaze On', the second set locks into a groove and never falters; it's a cohesive, feel-good stretch that taps into everything fans love about Phish. From the start, 'Blaze On' was destined to be a band and fan favorite. Debuting in 2015 and having a handful of impressive performances in that inaugural year, the song was part of 2016's opening tryptic ('Blaze On' > 'Carini' > 'David Bowie') when performed out of 'Auld Lang Syne' at the band's NYE show at MSG. The band were only able to play four full-length concerts in 2020, but on the third of those (on 21 February), the band delivered a 32-minute 'Bathtub Gin' > 'Shafty' > 'Bathtub Gin' > 'Blaze On' sequence that went to some interesting places. The jam moved from playful syncopation into darker, murkier textures during 'Shafty', then rebounded with renewed energy, eventually dissolving into the buoyant groove of 'Blaze On'. The following summer, when the post-COVID touring was fully underway, the band delivered an epic 'Blaze On' (coming right out of 'AC/DC Bag' on 6 August. That entire second set at Deer Creek is worth hearing, not just for the 'AC/DC Bag' > 'Blaze On' that starts things off, but also for the 'Wilson' > 'Simple' and the (to a slightly lesser degree) 'Harry Hood' > 'I Never Needed You Like This Before' that followed. Over 50 minutes of that second set from 6 August (the 'Simple' and the 'Blaze On') was later released on vinyl as *Live Phish On Long Play 06*.

After wrapping up the longest version of 'Blaze On' an audience had heard to date and one the band felt highly enough about to include as the opening track to their *Baker's Dozen* compilation, the band move into 'Twenty Years Later'. This version of the closing track off *Joy* does not reach the heights seen in

Chicago two weeks earlier; it does get into a groove that could have been ridden a lot further if the band did not have other songs on their agenda. Another great version of 'Twenty Years Later' was included in the previously mentioned 'Backwards Down The Number Line Concert' from 28 October 2021. A solid, unassuming version of 'Twenty Years Later' was also played at the 12 June 2010 concert at the Blossom Music Center. From their one-off performance of The Band's 'Look Out Cleveland' to their first of three performances of John Lennon's 'Instant Karma!', this Ohio concert is ripe for rediscovery.

The band then transition to the 'Alumni Blues' > 'Letter To Jimmy Page' > 'Alumni Blues' sequence that they have stuck with since bringing those songs back in the 3.0 era. With a couple of references to Mike's bass playing (and some fantastic keyboard work by Page), the opening portion of 'Alumni Blues' is especially fun. The middle 'Letter To Jimmy Page' section features a nice, long pause in-between the riffage. When 'Alumni Blues' comes around again to wrap things up, you can almost *hear* the smiles (and imagine how John Belushi might have danced to such a number in an alternate timeline). Focusing on just the 3.0 era, two great versions occurred on 25 June 2010 and 15 August 2011. For the 2010 show in New Jersey, the band opened their first set with a six-minute, window-rattling blast of 'Alumni Blues' > 'Letter To Jimmy Page' > 'Alumni Blues' (that was followed by an equally fierce 'Big Black Furry Creature From Mars'). That same set would eventually find the band playing a fun version of Joni Mitchell's *Court And Spark* classic 'Free Man In Paris' for the only time. For the 2011 show in Chicago, the band ended their opening set with 'Alumni Blues' > 'Letter To Jimmy Page' > 'Alumni Blues', setting the stage for the second set monster jam that is 'Sand' > 'Light' > 'Dirt' > 'Waves' > 'Undermind' > 'Steam' > 'Fire'.

'Meatstick' follows, and although it did not make the cut for either *The Story Of The Ghost* or *Farmhouse*, it is always a fan favorite. Although not commonly played, that popularity ensures 'Meatstick' never stays gone for too long. The first great 'Meatstick' was its debut performance on 25 June 1997. Playing France for the third-to-last time, the band included 'Meatstick' in a nearly hour-long jam of 'Down With Disease' > 'Piper' > 'Down With Disease' > 'Meatstick' > 'McGrupp And The Watchful Hosemasters' > 'Makisupa Policeman'. Almost three years later, on 9 June 2000, the band performed in Tokyo and honored their host nation by including some new lyrics in Japanese. These Japanese-language lyrics would eventually become a permanent addition to the song, but this would not be the only time the band applied a foreign tongue to 'Meatstick'. For the final song performed in 2010, Phish showcased how 'Meatstick' flavors our cultural stew, with African tribesmen, a mariachi band, Hasidic rabbis, Swedish ski bunnies and – finally – German Oktoberfest partiers all appearing to sing the song in their own languages. Numerous other jokes have been associated with 'Meatstick' performances, some more crass than others, but they are always delivered with a wink and a smile.

After the 'not quite right for *Farmhouse*' 'Meatstick', the band play a song that did find a home on *Farmhouse*: 'Dirt'. One of the darker songs on one of their sunnier albums, 'Dirt' is delivered in the expected manner and it works as a nice transition between the jokey 'Meatstick' and the epic 'Harry Hood' that concludes the set. Also included on the *Trampled By Lambs And Pecked By The Dove* project, 'Dirt' was added to the setlists during the summer of 1997 and stayed in a fairly consistent rotation until the 1.0 era ended. Since the reformation, it has made a handful of appearances each year (with 2003 holding the current record of five). Surprisingly, given how good of a song it is (and how well it can be delivered acoustically), it has never really gotten much play in Trey's solo acoustic shows. A good example of how it can be performed in an acoustic setting would be the opening set of the 27 February 2011 show in Chicago (with an electric set that followed also being solid) or the 12 February 2018 show in Pittsburgh. This show was entirely acoustic, and in addition to a fine 'Dirt', it delivered a great 'Harry Hood'.

For *The Baker's Dozen*, the band take 'Harry Hood' and, using its customary magic, turn the full set up to 11. This closing 'Harry Hood' elevates the set (not that any set that opens with that version of 'Blaze On' would need much help). Originally released on *A Live One* and subsequently released on at least a dozen other live albums, 'Harry Hood' is the definition of a 'crowd pleaser'. The 22 November 1997 version included on the *Hampton/Winston-Salem '97* box set is solid, but it is not as great as the version found on *A Live One*. For a version approaching that, listen to the second set included on the *Live Phish 02.28.03* CD. The second set starts off with a 'Tweezer' > 'Soul Shakedown Party' > 'David Bowie' sequence and then ends with a 'Round Room' > 'Harry Hood' pairing. It is one of the best five-song sets the band have ever delivered.

Encore

'Cinnamon Girl' (Young)

Although Night 7 did not include any debuts, it did feature the return of Neil Young's crunchy 'Cinnamon Girl'. Last played almost exactly 20 years earlier, on 31 July 1997, 'Cinnamon Girl' has only been played five times (to date). But, considering Neil's 'Powderfinger' has only made a single appearance, we should consider ourselves lucky to have had those five performances.

Above: An advertisement for *The Baker's Dozen* displayed outside Madison Square Garden. (*Live For Live Music*)

Below: Phish take a breather before their 13th (and final) encore to celebrate their achievement. (*Live For Live Music*)

Left: The front cover of 2018's *The Baker's Dozen Live At Madison Square Garden* compilation. (*JEMP Records*)

Right: The vinyl edition of *The Baker's Dozen* compilation featured 13 tracks spread over 12 sides. (*JEMP Records*)

Above: The 36-CD box set edition, titled *The Complete Baker's Dozen* and released in November 2018, featured every note from those 13 nights.

Below: The packaging for *The Complete Baker's Dozen* included an 86-page book, prints, memorabilia and signed artwork by Jim Pollock. (*JEMP Records*)

Above: Chris Kuroda, after taking guitar lessons from Trey, began work as a roadie for Phish before becoming their lighting director.

Below: To synchronize the lights with the band's improvisations, Chris must anticipate how a song will progress. This has earned him the honorarium of 'fifth member'.

Above: While bands typically place the drums towards the back, Fishman's are closer to the front of the stage to illustrate equality.

Below: Trey: 'I don't think any one of us has the greatest voice, but with barbershop, we can blend and make beautiful music.' (*Getty*)

Above: Mike Gordon primarily played his signature Modulus bass with a graphite neck and EMG pickups at *The Baker's Dozen*. (*Live Phish*)

Below: Page McConnell's keyboards at *The Baker's Dozen* included a grand piano, a clavinet, an organ, a Wurlitzer and a Moog One synthesizer. (*Live Phish*)

Above: Jon Fishman's drum kit contains over 20 pieces. These drums and cymbals are produced by over a dozen different manufacturers. (*Live Phish*)

Below: Trey Anastasio primarily played his Languedoc Koa 1, but his Koa 2 was played a handful of times when alternate tunings were required. (*Live Phish*)

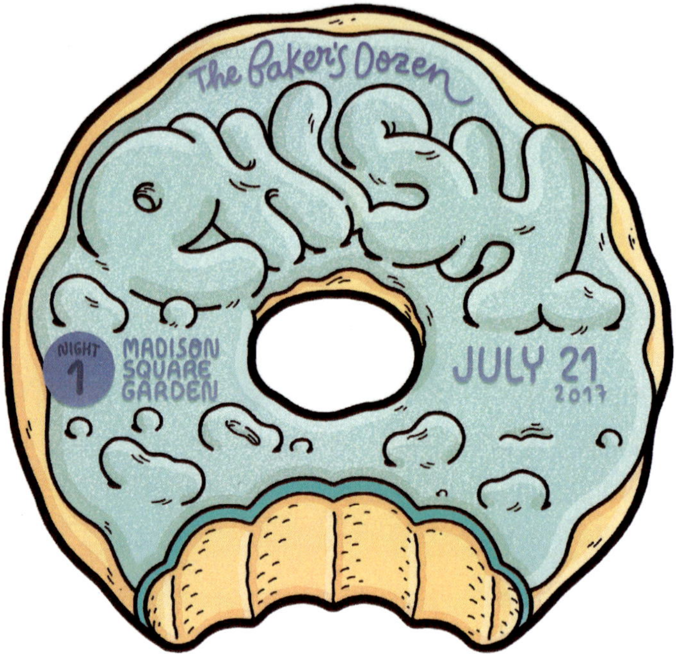

Left: Brosmind, the creative duo of brothers Juan and Alejandro Mingarro, designed donut-shaped tickets for *The Baker's Dozen*. (*Brosmind*)

Right: Because flavors were not announced until closer to showtime, the Brosmind donut designs did not align with each night's theme. (*Brosmind*)

Above: Brosmind's donut-shaped tickets were housed in a custom donut box. The inside of the lid featured 'Glaze On' – a homage to 'Blaze On'. (*Brosmind*)

Above: A playfully surreal imagining of a donut-shaped Market Square Arena in New York City. (*Live For Live Music*)

Above: Trey's luthier, Paul Languedoc, includes his signature on his headstocks. (*Getty*)

Below: Mike prefers a five-string bass because of the expanded range it affords his playing. (*Wallyography*)

Above: Page purchased James Brown's Moog Liberation keytar at a Christie's auction. It is primarily used for the band's version of Edger Winter's 'Frankenstein'.

Below: Page's Liberation keytar is also special because Moog produced fewer white versions.

Above: Working under the name Your Cinema, Ryan Besch produced a poster for the second weekend of *The Baker's Dozen* run. (*Ryan Besch/Your Cinema*)

Above: Artist Drew Millward produced a limited-edition poster that was available on 25 and 26 July. (*Drew Millward*)

Above: Federal Donuts chief Matt Fein worked overnight shifts with his crew to produce the thousands of donuts necessary for *The Baker's Dozen*. (*Alamy*)

Below: Beyond the unique flavors, Federal Donuts produced special edition Phish donut bags for *The Baker's Dozen*. (*Alamy*)

Above: Professional bassist and amateur donut delivery man, Mike Gordon. (*Billy Penn at WHYY*)

Below: One phan freeze-dried their donuts, encased them in plastic and listed them on eBay for $499.

Above: Brosmind also designed regular tickets for *The Baker's Dozen*. (*Brosmind*)

Above: Darin Shock created a limited-edition poster for the final weekend of *The Baker's Dozen*. (*Darin Shock*)

Night 8: Sunday 30 July ('Jimmies')

As Phish reminded the audience a week earlier (as if they needed reminding), 'Never miss a Sunday show!!'

Set 1

'The Curtain With' (Anastasio/Daubert) > **'Runaway Jim'** (Abrahams/Anastasio)

The eighth crazy night of *The Baker's Dozen* starts off with 'The Curtain With', and although it is not perfectly played, it is still an exemplary version (and a damn sight better than the version which concluded the 2.0 era). When Phish devoted their final encore (of what, to them, was to be their final concert) to 'The Curtain With', they made clear the song's significance. Unfortunately, during that 15 August 2004 performance, they started their final song off in the wrong key. The whole thing collapsed and they had to start their final number anew. For a band known for their musicianship, it was another painful reminder that it was time to separate. A much better version of 'The Curtain With' to revisit is the 17 September 2000 version from the Merriweather Post Pavilion. Listening to this first set-closing 'The Curtain With' > 'Chalk Dust Torture', you would be unable to believe that (in less than a month) they would be performing it as badly as they did. The Night 8 version is not quite the opposite of that 'farewell' performance, but it is at least professionally delivered, and it includes a nice segue into its follow-up, 'Runaway Jim'. This performance of 'Runaway Jim' is a nice introduction to the night's theme and it includes some excellent Type I jamming. Although not as explored as other versions (not that any version is likely to come close to the mammoth 59-minute version played on 29 November 1997, included on *Live Bait Vol. 03*), this version of 'Runaway Jim' is well-received and is worth revisiting. Other versions worth seeking out include the 7 August 1996 version, the version included on the *New Year's Eve 1995 – Live At Madison Square Garden* release, or (honestly) any version from 1993.

'Waking Up Dead' (Gordon/Murawski)

One of Mike's *Big Boat* contributions, 'Waking Up Dead' takes the band past the half-an-hour mark and helps fully launch the night's theme. For those that do not know, 'Jimmies' are tiny, colored sugar pellets placed atop donuts (or cookies, ice cream, cake, etc.). They are small, sweet and capable of elevating a routine treat into something special. The band spend most of the first set playing either short(-ish) songs or shorter versions of songs they have jammed out in the past ('Runaway Jim' is a fitting example of the latter). As for 'Waking Up Dead', it is well-delivered. Upon its *Big Boat* release, *PopMatters* wrote that Mike's 'Waking Up Dead' 'doesn't fit his usual funk or bluegrass templates; the song distances itself from the rest of *Big Boat* as a sort of gloomy psychedelic/prog number.' *The Baker's Dozen* version largely aligns with that assessment, although it does feature some isolated funk now and then.

Phish essentially abandoned 'Waking Up Dead' after *The Baker's Dozen* (not that it was in heavy rotation prior to this run). They played it twice more and then retired the number. Mike did not keep it in his solo setlists for long; only six more performances after *The Baker's Dozen*. For a great Mike Gordon show featuring 'Waking Up Dead', check out the 22 January 2020 performance at Chicago's Thalia Hall. It is a great two-hour show followed by a version of Rancid's 'Ruby Soho' as the encore. (Mike is not the only member of the jam-band scene to appreciate Rancid's Clash homage; Phish's jam-band peers Spafford periodically include 'Ruby Soho' in their shows.) Their 21 January 2023 performance at Washington D.C.'s 9:30 Club illustrates how their more concise take differs from Mike's version (which feels more indebted to the version Jimmy Cliff released on his excellent 2012 album, *Rebirth*).

'Esther' (Anastasio)

The first of three *Junta* tracks the band would tackle on Night 8, 'Esther' is another of their early 'story songs' featuring complex compositional components and a dark storyline. The song concerns a young girl who, on a trip to the fairgrounds, meets a foreigner who gives her the gift of a doll. One thing leads to another, and the girl eventually finds herself in a lake, the doll dragging the girl 'down through the eerie green deep' to her death. Beyond all that, 'Esther' also sets up a second theme of the night: song titles that include names. 'Esther' made its live debut in the late 1980s and, to this day, still receives a couple of performances annually. However, Night 8 would be its only appearance in 2017. Beyond *Junta* and *The Baker's Dozen*, a few other great versions of 'Esther' have received a physical release. The second half of the opening set on 21 February 1993 included an excellent sequence of 'Esther' > 'Dinner And A Movie' > 'Bouncing Around The Room' > 'Run Like An Antelope'. This 30-minute medley was included on the *Phish At The Roxy* box set that 'captures Phish right when they were putting a spit-shine polish on the live improvisation that would make them kings of the 1990s jam-band scene', according to *Rolling Stone* (in a four-star review). For the opening night of *The Clifford Ball* on 16 August 1996, the band included a great flow through 'AC/DC Bag' > 'Esther' > 'Divided Sky' (which, sadly, needed to be split across two sides of vinyl for the 2022 release).

'Home' (McConnell)

The second (and final) *Big Boat* song of the night is Page's 'Home'. In his 2016 review for *NPR*, Mike Katzif wrote that *Big Boat*'s producer, Bob Ezrin, 'reportedly challenged the band members to share more of themselves in their songs' and that this results in 'expressions of sadness, anger and earnest positivity, as well as themes of ageing and mortality.' He later remarked that

'Home' is McConnel describing 'his restlessness after a lifetime in motion.' Listening to either the *Big Boat* version or the Night 8 version, it is hard to disagree with Mr. Katzif's take. Another excellent assessment of *Big Boat* that, while not specifically about 'Home', definitely seems to apply is the take supplied by *Consequence Of Sound*. Sean Barry's B- review said the album was 'wonderfully accessible thanks to its relatable sense of communal fun.' Unfortunately, 'Home' (like its *Big Boat* brethren 'Waking Up Dead') was not destined for longevity. With only seven performances (one less than 'Waking Up Dead'), 'Home' was quickly dropped from contention. I can understand 'Waking Up Dead' not being a regular part of the rotation; it is an oddly structured song that does not go to too many interesting places. 'Home', however, seems like it could be slotted into the setlist whenever the band want to keep the energy simmering without losing focus – it is a mid-tempo anchor that deserves more stage time.

'Brian And Robert' (Anastasio/Marshall)
This is the only representation from *The Story Of The Ghost* for the night, but it is a great one. One of my all-time favorite Phish songs, especially the version later included on Trey and Tom Marshall's collaborative album, *Trampled By Lambs And Pecked By The Dove*, 'Brian And Robert' is a Phish song for those who appreciate the band's more concise moments. An overly reductive description of the song would mention it is named in honor of the two men who have worked with two of the more frequently mentioned artists in this book: Talking Heads and David Bowie. In addition to those collaborations and appearing on each other's solo albums (most notably Eno's best three-album run: *Here Come The Warm Jets*, *Another Green World* and *Before And After Science*), they also formed the musical duo Fripp & Eno. Under that title, and starting with *No Pussyfooting* in 1973, they have released four instrumental albums. Their music heavily features Eno's keyboards and synthesizers and Fripp's guitar with a tape delay technique called Frippertronics that is mirrored in some of Phish's Type II jams. Since expanding on their credits would take more space than this book permits, we will just say they were influential enough to warrant a song in their honor (and, if we are being honest, an honorary songwriting credit for Night 1's 'Seven Below'). Two great versions of 'Brian And Robert' to receive official releases are from Portland, Oregon (*Live Phish Volume 17, 7.15.98*) and the acoustic set at *Indio 8* (on 1 November 2009). Two versions that have yet to receive official releases include Trey's solo acoustic performances at the Newport Folk Festival on 2 August 2008 and the SiriusXM broadcast from his NYC apartment on 14 May 2021.

'Nellie Kane' (O'Brien)
The next 'name' song of the night is from the self-titled debut album of progressive bluegrass band *Hot Rize*. Written in the 1970s but sounding like it

could have been penned decades earlier, 'Nellie Kane' is one of the Phish's best covers (bluegrass or otherwise). A fun, lively number that picks up speed as it moves along, 'Nellie Kane' allows the band to have a bit of fun (musically) while Mike sings the lyrics without a wink. Only available physically on the *Hampton Comes Alive* box set, 'Nellie Kane' is well-represented in archival digital-only releases. Two of the best of those are from September 1999; the show on 14 September concludes its opening set with frenetic versions of 'Nellie Kane', 'Taste' and 'Rocky Top'. The 'Nellie Kane' from 29 September is a standard version, but once it concludes, the show really comes alive.

'Colonel Forbin's Ascent' (Anastasio) **> 'Fly Famous Mockingbird'** (Anastasio) **> 'David Bowie'** (Anastasio)

The final sequence of the opening set starts off with another 'name' song and the evening's first trip to *Gamehendge*. Telling the tale of the retired colonel who helped collect *The Helping Friendly Book* from Wilson, 'Colonel Forbin's Ascent' details how the song's titular character (and Icculus) built their plan around The Famous Mockingbird. The second song of the sequence, 'Fly Famous Mockingbird', covers the bird's flight into Wilson's castle and his acquisition of *The Helping Friendly Book*. This evening's performance also includes narration that pays tribute to The Beatles' 'Glass Onion' that reveals 'the walrus was Jimmy'. Presumably, since this is *Gamehendge*, this is the same Jimmy who owns a cat named Poster Nutbag. 'Colonel Forbin's Ascent' and 'Fly Famous Mockingbird' are (essentially) always paired together, and they are better for it. Since debuting in the spring of 1988 ('Fly Famous Mockingbird' making a solo flight on 7 February before being joined with 'Colonel Forbin's Ascent' on 12 March), there have only been a handful of times when one was played without the other, and those versions are only worth seeking out by completists. The standout sequence of 'Colonel Forbin's Ascent' > 'Fly Famous Mockingbird' > 'Character Zero', which fills much of Disc 2 of *Live Phish Volume 15*, is essential listening (as is the band's full performance of *Remain In Light*, their Talking Heads 'musical costume' performed that same night). A few years later, as the 1.0 era was winding down, the band played 'Colonel Forbin's Ascent > Fly Famous Mockingbird' during the 30 September 2000 performance captured on the *Live In Vegas* DVD. That night, instead of referencing Jimmy or The Beatles, Trey would thank the fans for the 'opportunity to do what we do, and we do love it' and he would also thank 'the greatest crew ever assembled in the history of music.'

After working through the composed sections of 'Fly Famous Mockingbird', the band move into the concluding 'name' song of the set, 'David Bowie'. Two archival releases (among the many included on the Live Phish app) that feature 'David Bowie' are 1 December 1992 and 8 May 1993. The second set of that December show in Ohio concluded with the band inserting a cover of

'Baby Elephant Walk' (by the mascot's best friend, Henry Mancini) into the middle of 'David Bowie'. The whole 'Dinner And A Movie' > 'David Bowie' > 'Baby Elephant Walk' > 'David Bowie' sequence lasts less than 24 minutes, but it is always interesting. For the band's show the following May in New Hampshire, the band took the scenic route in introducing 'David Bowie' to some of their influences. Running even shorter than December's Ohio show, Phish played through 'David Bowie' > 'Jessica Jam' > 'David Bowie' > 'Have Mercy' > 'David Bowie' in only 20 minutes. Beyond the numerous archival releases, 'David Bowie' was included on *Junta*, five of the 20 *Live Phish* collections (volumes 9, 12, 13, 19 and 20) and on the *Ventura* box set the band released in 2016. That *Ventura* version is even more incendiary than this Night 8 version, but that is not to say this version is lacking; this 'David Bowie' is tightly played and its Type I jam is a perfect set closer.

Set 2

'Drowned' (Townshend) **> 'A Song I Heard The Ocean Sing'** (Anastasio/Herman/Marshall)

Starting the second set with a song from The Who's concept album *Quadrophenia*, 'Drowned' tells of the protagonist's suicidal thoughts. It is a song the band played over 40 times previously (starting with their full album cover of *Quadrophenia* on 31 October 1995). Since that suicidal protagonist is a bellboy named Jimmy, this oft-deployed cover also fits in thematically. Containing the night's first epic jam, 'Drowned' contains enough elements to please fans of the band's Type I jams as well as those who prefer Type II. Although the band's initial attempt was a self-contained five-minute reproduction, the band's second performance of 'Drowned', included on the *New Year's Eve 1995 – Live At Madison Square Garden* collection, was an instant classic. Running about two-and-a-half times longer than its debut performance, that follow-up performance at MSG transitioned into a classic 'The Lizards' (and that initial one-two punch of 'Drowned' > 'The Lizards' was followed by an equally strong 'Axilla (Part II)' > 'Runaway Jim' combo). Post-*Baker's Dozen*, on 14 August 2021, 'Drowned' started off an interesting sequence of 'Drowned' > 'Ghost' > 'Scents And Subtle Sounds' > 'Chalk Dust Torture' > 'No Quarter' > 'Slave To The Traffic Light' > 'Suzy Greenberg'. This sequence of songs illustrates how the band can move in and out of tunes, stopping periodically when they discover a melody or texture worth exploring.

During Night 8, the 'Drowned' melody eventually moves into *Undermind*'s 'A Song I Heard The Ocean Sing' (which, honestly, sounds like it could be the title of another *Quadrophenia* song). With its extensive Type II jamming, 'A Song I Heard The Ocean Sing' allows the band to pass the 40-minute mark while still delivering two songs that are near-instantaneously praised. The band's confidence in 'A Song I Heard The Ocean Sing' is strong from the beginning. Its debut performance was also the opening song on the first night of their 2004 summer tours. That version was also included on the *Live In*

Brooklyn DVD, but it would be a different New York version that would be amongst the most memorable. For the New Year's Eve show on 31 December 2017, the band used 'A Song I Heard The Ocean Sing' to launch a sequence of songs ('The Moma Dance' > 'Prince Caspian' > 'Wading In The Velvet Sea' > 'First Tube') that continued nodding towards that night's nautical theme.

'Harpua' (Anastasio/Fishman) **> 'Also Sprach Zarathustra'** (Deodato) **> 'Golgi Apparatus'** (Anastasio/Marshall/Szuter/Woolf)
The next three-song sequence kicks off with another *Gamehendge* track, 'Harpua'. This one is a twisted tale of a fat, sweaty bulldog who kills Poster Nutbag, the beloved cat of Jimmy ... or is it The Walrus this time? After breezing through the intro lyrics, the band settle into a steady groove and launch into an 'improvised' monologue about life, the universe and everything. Long story short, the universe is shaped like a donut. 'Harpua' is always a welcome treat for phans, but this version features one of the band's more genuinely enjoyable digressions. For contrast, consider the performance from 16 August 2009, in Saratoga Springs, New York. Once the song's narration shifts to Jimmy and his Spirit Guide, Fishman channels Wesley Willis while singing Katy Perry's already-dated-by-2009 'I Kissed A Girl'. In the moment, Trey deadpans: 'That didn't work on so many levels.' Whether he was being facetious is debatable, and honestly, I could go either way on whether the bit lands. Someone who feels the moment did work, however, is Isaac Kandall Slone. His essay 'Exploring Jewishness And Queerness On Phish's Dance Floor' uses that Saratoga Springs 'Harpua' as a starting point for one of the best summaries of the Phish experience ever written:

> Phish take musical risks that leave them vulnerable to the potential for failure. These moments often occur during the band's improvisational jams, although other instances occur during shows: the performance of a gag or stunt, such as the aforementioned Katy Perry cover. Phish's openness to vulnerability resonates with me as an audience member. They are brave and authentic and reject mainstream expectations that a band play their hit songs in ways that resemble their recordings. With these risks comes the immense reward of a jam, song or stunt going well. In these instances, the band and audience both share in the newfound creative space. Fans often memorialize these moments as part of Phish's lore and often discuss them following the show.

The Night 8 'Harpua' likely won't inspire quite as many epiphanies, but it is still a great moment that eventually runs its course.

The band then take their interstellar donut talk into a version of the *2001* theme 'Also Sprach Zarathustra'. Initially performed by the band in 1993 and subsequently included on numerous *Live Phish* releases, 'Also Sprach Zarathustra' really came into its own during the 17 June 1994 show at the Eagles Ballroom in Milwaukee, Wisconsin. Coincidentally, this show was released as an Archival concert about a month before the start of *The Baker's Dozen*. The release notes described the importance of this release:

> This was the 'O.J. Show' performed during O.J. Simpson's slow-speed Bronco chase. Starting just before showtime and unbeknownst to the audience (O.J. had a cell phone in 1994, but most fans did not), the band were following O.J.'s progress along the freeways of Los Angeles. To say this affected the show would be an understatement. Phish channeled that crazy American energy and injected the juice into the music. The result is no secret – the O.J. Show is a classic introductory Phish tape.

As one of many highlights of the (at the time) most recently made available show, this 1994 classic was likely on numerous phans' minds that night in MSG.

For *The Baker's Dozen*, the band surf the *2001* groove all the way to the third (and final) *Junta* song of the night, 'Golgi Apparatus'. Written, as all great rock songs should be, by bored eighth-graders in an otherwise uninteresting biology class, 'Golgi Apparatus' was originally performed as the opening song to the band's 17 October 1986 show at Goddard College (the same show in which 'Wilson' made his debut). With its 'I saw you, with a ticket stub in your hand' lyric, it is ideal for smaller venues, but Night 8 demonstrates that it does just as well in larger arenas. Although included on almost half of the physical *Live Phish* releases, which is a drop in the bucket of its almost 500 total appearances, the most fun of these officially released versions might likely be the *Live Phish Volume 6, 11.27.98* show. That night, the Surfaris' 1962 hit 'Wipe Out' appeared in the setlist thrice, with the third time being the show-closing 'Golgi Apparatus' > 'Wipe Out'. For *The Baker's Dozen*, 'Golgi Apparatus' allows the band to rock out once more before the night ends.

'In The Good Old Summer Time' (Evans/Liles/Shields)

But the night isn't over yet. The second set closes with an a cappella, barbershop-style rendition of 'In the Good Old Summer Time', a Tin Pan Alley standard the band had debuted just two weeks earlier in Chicago. As of Night 8, it remains the last time Phish attempted the tune. If they ever bring it back, here's hoping for a full-blown cow-funk version, ideally modeled after the rendition performed by Chuck E. Cheese during the animatronic rodent's early-2000s Studio C lounge act. (Yes, that version of the song really existed, complete with slow-jam keyboard backing, disco lights and Chuck delivering the lyrics with all the laid-back swagger of a robot who's seen some things.)

Encore

'The Wind Cries Mary' (Hendrix)

The final song of the night is one last 'name song' and the first of four Jimi Hendrix songs the band performed during *The Baker's Dozen*. Speaking to a New York Post staff reporter during the last week of 1998, Trey said:

> My three all-time favorite guitarists are Jerry [Garcia], [Jimi] Hendrix and [Frank] Zappa. They are all totally unique from one another, yet oddly similar. They were all striving for this depth where a solo would take you on a journey. But the journey was their own vibe: Zappa was sarcastic, Hendrix was bluesy, Jerry was down home. I guess I have a suburban vibe. But I still want to get to the places that they got to.

Trey leans into the bluesy phrasing that he often praises in Hendrix's playing, and the crowd clearly feel it: cheers swell during his solos and there's a moment of almost reverent quiet before the applause rolls in at the end. To date, this remains the only time Phish have performed 'The Wind Cries Mary', but given the band's long-standing affection for Hendrix, there's a good chance it'll return.

Night 9: Tuesday 1 August ('Maple')

By the time the band got to Night 9, the 1980s were starting to become a footnote to their setlists. Of the 20 different songs performed for 'Maple', there were half as many that originated in the 1980s as there were that came from the 3.0 era.

Set 1

'O Canada' (Lavallee) **> 'Crowd Control'** (Anastasio/Marshall)

After taking a night off, the band kick off Night 9 ('Maple') with an instrumental take on the Canadian national anthem, 'O Canada'. Written originally in 1880 and with English-language lyrics incorporated in 1908 by Bob Weir (no, not that one), 'O Canada' allows the band to pay tribute to its maple-loving brethren, to the north and to Hendrix's Woodstock performance of the American national anthem. After promptly wrapping that up, they move into *Undermind*'s 'Crowd Control'. A show-opener in the 3.0 era (with the exception of this Night 9 performance and an isolated occurrence in 2022 when it followed their first 'Strawberry Fields Forever' since Night 2), 'Crowd Control', which *Rolling Stone* affixed the cumulative adjectives of 'joyous rock' in their 2004 review, allows the band to start Night 9 off with a midtempo party song that doesn't ask too much of the band or the audience. The next time they opened a show with 'Crowd Control', it was about a year later when the band were a hundred miles away in Camden, New Jersey. That 7 August 2018 show opened with 'Crowd Control', setting a relaxed but focused tone that carried through a second set packed with movement and momentum: 'Down With Disease' > 'Backwards Down the Number Line' > 'I Always Wanted It This Way' > 'Miss You' > 'Light' > 'Mike's Song' > 'I Am Hydrogen' > 'Weekapaug Groove'.

'Sugar Shack' (Gordon)

Mike's *Joy* contribution, 'Sugar Shack', the third song of the night, builds upon the energy the opening nine minutes provided. Mike wrote 'Sugar Shack' in October 2007 and was planning to include it on his next solo album. However, the song evolved into one of the funkier tracks on Phish's album *Joy*. Although there is a darkness to the lyric, the Caribbean-calypso chorus and melody give it a whimsical groove. A song Trey has had difficulties performing in the past (it might be the one Phish song where the number of inferior versions have a fighting chance of outnumbering the superior versions), the band deliver an uncharacteristically excellent version during *The Baker's Dozen*. The last version approaching the excellence of this Night 9 version was also the last time the band played 'Sugar Shack' at MSG. On 30 December 2016, with only two songs standing between them and the set break, they delivered a powerful 'Sugar Shack' and a strong 'You Enjoy Myself'. Those, plus the 'Bathtub Gin' that preceded them, were then overshadowed by the 'Tweezer' > 'Sparks' > 'Ghost' > 'Light' > 'Wading In The Velvet Sea' > 'Rocky Top' sequence that followed.

'When The Circus Comes' (Hidalgo/Perez)

The band then turn the mood introspective with their version of Los Lobos' 'When The Circus Comes' (from their stone-cold classic *Kiko,* produced, like 'Crowd Control' and the rest of *Undermind*, by Tchad Blake). In that same *New York Post* article in which Trey mentioned his appreciation of Garcia, Zappa and Hendrix, he was asked about songs he wished he had written. In his response, along with 'seven or eight Beatles songs', he mentioned Los Lobos' 'When The Circus Comes'. He explained: 'It's a great song, and when I play it, I feel like I wrote it.' Originally played by the band in the spring of 1997 and then played 14 more times just that year, 'When The Circus Comes' has been a routine occurrence ever since. For the band's *Phish Destroys America* tour, they expertly deployed 'When The Circus Comes' in Denver, Colorado, in an effort to cool down the room after an hour-long opening set which consisted solely of 'Tweezer', 'Reba', 'Train Song' and 'Ghost' > 'Fire', plus a second set that was already 50-minutes strong by the time the band got through 'Down With Disease' > 'Olivia's Pool' > 'Johnny B. Goode' > 'Jesus Just Left Chicago'. All of this, and more, was later released on *Live Phish Volume 11, 11.17.97.*

'Daniel Saw The Stone' (Traditional)

After once again cooling things down with 'When The Circus Comes', the band proceed to bring some fire and brimstone to the bluegrass spiritual 'Daniel Saw The Stone'. Delivered with its customary energy, this last (to date) version of 'Daniel Saw The Stone' gets the phaithful on their feet and moving again like it is Night 1. An even quicker version was performed by the band on 14 August 1993 and was immortalized on the previously praised *Live Phish Volume 7, 8.14.93*. The second disc of that edition (the one that includes 'Daniel Saw The Stone') deserves to be mentioned as one of the best discs in that entire 60-disc series.

'Army Of One' (McConnell)

The second of two *Undermind* songs performed on Night 9, 'Army Of One' is Phish in full-on The Band mode. Sounding like something that either Danko or Manual could have brought to the group and with a guitar solo ripped from Robbie Robertson's playbook, 'Army Of One' makes a perfect follow-up to the *Cahoots*-sounding 'When The Circus Comes' and the *Rock Of Ages*-indebted 'Daniel Saw The Stone'. For another strong version, made even stronger by the 'Poor Heart' > '46 Days' > 'Tube' > 'Character Zero' which flowed out of it, check out the 7 August 2010 show in Berkeley, California. That show, like this Night 9 version, illustrates how Page's ballad provides an island of introspection before the pace picks back up.

'The Wedge' (Anastasio/Marshall)

Speaking of The Band one last time, 'The Wedge' features a lyric that could be passed off as one of theirs: 'Take the highway through the Great Divide'.

Although not reaching the peaks hit by the 20 July 2014 version performed in Chicago (available to view on the *Live Phish* YouTube Channel), 'The Wedge' still has a nice, up-tempo jazz feel. Additional versions, beyond the ones included on *Rift* and *Hampton Comes Alive*, include the *Live Bait Vol. 6* version (from the 20 August 1993 show in Colorado) and the *Live Bait Vol. 13* version (from the Chicago show on 20 July 2014).

'Guelah Papyrus' (Anastasio/Marshall)**/'Maple Leaf Rag'** (Joplin)**/'Guelah Papyrus'** (Anastasio/Marshall)
Starting with one of the best opening verses in Phish's oeuvre ('Aboard a craft bereft of oar/I rowed upstream to find Lenore/Abducted by a bandit or/A king from some forgotten war'), 'Guelah Papyrus' maintains a consistent vibe – until it does not. Performed as a brief interstitial by Page, Scott Joplin's 'Maple Leaf Rag' is a momentary mood breaker. But then Trey starts 'Guelah Papyrus' back up again as if a ragtime breakdown is always inserted into the middle of the composition. The closest they had come to this kind of mid-song surprise was during the not-officially-released version from 14 June 1994 in Des Moines, Iowa. There, the band dropped into a slinky 'Guelah Papyrus' and, mid-performance, stepped away from their microphones to deliver an unamplified, barbershop-style 'Sweet Adeline'. After delivering this, and before returning to finish 'Guelah Papyrus', the band slipped in a brief but compelling 'Digital Delay Loop Jam' that could have lasted three times as long without wearing out its welcome. As far as officially released versions of 'Guelah Papyrus', there is the studio version included on *A Picture Of Nectar* and the archival release from the 7 November 1996 show in Lexington, Kentucky.

'McGrupp And The Watchful Hosemasters' (Anastasio/Marshall) **> 'Limb By Limb'** (Anastasio/Herman/Marshall) **> 'Walk Away'** (Walsh)
The second of the two *Gamehendge* songs about dogs, 'McGrupp And The Watchful Hosemasters' tells of Colonel Forbin's good dog, McGrupp, who makes a positive contribution to the Gamehendge story (as opposed to that bad dog Harpua). Always played more frequently than 'Harpua', 'McGrupp And The Watchful Hosemasters' appears to be heading towards an even greater lead in the song count tally during the 3.0 era. Especially noteworthy versions include the trombone-powered version from 29 July 1988, the still-unreleased 23 July 1996 performance in Hamburg, Germany, the 29 October 1998 version included on *Live Bait. Vol. 14* and the acoustic *Festival 8* version from 1 November 2009.

'Limb By Limb' is played somewhat quietly, and then right near the end, an excellent jam develops. Originally included on *The Story Of The Ghost*, 'Limb By Limb' was later well-represented by excellent versions included on the *Live Phish Volume 17, 7.15.98* CDs, the *IT* DVD and the archival release of the show in Japan on 16 June 2000. In the positive parts of their three-and-a-half-star review of *The Story Of The Ghost*, *Rolling Stone* used 'Limb By Limb' as an example of what the album does right: 'But the soul of *Story* reveals itself during the album's second half, where simplicity, directness and brevity prevail. 'Limb By Limb' layers voices into a call-and-response dialogue with a hint of reggae in the simmering syncopations.' When 'Limb By Limb' was performed at Deer Creek on 10 June 2000, the *Indianapolis Star* also praised the song (and reviewer Dave Lindquest provided similar reasons): "Limb By Limb' was perhaps the best tune of the night – a complete package of Anastasio and McConnel on alternating vocals, Fishman's syncopated drums and Gordon's propulsive bass.'

After this great Night 9 version of 'Limb By Limb', it sounds as if the band are going to end the late-breaking jam with a fade into the set break, but then a final burst comes before they pivot into The James Gang's 1971 hit, 'Walk Away'. Writer Matthew Greenwald described the original Joe Walsh-powered version as 'A melting pot of hard rock and funk, the song is almost a wielding of Stax and proto-heavy metal.' That is a description that can also be affixed to innumerable moments across Phish's concertography. As one of the band's best attempts at big, dumb rock 'n' roll, 'Walk Away' is always fun (either as a closer or as part of an extended sequence). See the previously praised *Live Phish Volume 18, 5.7.94, Live Phish Volume 7, 8.14.93* and *Live Phish Volume 4, 6.14.00* for exhibits A, B and C.

Set 2

'Golden Age' (Adebimpe/Bunton/Malone/Sitek/Smith)
After delivering a set heavy with shorter songs, the band begin the second set with the longest single song of the night. If Los Lobos' 'When The Circus Comes' is a song Trey feels like he wrote, then I can imagine a follow-up interview where Trey makes the same claim about TV On The Radio's 'Golden Age'. Talent recognizes talent, and songwriters are generally happy when their music is given exposure to corners of the world it might not have otherwise reached. Speaking to *The Hollywood Reporter,* TV On The Radio's frontman, Tunde Adebimpe, seemed indifferent on the matter, concluding his thoughts with 'It's still weird to me that anyone is listening to my stuff.'

Sounding like something the band would have written for *Joy*, 'Golden Age' demonstrates their ability to follow up optimistic lyrics with intense jamming that has no consistent leader. As one of the best things the band introduced in the 3.0 era, 'Golden Age' is almost always a highlight in any concert. Included on their 2008 release *Dear Science*, 'Golden Age' was described by *Pitchfork* in their Best New Music-stamped review as that album's 'fulcrum' and by *AllMusic* as 'brilliantly funky'. In her review for the latter site, Heather Phares wrote that 'Adepimbe sings 'there's a golden age coming 'round' without a trace of irony' and Phish deliver the lyrics the same way. Phans looking for more concise yet still exciting versions should look to 2019 and the concerts performed on 18 June and 30 November. For the

Canadian show that summer, the band delivered 'Golden Age' (complete with teases to 'Gotta Jibboo', the Spencer Davis Group's 'I'm A Man' and 'Crosseyed And Painless' by Talking Heads) as part of an underrated 67-minute second set sequence of 'Plasma' > 'The Final Hurrah' > 'Wingsuit' > 'Golden Age' > 'I Always Wanted It This Way' > 'Prince Caspian' > 'If I Could' > '46 Days'. For the autumn show in Providence, Rhode Island, the band delivered a completely different but better-rated 67-minute second set sequence of 'Bathtub Gin' > 'Alaska' > 'What's The Use?' > 'Piper' > 'Golden Age' > 'Plasma' > 'Harry Hood'. Phans looking for a lengthier 'Golden Age' should revisit October shows from 2016 and 2018. On 28 October 2016, the band took their Type II jam deep into the unknown, pushing 'Golden Age' into truly exploratory territory. For the 19 October 2018 show at the Hampton Coliseum, the band played for almost an hour with 'Carini' > 'Sand' > 'Golden Age' > 'Twist' before running aground.

'Leaves' (Anastasio/Marshall)
Although only debuted two weeks earlier in Chicago, this second-ever performance of 'Leaves'' almost doubled in length. With a quiet start by Trey, 'Leaves' gradually gains the other members of the band and then builds into something truly special. The band scaled it back slightly during its third and final 2017 appearance at Dick's Sporting Goods Park a month later. They then shelved the song until their post-pandemic tour of 2021 (not counting, of course, its studio debut on 2020's *Sigma Oasis*, which featured what Stephen Thomas Erlewine called 'a sideways glance at David Bowie on 'Leaves''). It would take until 2022 for the song to truly come into its own – I am looking at you 26 July – and it would make regular appearances throughout the year. Its presence has been slightly less frequent since then, but hopefully, this is a momentary dip and it will start appearing with greater regularity in the not-too-distant future.

'Swept Away' (Anastasio/Marshall) **> 'Steep'** (Anastasio/Fishman/Gordon/Marshall/McConnell) **> '46 Days'** (Anastasio/Marshall) **> 'Piper'** (Anastasio/Marshall) **> 'Possum'** (Holdsworth)
Night 9 was the 30th time the band started up 'Swept Away' and then moved into 'Steep'. Those songs have always been paired together – and who can argue with the results? Both were originally included on *Billy Breathes*, in that order, naturally, and were played somewhat regularly from their October 1996 debut until December 1997. The third set of the band's 1996 Halloween show (aka *Live Phish Volume 15, 10.31.96*) featured a strong 'Simple' > 'Swept Away' > 'Steep' > 'Jesus Just Left Chicago' > 'Suzy Greenberg' (that had been preceded by an equally strong 'Also Sprach Zarathustra' > 'Maze'). Of greater interest might be the percussive 'Brother', which starts Disc 4. A forgotten gem of the band's catalog, 'Brother' was ripe for a bust-out during *The Baker's Dozen*, but it did not make an appearance until the band returned to MSG for

their New Year's run. That 30 December performance was the first time they had played 'Brother' since 17 June 2012, a gap of 216 shows.

After making it through their longest-ever 'Steep', the band start up another of their epics, '46 Days'. Not following the same journey as the 29-minute version performed on 3 August 2003, this '46 Days' still manages to bring the Type I fun and provides a tease of The Rolling Stones' 'Can't You Hear Me Knocking', as all good jams do. It also provides Trey a chance to bring back his Marimba Lumina (and for Mike and Page to also join the percussion army). Included on the debut album of their 2.0 era, *Round Room*, '46 Days' received a special mention in the accompanying *Rolling Stone* review:

> After spending two years doing other things, playing music in un-Phish-like settings, the four musicians appear newly dedicated to changing the very temperature of their interactions. They're baiting one another, throwing down challenges, chasing gnarled conversations that don't resolve neatly and looking for new levels of engagement. Their exchanges transform the ordinary organ-funk pulse of '46 Days' into a lacerating workout.

With a bad version of '46 Days' being almost impossible to find, any of its performances are worth hearing. For a version slightly off the beaten path, check out the performance on 14 February 2020 by Trey's supergroup, Oysterhead. Les Claypool and Stewart Copeland (Primus and The Police, respectively) joined Trey to deliver a version that is impossible to pin down. Performed as part of a three-song encore, Oysterhead first debuted the *Zenyatta Mondatta* classic 'Voices Inside My Head', then moved right into the only version of '46 Days' to include elements of The Doors' 'L.A. Woman'. After a slight pause, they wrapped things up with their original composition 'Owner Of The World' (although to be fair, Messrs. Blackmore, Gillan, Glover, Lord and Paice deserve songwriting credit for the excellently deployed 'Smoke On The Water' that was teased when they rolled into the four-minute mark).

After '46 Days', the band keep the energy alive with the forever-sprightly 'Piper'. Frequently deployed as a transition song, yet without a consistent preceding or succeeding song, 'Piper' is a Type I jam that can go Type II if the show requires it (and, apparently, Night 9 required it). 'Piper' was originally included on *Farmhouse* and was later included as part of the second set sequence of 'Heavy Things' > 'Piper' > 'Rock And Roll' documented on *Live Phish Volume 5, 7.8.00*. Although never taken as far as the longest '46 Days', 'Piper' more than holds its own when compared to one another: per statistics maintained on Phish.net, as of this writing, '46 Days' has an average jam length of 11:58 and 'Piper' has one of 15:39. Both songs have reputations for going to some memorable places, and when adjacent to one another on the setlist, it is almost inevitable something special will occur. But that should not imply they need each other in order to succeed; in the year preceding *The*

Baker's Dozen, Phish had three especially memorable versions of 'Piper'. For their annual Labor Day run at Dick's, the band delivered a magnificent 'Crosseyed And Painless' > 'Steam' > 'Piper' > 'Light' > 'The Lizards' on 4 September 2016. For the show in Jacksonville, Florida, on 16 October, the band began the back half of the show with 'Crosseyed And Painless' > 'Steam' > 'Piper' > 'Wingsuit' before delivering back-to-back pairings of 'Sparkle > 'The Wedge' and 'Wading In The Velvet Sea' > 'Run Like An Antelope'. And, finally, for the second set of the second show of their Halloween run on 29 October, the band started things off with extended workouts of both 'Mercy' and 'Piper' (and then kept things going with 'Scents And Subtle Sounds' > 'Tweezer' > 'I Always Wanted It This Way' > 'The Horse' > 'Silent In The Morning' > 'Golgi Apparatus').

The band conclude the second set with 'Possum', another of their impossible-to-dislike numbers – especially if you subscribe to the 'Page Side – Rage Side' mentality, a reference to the tradition of enthusiastic fans positioning themselves on keyboardist Page McConnell's side of the stage, where the energy (or 'rage') is believed to flow strongest. Great versions are almost too numerous to mention, but I would be remiss if I did not point out the 1 November 2013 version from Atlantic City and the 7 December 1995 version the band commercially released less than two weeks later on the *Niagara Falls* CDs. In an interview with Oren Kroll-Zeldin and Ariella Werden-Greenfield for their book *This Is Your Song Too: Phish And Contemporary Jewish Identity*, the Disco Biscuits' bassist Marc Brownstein makes an insightful comment about Phish and their 'hits'. He states:

> It's funny to say that every song is a hit for a band that's had zero hits. But that's the thing. In our world, we call them 'jam-band hits'. A jam-band hit is a song that the fans accept as one of their own. And it doesn't even have to be on the radio. It could be 20 minutes long. It doesn't have to have any of the other characteristics of a hit song. But songs that 'hit' with fans make it into the repertoire. That's a jam-band hit … But if you're Phish, every song is a hit. They're all hits.

'Possum' is most definitely one of Phish's 'hits', and with close to 600 appearances, it will likely be included in the band's (eventual) final run of shows. If they (and especially Page) continue to play it as strongly as they did on Night 9, there will be zero complaints.

Encore

'Rock 'N' Roll Suicide' (Bowie)

Performed for the second (and final) time by Phish, 'Rock 'N' Roll Suicide' was the third (of four) David Bowie songs the band would perform during *The Baker's Dozen*. Once again slotting Bowie in the encore slot, 'Rock 'N' Roll Suicide' is, in the words of British novelist and playwright Deborah Levy in her essay for *Long Players: Writers On The Albums That Shaped Them*, a message that she (Levy) 'was not alone in (her) beautiful desolation, certainly not desperate enough to smoke (her) final cigarette and say goodbye.' The perfect way to come down from the sugar-high of 'Maple Night', 'Rock 'N' Roll Suicide' is the heaviest conclusion to any show in the run, although Trey's concluding remarks about how 'that was really fun' lighten the mood.

Night 10: Wednesday 2 August ('Holes')

Each night of *The Baker's Dozen* featured a specially themed donut courtesy of the band and Philadelphia-based Federal Donuts. In an interview with *NPR*, co-owner Felicia D'Ambrosio discussed how the band emailed her in advance of the run and asked about her shop's availability to provide thousands of complimentary donuts to concert-goers as they entered the venue. Roughly 12 hours before each show, the band's social media channels would announce that night's theme and provide an image of the doughnut and a brief description. As a 'lifelong Phish fan', D'Ambrosio described the opportunity as 'surreal to say the least.' She credits Federal Donuts' chef, Matt Fein, with the 'hard work' involved in the undertaking. Fein stated that each night, they would need to prepare the 'equivalent of nearly five days' worth of doughnuts.' Luckily, there were simple recipes intermingled with some of the more complex flavors requested. Night 3 ('Red Velvet') and Night 4 ('Jam Filled') were two of the most intensive nights. Matt Fein and his crew had to start work at 9 pm the night before in order to ensure everything was ready for the following night's show. For Night 10 ('Holes'), Federal Donuts provided doughnut holes covered with a dusting of peanut butter and chocolate.

Set 1

'Way Down In The Hole' (Waits)

Originally included on the concluding album of his mid-1980s trilogy for Island Records, Tom Waits' 'Way Down In The Hole' is likely best known for either being the theme song to *The Wire* (which was subsequently re-recorded for that show by The Blind Boys of Alabama, Steve Earle and others) or as the inspiration for Nick Cave and the Bad Seeds' 'Red Right Hand'. So far, the song has only been played once, but based on the audience response and the fun the band seem to be having, it seems likely to return at some point. This is not the only Tom Waits song the band have tackled as a 'once and done'; on 15 June 2010, they performed his *Mule Variations* classic 'Cold Water' (which their peers in Railroad Earth had also included on their 2001 debut, *The Black Bear Sessions*). In a listicle he wrote for his blog, covermesongs.com, writer Ray Padgett ranked this as the best cover Phish performed during *The Baker's Dozen,* and it definitely deserves to be in the conversation.

'Buried Alive' (Anastasio)

Phans who recognized the instrumental that follows 'Way Down in the Hole' as 'Buried Alive' were likely amused (which is not meant to imply that getting the 'joke' was a prerequisite to enjoying the moment). Previously, an especially frenetic version was sandwiched between two performances of 'Big Black Furry Creature From Mars' on the *Live Phish 07.15.03* release and an unusually epic version was performed on 29 July 1998 and included on the *Live Bait Vol. 08* compilation. *The Baker's Dozen* version is well-played, and even if it is a totally different type of song than 'Way Down In The Hole', they pair nicely together.

'Kill Devil Falls' (Anastasio/Marshall)

Referred to by *Rolling Stone* as 'a boogie-till-you-puke number whose title works as a metaphor for overindulgence', 'Kill Devil Falls' is another of *Joy*'s instant classics. Occasionally taken into Type II territory, the version from Night 10 is comparatively compact. For their Labor Day Run in 2024, the 31 August show featured a locked-in Phish spending over an hour running through an unbelievable 'Loving Cup' > 'Kill Devil Falls' > 'What's Going Through Your Mind' > 'Crosseyed And Painless' sequence. For another excellent yet compact version of 'Kill Devil Falls', the Long Beach Arena show from 15 August 2012 features a tight 'Cities' > 'Kill Devil Falls' (among other highlights). After wrapping up their *Baker's Dozen* trip to 'Kill Devil Falls', the band (and audience) take a moment of respite before starting up the first indisputable high point of Night 10.

'Guyute' (Anastasio/Marshall)

Another of Phish's animal-related songs – this time a hostile hog – 'Guyute' was included on *The Story Of The Ghost* and was later re-worked in an orchestral format for Trey's 2004 *Seis De Mayo* project. Originally performed by the band during their fall tour of 1994, 'Guyute' made a good enough impression on the band and fans that it was included on the New Year's run setlist. For the 29 December show, the sinister sow made a memorable impression and that version closes the opening disc of the *Live Phish Volume 20, 12.29.94* collection. Definitely continue on to the second disc, though, because it opens with a 'David Bowie' that's hard to beat. Although this portentous pig makes periodic appearances to remind folks he is still around, it has been years since he was a setlist mainstay.

'I Didn't Know' (Wright)

The band then launch into what passes for a quotidian version of 'I Didn't Know' – that is, one without vacuum solos, Fishman antics or extended detours. At least at first. As shown on the *Live In Vegas* DVD, the song's first official release, Phish typically repeat the chorus eight times in a row. On Night 10, you can hear the band start to crack up by the seventh, suggesting that even the most routine elements of this song can teeter into absurdity. Trey then makes an announcement – 'The more holes, the more complicated the vacuum cleaner' – and Fishman takes a 'solo' on his trusty hoover. It probably wasn't worth the price of admission, and nobody is going to compare Fishman's embouchure to that of a clean Miles Davis, but I'm sure everyone enjoyed being there in the moment.

'NICU' (Anastasio/Marshall)

An initially Trey-heavy 'NICU' provides the audience with an up-tempo moment, and even before receiving his 'Play it, Leo, play it!!' exhortation from Trey, Page makes his presence known. One of the things I love about Page is his humility. He can unleash dazzling runs of jazz-informed comping, funky clavinet riffs or rich layers of Rhodes textures, but he never demands the spotlight. Another keyboardist might turn those moments into solo showcases, but Page always seems more focused on deepening the groove or lifting the overall sound. Page is always in service of either the song or the band – he is not playing a thousand notes for himself; he is playing them because that is what the moment needs.

'NICU' is another of the band's staples that has never made an appearance on a studio album, but that is okay because it has been on several of their classic live albums. Beyond appearing on *The Clifford Ball*, *Hampton Comes Alive* and *IT*, 'NICU' makes an appearance on the fourth disc of *Live Phish Volume 16, 10.31.98*. This 'filler' disc contains the second set (plus the encore) of the show that preceded their legendary musical costume of the Velvet Underground's *Loaded*. But these tracks are anything but 'filler'. This 78-minute stretch from 'Run Like An Antelope' through 'Freebird' is one of my all-time favorite performances, and the 'NICU' performed that night is a large part of the reason why.

'Meat' (Anastasio/Fishman/Gordon/Marshall/McConnell) **> 'Maze'** (Anastasio/Marshall)

The Story Of The Ghost's 'Meat' is next and it is a great version that becomes even better when, after the two-minute mark, Fishman misses the transition to the next section and, after apologizing to the band and audience, leads the recovery efforts to get the song back on track. After some Type II explorations, 'Meat' greets 'Maze' for only the fourth time (and for the first time with the '>' designation). This 'Rift' classic is no longer jammed as hard as it was during its first decade or so, but this version is still excellent and it reaches a solid peak before its conclusion. The band would wait over a year to revisit 'Meat', but when they did (on 12 August 2018), it was another strong version. For 'Maze', the wait was not quite as long – it was played when the band returned to MSG for their New Year's run in December. Both 'Meat' and 'Maze' are included on the *Star Lake 98* DVD. That 11 August 1998 performance included a well-received first set – 'Fee' > 'Maze' – and a second set – 'Meat' > 'Limb By Limb' – that unfairly pales against the 'Runaway Jim' that precedes it.

'Ginseng Sullivan' (Blake)

Written by Norman Blake (the *Oh, Brother Where Art Thou* one, not the Teenage Fanclub one), 'Ginseng Sullivan' is another of the band's bluegrass classics. Tightly delivered in under three-and-a-half minutes, 'Ginseng Sullivan' almost seems to have replaced 'Destiny Unbound' in Phish's setlists (but during the 3.0 era, they have received more equitable representation). On 10 and 11 August 1997, the band did back-to-back shows at Deer Creek. In his overly harsh ½ star review of the first show for the *Indianapolis News*, Marc

Allen does manage to find something nice to say about 'Ginseng Sullivan', calling it 'a toe-tapping, straight country song' that 'contained pretty harmonies and had some focus.' Those adjectives could be applied to this *Baker's Dozen* performance (or to the version also included on that 'all killer, no filler' *Star Lake 98* DVD).

'Waiting All Night' (Anastasio/Fishman/Gordon/McConnell)
Fuego's 'Waiting All Night' is Phish dialing back some of the 'Ginseng Sullivan' energy while simultaneously dialing up the emotion. Initially characterized as 'a dreamy classic rock tune' by *NPR* legend Bob Boilen, this version of 'Waiting All Night' lives up to that descriptor. Performed slower here than on that initial *Wingsuit* performance on 31 October 2013, 'Waiting All Night' is the perfect song to play before things start to (gradually) pick back up. Another version that was expertly positioned was the encore performance from 1 November 2014. After taking a well-deserved break (which they had earned after opening with 'Possum' and running through an impressive sequence of 'Crosseyed And Painless' > 'Light' > 'The Dogs' > 'Lengthwise' > 'Twist' > 'Wading In The Velvet Sea' > 'Harry Hood' > 'Golgi Apparatus' > 'Backwards Down The Number Line'), the band returned to the stage for a beautiful three-song encore. 'Waiting All Night', 'Sing Monica' and 'The Star-Spangled Banner' capped off a fantastic show. For *The Baker's Dozen*, the band follow 'Waiting All Night' with one of their bigger 'hits' and a song that helps get the blood flowing once again.

'Heavy Things' (Anastasio/Herman/Marshall)
The sole single from *Farmhouse*, hitting number 29 on *Billboard*'s Adult Pop Airplay chart on the week of 29 July 2000, 'Heavy Things' is Phish at their most accessible (which, ironically, turns off a certain segment of phandom). As someone who unequivocally loves this side of Phish, I find 'Heavy Things' to be a joy to hear. In their largely positive review of *Farmhouse*, which was accompanied by a group picture in which Fishman reps King Crimson, *Spin Magazine* (in a seven out of ten review) opines that 'In the buoyant alterna-shimmy 'Heavy Things', the Happy Mondays have group sex with the Steve Miller Band.' It is assumed that this was a compliment and it elevated their score by at least one full point. Beyond *Farmhouse*, excellent versions of 'Heavy Things' were included on two of the earliest archival releases, *Live Phish Volume 4, 6.14.00* and *Live Phish Volume 5, 7.8.00*.

'Run Like An Antelope' (Anastasio/Pollak)
The longest single song of the opening set, *Lawn Boy*'s 'Run Like An Antelope' closes things out. With an energy that never lags, the band stay tight and focused throughout the entire performance (and Page especially deserves to be commended for cutting through the whirlwind with sharp, rhythmic comping and bursts of melodic color that elevate the tension

without stepping on anyone else's toes). For additional examples of how great this song can be, check out pretty much any version performed in the Midwest during the early-to-mid-1990s. The version performed at the Murat Theater in Indianapolis, Indiana, on 24 June 1994 was included as a bonus track on *Live Phish Volume 10, 6.22.94* because of how the band incorporated assorted Type II moments into a cohesive whole. The more Type I version from the band's Madison, Wisconsin performance on 24 October 1995 has not been officially released (yet) but is easily available to hear online. Of course, the king of Midwest 'Antelopes' might be the version included on *Live Phish Volume 7, 8.14.93*. As mentioned on Night 6, the band take the audience in and out of the song as they make a 35-minute trip through 'Also Sprach Zarathustra' > 'Run Like An Antelope' > 'Sparks' > 'Walk Away' > 'Run Like An Antelope' > 'Have Mercy' > 'Run Like An Antelope'.

Set 2

'Mike's Song' (Gordon) **> 'O Holy Night'** (Adam/Clappeau) **> 'Taste'** (Anastasio/Fishman/Gordon/Marshall/McConnell) **> 'Wingsuit'** (Anastasio/Fishman/Gordon/McConnell) **> 'Sneakin' Sally Through The Alley'** (Toussaint) **> 'Weekapaug Groove'** (Anastasio/Fishman/Gordon/McConnell)

After an opening set comprised almost entirely of individual songs, the night's second set consists of one long medley. Starting with a 'Mike's Song' that some would consider an all-timer or at least a worthy successor to its MSG debut on 31 December 1995 or the Doors-referencing ('Mother, I want to cook you breakfast') version included on *Slip Stitch And Pass*, this entire second set is a microcosm of what Phish can do on any given night.

This night's epic 'Mike's Song' includes clever and inventive Type I jamming before moving into Type II territory as they find their way into an 'O Holy Night' that would not be out of place during one of their famed Halloween shows. Delivered with an eeriness that is difficult to define and a beauty that is hard to overstate, this 'O Holy Night' demonstrates how much effort the band put into one-off performances that, to be honest, were only included to satisfy a self-imposed 'theme'. Writer Elissa Goldstein's first Phish concert was during *The Baker's Dozen*, and in response, she tweeted, 'Okay, I'm starting to get it; this is a megachurch for secular software developers.' Goldstein's tweet succinctly satirizes and summarizes the scene: Phish fandom can feel like a full-blown belief system for tech-adjacent music fans, one that is not built around doctrine but around improvisation, playfulness and the obsessive pursuit of musical moments that only exist once.

After the homiletic conclusion to 'O Holy Night', the band stretch *Billy Breathes*' 'Taste' farther than they ever have before. In his two-and-a-half-star review of *Billy Breathes* for the *Chicago Tribune*, Greg Kot points to 'Taste' as something that does not work as well as the band intended. He writes: 'The band still undercut some of their best ideas with pointless ones, as when the polyrhythms of 'Taste' are derailed by goofy vocal harmonies.' But when it comes to the *Baker's Dozen*, I've found no one citing such goofiness, suggesting the band may have finally struck the balance Kot found lacking. The band had, on previous occasions, nudged 'Taste' beyond its usual boundaries. Their 5 December 1999 show in Rochester, New York, features one of the best examples of this. That same show also debuted 'Jennifer Dances', a song with real potential – if only someone had trimmed those opening lines: 'The workers they come back from their day in the field/ Jennifer dances and she cooks me a meal/A little less salt in the gravy tonight'. Not performed during the *Baker's Dozen*, 'Jennifer Dances' was later resurrected (sort of) as part of an in-joke during the 27 July 2014 show at Merriweather Post Pavilion. Still, the original 1999 version is worth a listen – at least once – for the curious and the completists alike. For another great 'Taste', the 8 November 1998 show in Chicago should be heard. Starting off the first set with 'Taste' and concluding the show with an encore consisting of just the Jane's Addiction classic 'Been Caught Stealing', the whole show is a treat.

The back half of Night 10 is past the 40-minute mark when they finally move out of 'Taste' (only their third song of the set). Next comes 'Wingsuit', and with its signature introspection, the band settle into a contemplative mood until it's time to shift gears and get down to Allen Toussaint's funky classic, 'Sneakin' Sally Through The Alley'. Originally set to be the title track for the album which became *Fuego*, 'Wingsuit' would be re-recorded (beautifully) by Trey and Mike for their *December* release. Performed regularly by the band during its first few years, 2017 is when 'Wingsuit' became more of a rarity. A great latter-day version was on 31 July 2022 when the band spent roughly 45 minutes going through 'Halley's Comet' > 'Tweezer' > 'Wingsuit' > 'Tweezer' > 'Birds Of A Feather'.

'Sneakin' Sally Through The Alley', originally recorded by Lee Dorsey (and backed by The Meters), allows the band to take the tempo up a notch and work their way into the set-closing 'Weekapaug Groove'. Although included on the *Alpine Valley* DVD (which documents the 14 August 2010 performance), the best physical release of 'Sneakin' Sally Through The Alley' is the 'Sneakin' Sally Through The Alley' > 'Chalk Dust Torture' > 'Lawn Boy' sequence on *Live Phish Volume 16, 10.31.98*. Of course, this being Phish, most of the best versions are only available digitally (through either official or unofficial channels). The band's archival release of the 30 December 1994 show at Madison Square Garden started with 'Sneakin' Sally Through The Alley' > 'Taste', and then, for an encore that ran for almost half an hour, they performed 'Carini' > 'Black-Eyed Katy' > 'Sneakin' Sally Through The Alley' > 'Frankenstein'. In between that opening 'Sneakin' Sally Through The Alley' and the concluding 'Frankenstein', the band delivered what might be the best night of their 1997 New Year's Eve run. Another fantastic archival release, the *1998 Island Tour*, which followed that NYE run, documents the 'Wolfman's

Brother' > 'Sneakin' Sally Through The Alley' > 'Frankie Says' > 'Twist' > 'Sleeping Monkey' > 'Rocky Top' the band performed on 2 April 1998. For a great version that has yet to see an official release, check out the 8 August 1998 show at the Merriweather Post Pavilion. With a 'Sneakin' Sally Through The Alley' > 'Guyute' in the first set, a 'Cavern' > 'Also Sprach Zarathustra' > 'Tela' > 'Piper' (and an excellent 'Harry Hood') in the second set and the debuts of both 'Sweet Jane' and 'Sabotage', this show will likely see an official release someday.

For the closing 'Weekapaug Groove', which has a gallop that is about as far from the strange, mysteriousness of 'O Holy Night' as a band could get, the band conclude the set that began an hour earlier with 'Mike's Song'. Because of the path the band took to get from 'Mike's Song' to 'Weekapaug Groove' ('Mike's Song' > 'O Holy Night' > 'Taste' > 'Wingsuit' > 'Sneakin' Sally Through The Alley' > 'Weekapaug Groove'), the band omitted 'I Am Hydrogen'. This makes the oft-utilized segue track ('Mike's Song' > 'I Am Hydrogen' > 'Weekapaug Groove') the most-played Phish track (well over 300 performances prior to Night 10) to not be included in the *Baker's Dozen* setlists. With dozens of official releases, including its debut release on *Slip Stitch And Pass*, there are enough versions to keep fans in a Weekapaug groove for days. For a yet-to-be-released version, search out the 14 May 1992 performance at the Capital Theater.

After delivering the final performance of *A Picture Of Nectar*'s 'Eliza', the band played a fun run of 'Mike's Song' > 'I Am Hydrogen' > 'Weekapaug Groove' > 'Wait' > 'Weekapaug Groove'. Subsequent years would also see great versions. For the 16 August 1993 show in St. Louis, the band performed an excellent run of 'Mike's Song' > 'Faht' > 'Weekapaug Groove' (and during that same show, they followed in Sun Ra's footsteps and performed a version of Duke Ellington's 'Take The 'A' Train'). On 2 July 1994, they took a New Jersey crowd all the way from 'Also Sprach Zarathustra' > 'Mike's Song' > 'Simple' > 'Mike's Song' > 'Yerushalayim Shel Zahav' > 'I Am Hydrogen' > 'Weekapaug Groove', a journey that rivals the one taken on Night 10.

Encore

'A Day In The Life' (Lennon/McCartney)

Phish dropped their third and final Beatles cover during this single song encore. With its reference to the 'four thousand holes in Blackburn, Lancashire', 'A Day In The Life' was the ideal choice to close the (w)hole night. 'A Day In The Life' was originally performed by Phish during their 1995 summer tour (over seven months after the band performed The Beatles' 'White Album' in its entirety during the Halloween 1994 show). Generally, 'A Day In The Life' works best for the band as either a set closer or as an encore. However, there are two notable exceptions. For the 19 November 1996 show in Kansas City, Missouri, the bulk of the second set consisted of 'A Day In The Life' > 'Bathtub Gin' > 'The Vibration Of Life' > 'You Enjoy Myself'. Admittedly,

'A Day In The Life' is the weakest part of that sequence, but it is the starting point that made the subsequent songs possible. The second and chronologically earlier exception was the third set of the band's Halloween 1995 show. After having already performed a set of Phish classics and a complete run-through of The Who's *Quadrophenia*, the band delivered an epic 40-minute 'You Enjoy Myself' and one of the all-time great versions of 'Jesus Just Left Chicago'. The band then started up 'A Day In The Life' and took the closing cacophony straight back into a 'Suzy Greenberg' they had been revisiting throughout the night. This four-song set was even more impressive, considering that it was delivered after the band had already debuted 17 new songs in the previous three hours.

Night 11: Friday 4 August ('Lemon')

The band's final weekend started off with a strong showing of the group's 1980s material. In fact, ten of the night's 18 songs were from the 1.0 era.

Set 1

'See That My Grave Is Kept Clean' (Jefferson)

With 'See That My Grave Is Kept Clean', Phish open their 'Lemon'-themed night with a song the Grateful Dead covered early in their career (and that both Jerry Garcia and Phil Lesh would cover during solo gigs). Besides giving the keyboards a more prominent role, another differentiator between the Phish and Grateful Dead versions is the title. Phish utilized the original Blind Lemon Jefferson title, while the Grateful Dead used the title 'One Kind Favor' (likely owing to the fact that the Dead learned the song from Lightning Hopkins and that was the title he preferred). Interestingly enough, Bob Dylan used the 'See That My Grave Is Kept Clean' title for his self-titled 1962 debut and 'One Kind Favor' for the version he eventually released with The Band on *The Bootleg Series Vol. 11: The Basement Tapes Complete.* Regardless, Phish get the night off to a strong start by aligning their one-and-only performance of this 1920s classic with their strengths.

'Punch You In The Eye' (Anastasio) **> 'Party Time'** (Fishman)

Telling the tale of a tourist passing through Gamehendge, 'Punch You In The Eye' is a reminder that, in the story of *Gamehendge*, Wilson is the villain of the piece ('When Wilson knew that I was loose/I'd surely be subjected to some real abuse/Maybe end up hanging from the nearest tree'). Although not included on any of their studio albums, 'Punch You In The Eye' is another of their oft-performed classics. Played with customary zeal, the band deliver a version worthy of all its predecessors, and, of course, when the song nears the 4:20 mark, Trey and Mike take about 15 seconds to delight the audience with their choreographed dance moves. The band included a strong version during their 13 August 1996 show at Deer Creek and an even stronger version a few months later on 30 November in Sacramento, California, both available to hear on subsequent releases. The former was included as part of *Live Phish Volume 12, 8.13.96* and the latter was made available by the band as an archival release.

The band then move into the title track to *Joy*'s companion album, *Party Time*. Paul Williams, in his book *Bob Dylan, Performing Artist*, wrote that 'Rainy Day Women, #12 & 35' is a 'combination drunk party/revival meeting.' He could have also been referring to the Fishman-written 'Party Time'. Never performed with any real regularity, 'Party Time' is still performed a few times each year and is typically delivered as a fun burst of energy. On two occasions (8 July 2012 and 11 August 2018), the band even managed to extend the party slightly past curfew, but those are the exceptions that prove the rule.

'Big Black Furry Creature From Mars' (Gordon)
Phish's hardcore classic is always a nice reminder that when the band formed at the University of Vermont, punk bands like Minor Threat and Husker Du were doing their part to create 'college rock'. Although included on *Hampton Comes Alive*, *At The Roxy* and the *Alpine Valley* DVD, the best versions of the song tend to reside on the archival releases. Examples include the encore of 'Uncle Pen' > 'Big Black Furry Creature From Mars' on 31 October 1990; the second set pairing of 'Runaway Jim' > 'Big Black Furry Creature From Mars' from 22 November 1994; and the run from 'Tweezer' > 'Big Black Furry Creature From Mars' > 'Makisupa Policeman' > 'NICU' > 'Tweezer' > 'Jesus Just Left Chicago' > 'Harry Hood' from 1 December 1994. But great unreleased versions do still exist. Considering the band played 14 shows in December 1997, and six have already been released in one format or another, it seems inevitable that they'll eventually unleash 11 December's monster sequence of 'Drowned' > 'Roses Are Free' > 'Big Black Furry Creature From Mars' > 'Ghost' > 'Down With Disease' > 'Johnny B. Goode'.

'Dinner And A Movie' (Anastasio/Pollak)
Played well over 100 times during the 1.0 era, 'Dinner And A Movie' was only played once during the 2.0 years, and during the 3.0 era, this was only its eighth appearance. In the studio version included on *Junta*, 'Dinner And A Movie' is almost Phish's version of The Beatles' 'Let It Be' B-side 'You Know My Name (Look Up The Number)' (but with Phish incorporating subtler sound effects). For a 1.0 version of 'Dinner And A Movie', the entire 1 March 1997 show that was abridged for the *Slip Stitch And Pass* release is worth hearing. For its 2.0 appearance, the *Live In Brooklyn* DVD is fun. Beyond a 3.0-era 'Dinner And A Movie', the 29 June 2012 show from Deer Creek features a fantastic opening set: you get songs by Lou Reed, David Bowie, The Beatles and pairings of both 'Limb By Limb' > 'Possum' and 'The Mango Song > Big Black'. During the pandemic lockdown of 2020, Phish released livestreams of shows, accompanied by a band-provided recipe. The intention was for phans to isolate, make a common meal and then watch a simulcast from the band's vast video archive. Many individuals loved this experience and it was a phenomenal way to stay connected (and optimistic) during lockdown.

'Ocelot' (Anastasio/Marshall)
Another song delivered as a standalone, 'Ocelot' debuted at Fenway Park on 31 May 2009, near the start of the 3.0 era, and since then, it has passed the '100th performance' milestone. During its second (and, so far, final) Fenway Park appearance, the band placed 'Ocelot' as the fulcrum of an excellent performance of 'Halfway To The Moon' > 'Ocelot' > 'Rift'. The band also included a strong 'Ocelot' in their great performance in George, Washington, on 27 July 2013. In their blog post, 'More Heat: Gorge 2 Recap', for phish.net, Multibeast wrote: "Ocelot' drops in next, keeping the vibe somewhat mellow.

This is an above-average version, with Mike leading the way with his bouncy basslines. The Trey and Fish interplay yields some really great moments here and the end takes off to an apex that would make Jerry proud of this 'Tennessee Jed' knock-off. I kid!' Although I do agree in theory that 'Ocelot' can be closely associated with the Grateful Dead's 'Tennessee Jed' (with its loping rhythm and story-song groove), I can live with that and will continue to love its periodic appearances. One hundred and counting as of this writing! Of course, even if your opinion of 'Ocelot' aligns closer to Multibeast's, I'm hopeful that you'll still stick around for the second set of that 27 July 2013 show and its 'Down With Disease' > 'Undermind' > 'Light' > 'Sneakin' Sally Through The Alley' > 'Also Sprach Zarathustra' > 'Walls Of The Cave' > 'Fluffhead' > 'Run Like An Antelope'. Conflicting opinions of 'Ocelot' bring to mind the general reception *Joy* and 'Ocelot' received upon their release. Reviewers tended to praise *Joy*, even if they did not give special mention to 'Ocelot'. But I would like to think that 'Ocelot' is the track Wil Hermes was thinking of when he started to conclude his four-star review in *Rolling Stone*: 'If you can't enjoy *Joy*, you will probably never enjoy Phish.'

'Poor Heart' (Gordon)
After almost tripling the studio length of 'Ocelot', the band decide that another short, fast number is called for, opting for one of Mike's bluegrass originals. Included on *A Picture Of Nectar* and then a handful of the band's live albums, 'Poor Heart' is, in the words of *Noiseless Chatter* blogger Philip J. Reed:

> A simple bluegrass ditty by bassist Mike Gordon about somebody swiping his tape recorder ... It's not bad. It's fun. It's a bit of a one-note experiment, but it's brief and toe-tapping enough that it doesn't overstay its welcome ... It's just sort of there, and it's nowhere near Mike Gordon's best composition or the band's best dalliance with bluegrass. (See the next album's 'Fast Enough For You' for that honor.)

There is nothing inaccurate in that write-up, but I think the positives ('fun', 'toe-tapping', 'doesn't overstay its welcome') drastically outweigh any negative impressions provided. For the 22 November 1994 show at the University of Missouri (the same show with the aforementioned 'Runaway Jim' > 'Big Black Furry Creature From Mars'), the band opened with a fantastic 21-minute sequence of 'Buried Alive' > 'Poor Heart' > 'Horn' > 'Foam'. The high-octane burst of 'Poor Heart', placed between the dark instrumental intensity of 'Buried Alive' and the delicate melancholy of 'Horn', served as a jolt of breakneck bluegrass energy that reset the mood and sharpened the dynamics.

'Winterqueen' (Anastasio/Marshall)
Professionally delivered, 'Winterqueen' is another of the band's excellent midtempo 3.0 numbers. In a rare moment of positivity in a largely negative

review for *Tiny Mix Tapes*, Will Neibergall commented on the 'uncommon catchiness relative to the rest of Phish's studio discography' of 'Winterqueen' (and he lumped in 'The Line' and 'Wombat' for that same 'praise'). The *Baker's Dozen* performance of 'Winterqueen' was not as strong as the version played in Chicago just prior to the run, but few versions will be able to match that 15 July sequence of 'Corona' > 'Simple' > 'Winterqueen' > 'Light' > 'Scents And Subtle Sounds' > 'Cities' > 'Slave To The Traffic Light'.

'Bold As Love' (Hendrix) **> 'First Tube'** (Anastasio/Lawton/Markellis)
Fuego's closing track, 'Winterqueen', helped carry Night 11's opening set to its two-song conclusion. Delivered with as much passion as 'See That My Grave Is Kept Clean' (but with lead vocals by Page instead of Trey), their version of the Hendrix classic 'Bold As Love' starts the opening set's conclusion. With passion to spare, the band deliver a version that is faithful to the Hendrix original and that compares favorably to the classic version they delivered on their own *Hampton Comes Alive* box set. The band carry the song's instrumental outro into their original instrumental number: the *Farmhouse*'s 'First Tube'. Played occasionally as an opener during the 1.0 and 2.0 eras and generally acting as a closer in the 3.0 era, 'First Tube' allows the band to demonstrate that they deserved that Grammy nomination for Best Rock Instrumental Performance. 'First Tube' often takes on a life of its own in Colorado, especially at iconic venues like Red Rocks (1 August 2009) and Dick's Sporting Goods Park (4 September 2016 and 31 August). The song often hits with even more intensity when played by the Trey Anastasio Band – just listen to the electrified versions on *Plasma* or *Burn It Down* for proof. But, for *The Baker's Dozen*, the band deliver a version that can stand next to any of those. With tight, bombastic playing by all four members, the Night 11 'First Tube' is the sound of a band that have been pacing themselves and are ready to kick the remainder of the final weekend into overdrive.

Set 2

'Dem Bones' (Traditional)
Opening a set with an a cappella number is almost a *Baker's Dozen* tradition by Night 11. But, when the opening set concludes with one of the run's best instrumental numbers, the subsequent a cappella opener is doubly earned. Performed by the band for just the third time, 'Dem Bones' is a song that most have heard, even if they are unaware of its ethnomusicology. The song was originally written in 1928 by brothers James Weldon Johnson and J. Rosamond Johnson (two Johnson brothers who should not be mistaken for the Brothers Johnson – George 'Lightnin' Licks' Johnson and Louis E. 'Thunder Thumbs' Johnson – who topped the charts with the previously discussed 'Strawberry Letter 23'). With its reverence and humor, 'Dem Bones' establishes two recurring themes for the rest of the set.

'No Men In No Man's Land' (Anastasio/Marshall) **> 'Everything In Its Right Place'** (Greenwood/Greenwood/O'Brien/Selway/Yorke)

Following a song heavy with subtext with a follow-up song that keeps its denotation solidly on the surface is almost another *Baker's Dozen* tradition. 'No Men In No Man's Land', another of the *Big Boat* tracks, was jammed especially hard in 2017. Although the Night 11 version is not as praised as the prior month's version in Chicago (or the versions that would appear later in the year during the Labor Day and New Year's Eve runs), it is still a solid version. The band felt it was good enough to include as the opening track to the third disc of their *Baker's Dozen* compilation. Besides the aforementioned 2017 performances (14 July, 1 September and 28 December), another solid version that might be a little under the radar is the 30 December 2022 performance. Delivered as a standalone song to open the second set, it is a 'No Men In No Man's Land' that says what it needs to say and then gets out of the way.

After wrapping up the *Baker's Dozen* version of 'No Men In No Man's Land', Phish move into another debut: a cover of Radiohead's 'Everything In Its Right Place'. Although never again played by the band, elements of this *Kid A* classic would reappear throughout the remainder of the night. Full disclosure: I started this project with this song being my least favorite of the entire run, and while it has not since become my favorite, it has risen substantially (and it is not outside the realm of possibility that it is a segment of the phandom's favorite). Even at its lowest, I still awarded it three-and-a-half stars out of five, and anyone who gives it anything lower can suck a lemon.

'What's The Use?' (Anastasio/Fishman/Gordon/McConnell) **> 'Scents And Subtle Sounds'** (Anastasio/Herman/Marshall) **> 'Prince Caspian'** (Anastasio/Marshall) **> 'Fluffhead'** (Anastasio/Pollak)

The band then unleash the main component of the second set. This four-song run lasts close to an hour and encompasses several different elements of the band's repertoire. If 'Everything In Its Right Place' is the band tipping their hat to Radiohead, 'What's The Use?' is them playing in the same sandbox as *The Division Bell-/The Endless River*-era Pink Floyd. (Of course, at the time this *Siket Disc* track was recorded and released, *The Endless River* was not even a title under consideration by Pink Floyd.) Several substantial versions exist, and two of the best occurred on August nights and were preceded by 'Down With Disease'. For the 14 August 2010 show included on the *Alpine Valley* DVD, the band included a phenomenal triptych of 'Down With Disease' > 'What's The Use?' > 'Scent Of A Mule' in their second set. For the 30 August 2014 show at Dick's Sporting Goods Park, the band used the second set opening of 'Down With Disease' > 'What's The Use?' to set up the 'Carini' > 'Light' > 'Fuego' > 'Slave To The Traffic Light' > 'Meatstick' > 'Bold As Love' that follows.

The first consequential jam of the night, 'Scents And Subtle Sounds', follows. Originally recorded for *Undermind* and later featured on *The Baker's Dozen* compilation, 'Scents' begins with a lush, rising chord progression and rhythmic feel that evokes *Quadrophenia*-era Who before settling into a reflective, melodic space as the lyrics unfold. Thematically, it feels like a spiritual sequel to the Grateful Dead's 'Scarlet Begonias'. Where the Dead offered the now-iconic line, 'Once in a while, you get shown the light/In the strangest of places if you look at it right', Phish counters with their own existential nudge: 'If you would only start to live one moment at a time/You would, I think, be startled by the things that you would find'. Both lines grapple with the idea of hidden revelation, but where the Dead's version leans into cosmic surprise, Phish's take is more rooted in mindfulness and presence. The *Baker's Dozen* version stretches past 16 minutes and feels less like a fixed composition and more like a wide-open canvas. After the song's composed section, the jam doesn't just drift – it searches. The band move from gentle ambience into more abstract territory, with Fishman subtly shifting the groove beneath Page's cascading piano lines and Trey using delay and loop textures to blur the edges. It's not about big peaks but it is about mood, motion and space. In that sense, it acts as a precursor to later versions, such as those from 6 December 2019 and 2 August 2022 (both of which also abandon the traditional structure and opt for extended improvisation). Those later takes explore similar terrain: loosely structured, harmonically adventurous and open-ended in ways that make 'Scents' feel less like a standalone tune and more like a launchpad.

It is then time for the second of the night's 'big jams': 'Prince Caspian'. On Night 11, the instantly legendary Pittsburgh version was less than a month old and this 'Prince Caspian' had big shoes to fill. Spoiler alert: he did. Included on *Billy Breathes*, 'Prince Caspian' is a song that can shine as either a compact mid-set moment or as a centerpiece. On 3 December 1997, the band's second set included a stellar 'Prince Caspian' in the midst of a 'David Bowie' > 'Possum' > 'Jam' > 'Prince Caspian' > 'Frankenstein' > 'Harry Hood' sequence. Just over a year later, during the second set of 30 December 1998, 'Prince Caspian' stood by himself in between the opening 'Down With Disease' > 'Piper' and the concluding 'The Squirming Coil' > 'Slave To The Traffic Light'. And in between those two December shows, the band somewhat split the difference with the 'Prince Caspian' > 'Harry Hood' included on the *Ventura* box set.

The second set concludes with another of the band's epic, multipart compositions, 'Fluffhead'. Included on *Junta* and played consistently since then, 'Fluffhead' is a surefire way to grab the attention of anyone whose mind might have started to wander. One of the many reasons the band's 13 August 1993 debut performance at the Murat Theatre in Indianapolis, Indiana, was released as an archival title is the fun 'Ginseng Sullivan' > 'Fluffhead' > 'My Mind's Got A Mind Of Its Own' included towards the end of the opening set. For the band's final (to date) set at the Bonnaroo Music & Arts Festival, they included a nice 'Fluffhead' for the phaithful. But two of the best versions of

'Fluffhead' occurred at Alpine Valley. On 24 July 1999, the band unleashed a version of 'Fluffhead' that more than earned its subsequent placement on the *Live Bait Vol. 19* sampler. A lifetime later (not that they had not already had several lifetimes before the previously mentioned Alpine Valley performance), they opened their 13 August 2022 show with an exceptionally fun '1999' > 'Fluffhead' > 'Saw It Again' run. Even after having already delivered over 250 performances of 'Fluffhead', the band stayed present and in the moment throughout this *Baker's Dozen* performance. It was not perfectly executed, but it was delivered by a band who knew their audience.

Encore

'Frankenstein' (Winter)

Phish occasionally use the encore to turn the 'fun' up to 11. When Page grabs his keytar and the band launch into The Edgar Winter Group's marching band classic, the band do exactly that. With its multipart structure, 'Frankenstein' is not dissimilar to many Phish songs. That, coupled with the audience response, is likely why it gets inserted into periodic setlists. Although my dream setlist has never been and likely never will be played, it features a 'Frankenstein' closer. An instrumental set running 'Peaches En Regalia' > 'The Landlady' > 'Cars Trucks Buses' > '2001' > 'First Tube' > 'Frankenstein' is the kind of once-in-a-lifetime sequence I can imagine Phish pulling out on a random midweek summer night.

Night 12: Saturday 5 August ('Boston Cream')

Assuming a concert is comparable to an album, and it most definitely is when discussing Phish, Night 12 brings to mind Tom Gatti and his book *Long Players: Writers On The Albums That Shaped Them*. He writes:

> Albums can alter the architecture of our minds. The ones that speak to us, we listen to hundreds of times over decades; we know them far better than any novel or film. They are faithful companions, with us from the first time we lower the needle to the last time we hover a thumb over the screen. They are, truly, long players.

Night 12 fits Gatti's description with uncanny precision. With its pacing, emotional textures and narrative shape, it unfolds like a concept album. Rather than just a collection of songs, the show is comprised of movements that build, stretch and resolve in ways that reward deep, attentive listening. Like any great record, it balances the familiar and the unexpected, creating tension and release through thoughtful sequencing and tonal contrast. Themes intentionally emerge and evolve over the course of the night. And, as with the albums we return to for years, this show reveals more each time you revisit it. A shift in energy here, a subtle textural choice there ... it is the kind of musical architecture that doesn't demand your attention but earns it. Night 12 isn't just a concert. It's a long player in spirit and structure – a sonic document worthy of shelf space alongside Elton John's *Blue Moves*, Joni Mitchell's *Hejira* and David Bowie's *Station To Station*.

'Soul Shakedown Party' (Marley)

Phish start their penultimate party with Bob Marley's 'Soul Shakedown Party'. Originally released as a single and as the opening track to their 1971 studio album *The Best Of The Wailers*, this was the 11th time in just over 20 years that the band had tackled this one (and the eighth instance in which it had opened a set). From its debut performance on 17 February 1997 (included on the *Amsterdam* box set) to the 28 February 2003 concert released as the *Live Phish 02.28.03* CD, 'Soul Shakedown Party' has never disappointed an audience. For the former, the band open their first Amsterdam show with a roughly 18-minute 'Soul Shakedown Party' > 'Divided Sky', and for the latter, the party breaks out between two titans. The whole 'Tweezer' > 'Soul Shakedown Party' > 'David Bowie' sequence runs nearly an hour and the party never stops.

'Uncle Pen' (Monroe)

Another of the Mike-sung bluegrass numbers, 'Uncle Pen' made over 200 appearances during the 1.0 era before being ostensibly shelved. It did not appear at all during the 2.0 years, and so far in 3.0, this *Baker's Dozen* performance is the eighth (and final) one. It is a fantastic number and – no disrespect to either original composer Bill Monroe or Jerry Garcia's *Old And In*

The Wayside project – much more fun than other versions. Beyond the previously mentioned 31 October 1990 encore of 'Uncle Pen' > 'Big Black Furry Creature From Mars', great versions have been included in numerous archival releases. The 29 October 1994 show in Spartanburg, South Carolina, is more effective because of the songs which surround 'Uncle Pen', but the song more than holds its own. That night, 'Uncle Pen' was cleverly nestled between The Who's instrumental firestorm 'Sparks' and the sprawling complexity of 'You Enjoy Myself'. It acted as a kind of musical reset, a stripped-down, rootsy reprieve before the band launched into one of their most ambitious compositions. The contrast was striking, but rather than feeling like a throwaway interlude, 'Uncle Pen' shone on its own terms. With crisp harmonies and razor-sharp picking, it held the energy and briefly grounded the audience in something warm and familiar. For the Sacramento show on 30 November 1996, the band invited the Nitty Gritty Dirt Band's John McEuen (and his banjo) to join them on 'Old Home Place' and 'Uncle Pen'.

'The Sloth' (Anastasio)
Things finally start to get heavy with 'The Sloth', another of Trey's *Gamehendge* numbers. Even taken out of the context of *Gamehendge*, 'The Sloth' is an excellent song (and another that would not have been out of place on The Beatles' self-titled 'White Album'). Although performed much less frequently than it once was, knockout versions of 'The Sloth' have occurred in both the 1.0 and 3.0 eras. For the 2 September 2011 show at Dick's Sporting Goods Park, the band slotted 'The Sloth' between 'Sparkle' and 'Sweet Virginia' in its 'every song starts with 'S'' show. Back in 1995, two great versions of 'The Sloth' appeared. For the 31 December 1995 show documented on the *New Year's Eve 1995 – Live At Madison Square Garden* CDs, the band's performance of 'The Sloth' > 'Reba' in the opening set laid the groundwork for a fantastic night of music. Just over six months earlier, on 26 June, the band included versions of 'NICU' > 'The Sloth' in a different New York concert. Recorded at Saratoga Springs and subsequently released as an archival title, that summer of 1995 concert is worth hearing in its entirety. Beyond the hot 'NICU' > 'The Sloth' pairing, it also features an exclusive-to-Summer-of-1995-song, 'Don't You Want To Go?'. Originally released in 1966 by Della Reese and her group The Meditation Singers, 'Don't You Want To Go?' was the opening track to their funk-soul-gospel classic. Dropped by Phish after that summer tour, 'Don't You Want To Go?' will hopefully make another appearance in the future.

'Gotta Jibboo' (Anastasio/Lawton/Markellis)
Another *Farmhouse* track that could've easily landed on *The Story Of The Ghost*, 'Gotta Jibboo' thrives on a loose structure that invites the band to stretch out the groove between its breezy, low-stakes verses. How far they stretch it, of course, depends on how much they think the audience need to dance it out. At the 4 July 2000 show, the answer was apparently 'a lot'.

Clocking in at nearly 40 minutes when later released on *Live Bait Vol. 14* ('Gotta Jibboo' > 'Saw It Again' > 'Magilla'), this version wanders, soars and drags the audience along with gleeful insistence. Two months later, on 20 September in Cincinnati, Ohio, the band delivered a shorter – but in many ways more playful – version of 'Jibboo'. Where the 4 July rendition was sprawling and exploratory, the Cincinnati take was sharper, funkier and full of mischief. The band locked into a tighter pocket, trading rhythmic ideas and melodic teases with a looseness that felt more like a conversation than a journey. Instead of building toward transcendence, this version seemed more interested in poking fun, flashing grins and inviting the audience into the inside joke. It's a masterclass in how less can sometimes be a whole lot more fun. At the *Baker's Dozen*, 'Jibboo' makes yet another impression. Page puts in overtime to make sure it doesn't slip into 'jam for jam's sake' territory – and he nails it. The whole band keep the groove compact but still give the crowd plenty of room to move.

'Fuck Your Face' (Gordon)
Residing at the midpoint between Led Zeppelin and Primus, Mike's 'Fuck Your Face' is another fun bit of juvenilia from the band. Although at times it can sound like a poor man's version of Frank Zappa's 'My Guitar Wants To Kill Your Mama', for the *Baker's Dozen*, Mike keeps his original composition from devolving into a pale imitation. No recap of 'Fuck Your Face' would be complete without a shout-out to the band's 31 August 2012 show at Dick's Sporting Goods Park. With an opening set consisting of 'First Tube', 'Uncle Pen', 'Carini', 'Kill Devil Falls', 'You Enjoy Myself', 'Ocelot' and 'Undermind', studious Phans keeping track in real-time noticed the first letters spelled out 'FUCK YOU'. Of course, during the second set, the band started off with 'Runaway Jim', 'Farmhouse', 'Alaska', 'Chalk Dust Torture' and 'Emotional Rescue' in order to transform that contemptuous remark into an inside joke for those still paying attention. After spelling it out for them, they then closed the second set with 'Fuck Your Face' (and, to double down on the joke, encored with 'Grind' and 'Meatstick'). For the *Baker's Dozen*, this *White Tape* classic is delivered with a perfect amount of boyish humor as well as a shout-out to The Rolling Stones' all-too-often unfairly maligned compilation *Sucking In The Seventies*.

'Sunshine Of Your Feeling' (Baker/Clapton) (Scholz)
The audience's excitement when Phish start up Cream's 'Sunshine Of Your Love' is palpable. It appears to be a fun way for the band to acknowledge the Night 12 theme. Of course, it is not 'Cream-Filled' night, but rather it is 'Boston Cream' night, so when they get to the chorus, they pivot into 'More Than A Feeling' (or should that be, 'More Than A Filling'?!). After getting through the best parts of 'More Than A Feeling', the band return to 'Sunshine Of Your Love' (after a brief detour through a spoken-word portion of Cream's

'Tales Of Brave Ulysses'). Before the song is done, they also interpolate Cream's 'White Room' and Boston's 'Foreplay/Long Time'. Once finished, Trey announces, 'Tomorrow's donut will be 'Kansas/Metallica flavor'.' Fishman follows it up with, 'We've been waiting for that joke for 20 years. Really, seriously.' Trey weighs in again, 'This whole thing was just so we could do that. We're out of here!' Although the band have performed more elaborate jokes within their setlists (the 'Fuck Your Face' and 'All 'S" shows, for example), the 'Sunshine Of Your Feeling' gag bests them when it comes to playing the long game.

'Frost' (Anastasio/Marshall) **> 'Scent Of A Mule'** (Gordon)

After taking a little bit of time to enjoy their moment, the band start up their second-ever performance of Trey's *Traveler* ballad, 'Frost'. A song Trey routinely performs during his solo acoustic shows with his Trey Anastasio Band and with the occasional symphony orchestra (appropriate given the funereal strings included on the studio version), 'Frost' is almost a precursor to the types of songs he'd include on his *Ghosts Of The Forest* project nearly a decade later. Careful attention should be paid to the lyrics of 'Frost', both because of their beauty and because of how the final line of the verses can change slightly from night to night. The song describes three scenes – and each concludes with someone leaving. Sometimes delivered as 'Maybe he would sail away' and sometimes as 'Maybe he was sent away', the difference between 'sail' and 'sent' is the difference between leaving of your own accord and being sent packing against your will. Personally, considering how the leaving characters are described in their preceding couplets, I prefer 'sent away' in the first two verses and 'sail away' in the third. For Night 12, Trey delivers the line as 'Maybe he was sent away' all three times.

If 'Frost' is melodic and mellow, 'Scent Of A Mule' is rambunctious and upbeat. Originally included on *Hoist*, 'Scent Of A Mule' is (yet) another of Mike's bluegrass numbers. Although it is not thematically dissimilar to The Byrds' 'Mr. Spaceman', musically speaking, 'Scent Of A Mule' is what that Roger McGuinn song might have sounded like if it had been written two years later. Any other band with a song as strong as 'Scent Of A Mule' would ride its traditional arrangement as far as they could, but Phish have taken to using it as a launch pad for their more eccentric impulses. A splendid example of this is included on the band's YouTube channel. The mid-song jam during the 20 July 2014 'Scent Of A Mule' features Trey on drums, a fantastic keyboard solo by Page and a candle-lit Fishman on the Marimba Lumina (the MIDI-controlled instrument discussed during the Night 2 version of 'I Always Wanted It This Way'). The version performed during *The Baker's Dozen* might not go quite as far as that 2014 version, but it does feature a shout-out to 'Sunshine Of Your Love' and some damn fine Klezmer. 'Scent Of A Mule' was the band's second and final mule-centric song of the run – their long-dormant cover of Taj Mahal's 'She Caught The Katy And Left Me A Mule To Ride' remained on the shelf.

'Fire' (Hendrix)
Even though the band allow themselves a quick moment to catch their breath, 'Fire' maintains the energy started by 'Scent Of A Mule'. Delivered with a technical proficiency missing from most of the garage rock bands who covered it back in the day, this (the third of the four Hendrix songs the band would perform during the run) is the right song at the right time. It is especially appropriate considering Hendrix himself had covered 'Sunshine Of Your Love' (and, maybe less appropriately, because the 'Frost' played earlier always puts me in the mind of Hendrix's 'The Wind Cries Mary', which the band performed on Night 8).

The band's first version of 'Fire' was on 1 December 1984. A soundboard recording of this performance at Burlington, Vermont's famed Nectar's has not been officially released, but it is available online. It is worth listening to for its historical value as well as how the band fit their version of 'Fire' in between their versions of 'Scarlet Begonias' and 'Fire On The Mountain'. The Jerry Garcia iteration of The Grateful Dead performed this 'Scarlet Begonias' > 'Fire On The Mountain' pairing over 250 times and never once did they include a 4:20 'Fire' in the middle of it. Altogether, it is a great 20 minutes that does a wonderful job of showing how the band were playing as an ensemble during those earliest years. For another fun version of 'Fire', check out the 14 August 2015 encore. The band deliver a version of 'Farmhouse' that does not fully take off because of issues with Trey's guitar (but, of course, Page steps up to the plate). They then launch into an especially incendiary 'Fire' that shows Trey's guitar is not quite done for the night (and, of course, his playing has evolved substantially in the intervening 30+ years).

'Alaska' (Anastasio/Marshall) **> 'Plasma'** (Anastasio/Herman/Marshall)
Reminiscent of The Band's 'Up On Cripple Creek', 'Alaska' is their most frequently played song from the *Party Time* release. A few years later, the band would deliver a bombastic 'Alaska' during another donut-related show. When performing a 30 November 2019 show at the Dunkin Donuts Center in Providence, Rhode Island, the band used 'Alaska' to kick things up a notch as they gradually worked their way towards the set break. That night's sequence of 'Bathtub Gin' > 'Alaska' > 'What's The Use?' > 'Piper' > 'Golden Age' > 'Plasma' > 'Harry Hood' is indicative of how strong the band were on any given night in the late 2010s.

After working their way through 'Alaska', the band close out the first set with 'Plasma', the final song – and final jam – of the night's opening frame. Compared to some of the looser, funkier takes that the Trey Anastasio Band have laid down on tape, the *Baker's Dozen* 'Plasma' is more restrained, keeping its energy coiled rather than unleashed. Though 'Plasma' served as the title track of Trey's 2003 live album, the version released on 2020's *Burn It Down* raised the bar even higher. And post-*Dozen*, Phish themselves started pushing 'Plasma' further, making it a genuine set-piece. By the time they kicked off their 2024 Sphere residency in Las Vegas, the song had fully bloomed. On the final night of that run, they opened with a version so expansive and confident that it bumped every earlier rendition down a slot in the imaginary (but very real) 'Plasma' rankings. That's not to say the *Baker's Dozen* take is a slouch; it is solid, smartly played and serves its role in the set with confidence. But if we're being honest, it plays things a bit safe. The jam hints at open space but never quite steps out into it. There's a sense that the band are testing the waters rather than diving in, stretching the groove just enough to remind you of what 'Plasma' can do but not quite enough to let it fully bloom. It's a version that knows its place, closing out the set without stealing the whole show. In the grand scheme of 'Plasma' history, it's respectable ... but probably fighting for third place at best. Topping the list is the commanding opener from the final night of the 2024 Sphere run, a version that redefined what the song could be in the modern era: layered, patient and unafraid to push past expectations. A close second? That'd be the 29 November 2019 Providence rendition, which walked the line between menace and bliss so well that it might've needed a warning label. Against those titans, the *Baker's Dozen* 'Plasma' is more of a strong suggestion than a definitive statement, but one that still holds its head high.

Set 2

'Ghost' (Anastasio/Marshall) **> 'Petrichor'** (Anastasio) **> 'Light'** (Anastasio/Marshall) **> 'The Lizards'** (Anastasio)

The closing set of the penultimate night of *The Baker's Dozen* is divided into two extended sequences (each four songs long). The second set opens with a sprawling, scene-setting 'Ghost' that immediately signals the band aren't easing into things. From the first few minutes, it's clear they've got big plans, and this jam is the opening statement. Listening to 'Ghost' on *The Baker's Dozen* album brings to mind Raymond Chandler's *Farwell, My Lovely*: 'Time passed ... I don't know how long. I had no watch. They don't make that kind of time in watches anyway'. It might be the best 'Ghost' since the *Live Phish Volume 11, 11.17.97* version recorded at the McNichols Sports Arena. Almost four years after *The Baker's Dozen*, on 4 August 2021, the band would unleash another 'Ghost' at Nashville, Tennessee's Ascend Amphitheatre. Running 'Ghost' > 'Bathtub Gin' > 'Also Sprach Zarathustra' > 'Split Open And Melt', this sequence showcases the band operating at one of their many peaks.

After wrapping up the *Baker's Dozen* 'Ghost', the band move into the opening section of 'Petrichor'. Trey's song suites often oscillate (stylistically) between 'Terrapin Station'-like sequences or *Abbey Road*-like medleys. Because of its lyrical consistency, 'Petrichor' is closer to 'Terrapin Station'. Despite differing opinions on *Big Boat* as a whole, reviewers tended to agree that 'Petrichor' was a standout track. *Consequence Of Sound* praised its display of the band's jamming skills and individual talent, describing it as a bright, confident journey through melodies. Sam Sodomsky (writing for

Pitchfork) called it an 'immaculately arranged prog opus' while *PopMatters* highlighted its epic nature, emphasizing Trey Anastasio's intricate guitar work and emotional vocals, comparing it to classic tracks like 'Divided Sky' and 'Tweezer'. In concert, 'Petrichor' often gets a lukewarm reception (especially when it's seen as awkwardly placed within a set). At the 8 December 2019 show in North Charleston, South Carolina, it closed the second set as part of a three-song run: 'Petrichor' > 'Boogie On Reggae Woman' > 'Rise/Come Together'. Some reviewers argued the set couldn't recover after 'Petrichor', suggesting it stalled the show's momentum. I'd disagree. That final stretch may not have been explosive, but it didn't detract from the show's overall impact. The argument could be made that it added a kind of graceful decrescendo that worked on its own terms.

As the band approach Night 12's 40-minute mark, they open up 'Light'. Another of *Joy*'s optimistic-slash-introspective tracks, which provided director Steven Cantor with the title of his 2019 documentary about Trey (*Between Me And My Mind*), 'Light' features lyrics that can either be sung or shouted depending on how much muscle is being applied to the melody. When previously played at Madison Square Garden on 30 December 2016, 'Light' was included as part of a set-long series of songs consisting of 'Tweezer' > 'Sparks' > 'Ghost' > 'Light' > 'Wading In The Velvet Sea' > 'Rocky Top'. This 70-minute sequence was a highlight of that New Year's Eve Run and its 'Light' raised expectations for its eventual inclusion in *The Baker's Dozen*. Although not as exploratory (or, frankly, as strong) as the earlier version, the Night 12 version has nothing to be ashamed of.

The final song in this opening sequence, 'The Lizards', brings listeners back to *Gamehendge* one last time. A cornerstone of the narrative arc, 'The Lizards' is built on intricate melodic phrasing and some of the most whimsical, singable lyrics in Phish's catalog. It is an oddball anthem that still manages to feel emotionally resonant. Last performed during the previous year's Labor Day run at Dick's Sporting Goods Park, its return is met with genuine enthusiasm and not just because of the long absence. As the segue from 'Light' into 'The Lizards' begins to materialize, the entire crowd are locked in, ready for the ride. This rendition isn't flawless (Trey stumbles over a few lines and some transitions are a little wobbly), but the collective willingness of the audience to 'surrender to the flow' carries the moment. It is a reminder that, at its core, 'The Lizards' is as much about shared energy as it is about precision. Among its many appearances over the years, two especially stand out: 21 October 1995 and 9 July 2016. In the former, during a first set in Lincoln, Nebraska, the band dropped 'The Lizards' into what might have otherwise been seen as a low-stakes show in a smaller market. Instead, the entire performance glows, and when it subsequently earned an official release, it served as proof that Phish never phone it in, no matter the venue or zip code. Two decades later, in Hartford, Connecticut, The Lizards returned as part of a two-song encore alongside 'Loving Cup'. Either song would've made for a memorable closer on its own, but once again, Phish went above and beyond and left the audience with a double dose of joy and a reminder that the unexpected is always in play.

'The Horse' (Anastasio/Marshall) **> 'Silent In The Morning'** (Anastasio/Marshall) **> 'Quinn The Eskimo (The Mighty Quinn)'** (Dylan) **> 'Rocky Top'** (Bryant/Bryant)

Phish ride 'The Horse' into the night's concluding sequence. Paired, as it always is, with 'Silent In The Morning', this *Rift* duo is so strong that it almost requires an act of God to be torn asunder. It also provides a nice breather before the band start to crank the energy back up. Versions of 'The Horse' > 'Silent In The Morning' from almost 15 years earlier were released just prior to *The Baker's Dozen* as part of the *St. Louis '93* box set. Beyond that excellent pairing, that 14 April 1993 show features a 'You Enjoy Myself' > 'Spooky Jam' > 'You Enjoy Myself' progression which deserves to be heard. Additionally, although it was released years earlier, the *At The Roxy* box set features an excellent 'The Horse' > 'Silent In The Morning' > 'Fluffhead' that was recorded less than two months prior to that *St. Louis '93* version.

After the conclusion of 'The Horse' > 'Silent In The Morning', the band kick things up a notch with their version of Bob Dylan's 'Quinn The Eskimo (The Mighty Quinn)'. Originally heard by a sizable portion of phans on the *Hampton Comes Alive* box set, this *Baker's Dozen* performance is even stronger than that November 1998 version. Originally recorded by Dylan and The Band in 1967 and subsequently re-recorded and released in assorted ways over the course of 50 years, that initial take would remain unreleased until 2014. Although recorded during the private sessions that eventually resulted in *The Basement Tapes*, 'Quinn The Eskimo (The Mighty Quinn)' was not included on 1975's Columbia-sanctioned compilation (perhaps because alternate versions had already been released on *Self Portrait* and *Greatest Hits Vol. II*). In an interview with *Relix*, the band listed some albums (Gillian Welch's *Revival*, Brian Eno's *Another Green World* and Bruce Springsteen's *The Wild, The Innocent And The E Street Shuffle*, among others) that they had encouraged each other to listen to during their 2003 summer tour. Trey included the 'Quinn The Eskimo (The Mighty Quinn)'-free *Basement Tapes* as one of his, saying, 'I spent the entire tour listening to this. I think I like it better than anything Dylan or The Band did separately. If we had done Halloween this year, I was going to argue heavily for this album.' For what it is worth, Fishman also included a CD by The Band, but he went with their *Greatest Hits* compilation from 2000. Per Fishman:

> The Band's highs were like a career's worth of highs in each song, but their lows were total garbage, like a bad garage band. So, for me, The Band really are a greatest hits package because there's a lot of stuff that just wasn't that great in my humble opinion. Every song on here – 'Tears Of Rage', 'The

> Night They Drove Old Dixie Down', 'Stage Fright', 'Ophelia' – is unbelievable. Robbie Robertson was on a par with the best of them as far as lyrics go; one of the greatest musical storytellers of all time.

Hopefully, Phish will eventually reach a consensus on The Band album (with or without Dylan) they should tackle during a concert. Until then, we will always have 'Quinn The Eskimo (The Mighty Quinn)'.

Because of how hard it is to top, audience members would be forgiven for thinking that 'Quinn The Eskimo (The Mighty Quinn)' would be the set closer. But if any song can one-up 'The Mighty Quinn', it is 'Rocky Top'. Although the 17 February 1997 version of 'Sleeping Monkey' > 'Rocky Top' included on the *Amsterdam* box set is worth hearing, there is a never-to-likely-be-released version also worth tracking down. A crowd recording of the 2 December 1990 show includes a rambunctious 'Rocky Top'. As mentioned, the show is likely to remain unreleased since substantial portions of the show are not available (and the existing recordings suffer from poor audio). But it is a fun show that is enhanced by the joy that the audience bring to the proceedings. Speaking of joy...

Encore

'Joy' (Anastasio/Marshall)

The band bring one last bit of happiness to the night with their 'Joy' encore. The title track to their 3.0 comeback album, 'Joy' is upfront about its dueling inspirations, and considering one is birth and the other is death, 'Joy' is almost the band's version of Bob Weir's 'Cassidy'. Later re-recorded by Page and Trey for their *December* release, 'Joy' is an excellent summation of the band's ethos, and its lyrical conclusion – 'We want you to be happy 'cause this is your song too' – is the perfect way to end a concert.

Night 13: Sunday 6 August ('Glazed')

As mentioned up front, the band's final night concluded without them having performed the same song twice. Although Mike states (in an interview with *Gothamist*) that Trey did float the idea of repeating songs, they quickly decided not to because performing a song more than once would be 'the wimpier choice.' However, it was stressed during Night 3 ('Red Velvet') and Night 8 ('Jimmies') that you should 'Never miss a Sunday show!!'

Set 1

'Dogs Stole Things' (Anastasio/Marshall)

The final night of the run kicks off with the fourth performance of 'Dogs Stole Things' of the 3.0 era. A fun, easygoing number, 'Dogs Stole Things' allows the band to ease into their final night of the run. Surprisingly, this was only the third time the band opened a concert with 'Dogs Stole Things'. This popular, midtempo number has never appeared on a studio album, but it does close out Trey and Tom's *Trampled By Lambs And Pecked By The Dove* in a version that is much slower (and with much less shuffling) than the version to which Phans are accustomed.

'Rift' (Anastasio/Marshall)

The title track to *Rift* is an exciting number; due to its compositional complexity, it is not one that the band can easily coast through. There are too many moving parts in that song for anyone to put themselves on autopilot. But, as Richard Cromelin wrote about Yes's fourth album, *Fragile*, in *Rolling Stone*: 'Complex isn't the same thing as inaccessible.' Beginning as a late-1980s instrumental section of 'The Curtain With', 'Rift' was transformed by the early 1990s into one of the band's most frequently played songs. Usually placed mid-set (when energy is sometimes required), the band's exploration of a strained relationship benefits from Trey and Page's alternating vocals (and, on its best nights, their dueling piano/guitar showcase brings to mind Donald and Daffy Duck performing Hungarian Rhapsody No. 2). The version included on the *Chicago '94* live album is worth checking out because 'the level of energy put forth over the course of *Chicago '94* is undeniable, and the high points are some of the most brilliant in the band's catalog', according to *AllMusic* upon its release.

'Ha Ha Ha' (Fishman)

A simplistic riff and even simpler lyrics make 'Ha Ha Ha' a fun number to insert into any proceedings. If a band were punch-drunk after having already performed a dozen shows at MSG, it might be just what the doctor ordered. Another song not represented on a studio album, 'Ha Ha Ha' is (like 'Dogs Stole Things') available on the *Hampton Comes Alive* box set. On that collection, Fishman's 'Ha Ha Ha' helps anchor the back half of the sixth disc (which, arguably, is the best CD in the box). Another fantastic version is the aforementioned 30 October 2010 performance in Atlantic City, New Jersey. 'Ha Ha Ha' was one of the six songs played that night that teased Led Zeppelin's 'Whole Lotta Love'.

'Camel Walk' (Holdsworth)
Another slightly silly song that has never made it onto a studio album, 'Camel Walk' keeps the party going with more of the old-school fun that only Phish can deliver. Included in the setlist of one of their earliest gigs (and, like Night 9's 'Possum', written by early Phish singer-guitarist Jeff Holdsworth), 'Camel Walk' would later show up on their *Live In Vegas* DVD. It is also one of the many highlights of Trey's 2020 *Burn It Down* compilation. Just over four years after *The Baker's Dozen*, the band performed one of the all-time great 'Camel Walks'. The smoking 'Camel' played at the Gorge Amphitheater on 27 August 2021 led directly into an equally fierce 'Chalk Dust Torture'.

'Crazy Sometimes' (Gordon/Murawski) **> 'Saw It Again'** (Anastasio/Marshall) **> 'Sanity'** (Anastasio/Fishman/Gordon/McConnell/Pollak) **> 'Bouncing Around The Room'** (Anastasio/Marshall)
The first extended sequence of the night starts off with the band's second performance of Mike's 'Crazy Sometimes'. A high-point on one of Mike's stronger solo albums, the studio version of 'Crazy Sometimes' brings to mind David Byrne and Brian Eno's *My Life In The Bush Of Ghosts*, only with the sampled grooves replaced by actual in-studio recordings. For this *Baker's Dozen* performance, the band dial back the rhythm (a bit) and focus on the top melody. Both versions are solid, but this live version is more effective because Page's keyboard work and the power of everyone's backing vocals cannot be denied.

Once they have reminded the audience that there is a little Jack Torrence in everyone, the band work their way into an angry 'Saw It Again'. This unrecorded song, like 'Camel Walk', is available on the *Live In Vegas* DVD. With that being said, fans looking to see 'Saw It Again' should check out the *Live In Utica* DVD. This 20 October 2010 performance includes the band taking 'Saw It Again' straight into the greatest version of 'Run Like An Antelope' from the 3.0 era. For the *Baker's Dozen* version of 'Saw It Again', the band take the briefest of moments to fully introduce the song, but when they do, there is no turning back (especially once they hit the 90-second mark).

Eventually, the band work their way into 'Sanity', which has moments that sound even angrier than the 'Saw It Again' that preceded it (plus a few teases to both the aforementioned tune and the 'Everything In Its Right Place' played on Night 11). 'Sanity', included on the *Junta* album, was never a song that featured heavily in their setlists. In fact, its biggest year was in 1989 when the relatively-song-strapped band played it seven times. On Night 13, 'Sanity' features something not in the 1989 Phish arsenal: an explosion straight out of 'The Very Long Fuse'.

Finally, the band roll into 'Bouncing Around The Room'. With characteristically delicate vocals and its gently looping melody, the song cools down the room and wraps the set in a familiar warmth. It's grounding and nostalgic, leaving the audience in a state of calm, open-hearted anticipation for the final debut of *The Baker's Dozen*. When it comes to Phish songs that even non-phans know, 'Bouncing Around The Room' might be in the running for 'Most Popular'. With a melody that closely aligns with the titular bounce and lyrics that are simple (yet never simplistic), 'Bouncing Around The Room' deserves the widest possible audience. One of the most frequently played songs, 'Bouncing Around The Room' is played at roughly 25% of the band's shows (and occasionally during one of Trey's solo acoustic shows). Speaking of acoustic, the Festival 8 performance (1 November 2009) is worthwhile. But the most famous version is likely the one that convinced a generation that there was something to Phish: the version included on *A Live One*. Described by Walter Holland (in his indispensable 33 1/3 contribution) as a 'gorgeous chamber pop tune' with 'Senegalese rhythm rings and romantic/aquatic imagery', the 31 December 1994 performance at the Boston Garden is 'first among equals' when it comes to 'Bouncing Around The Room'. This era of 'Bouncing Around The Room' is approximately when future members of alt-country icons Old Crow Medicine Show began to take notice of the band. These at-the-time teenagers would see the band in Richmond, Virginia and Washington, D.C. and soak up that influence. In fact, roughly one year after *The Baker's Dozen*, Old Crow Medicine Show headlined a Vermont concert and they used that opportunity to pay tribute to that influence. Outside of the extended introduction, which included the 'First Tube' riff, Old Crow's version of 'Bouncing Around The Room' was as playful as the original. The band have an irregular habit of covering Phish when in Vermont. Previous stops to the Green Mountain Stage have included performances of 'Lawn Boy' and 'Poor Heart'.

'Most Events Aren't Planned' (Batiste/Burbridge/Dillof/McConnell)
In 2002, during the band's initial hiatus, Page formed a trio with Funky Meters drummer Russell Batiste and sometime Allman Brothers bassist Oteil Burbridge. The opening track to Vida Blue's self-titled album, 'Most Events Aren't Planned' telegraphed their intent. As Kerry L. Smith noted in their contemporaneous *Rolling Stone* review, Vida Blue 'digs deep into a 1970s-era rock-funk-jazz-fusion candy jar' and Phish did the same when they finally gave this underappreciated gem a full-band airing. Beyond being a high point of the opening set, it also made the perfect concluding track on *The Baker's Dozen* compilation. Phish would return to 'Most Events Aren't Planned' when they held their Labor Day Weekend run at Dick's Sporting Goods Park in Colorado. Once again, the song *Rolling Stone* said was 'enough to hook Phish

fans, as well as loyal followers of Herbie Hancock and the Headhunters' was well-received. Sadly, 'Most Events Aren't Planned' has been placed on the back burner; it has only been played by the band 11 times since those two successful Sunday appearances.

'Bug' (Anastasio/Marshall)

Phish then went back to the *Farmhouse* one last time and brought back another rustic, melodic gem. The song, which 'Doctor_Smarty' ingeniously refers to on Phish.net as 'a hybrid of Velvet Underground's 'Oh! Sweet Nuthin' and the Marshall Tucker Band's 'Can't You See'', is another Anastasio/Marshall composition that works best when the moment calls for something mellow. That is not to say that 'Bug' will put a listener to sleep; it may start off with semi-introspective lyrics, but it ends with the instruments doing the talking. This *Baker's Dozen* performance, as well as the Big Cypress version from 31 December 1999 and the second set-closing Alpine Valley version from 14 August 2010, is especially good at reshaping the mood. By the time the band reach the final, repeated mantra of 'It doesn't matter', it no longer feels like resignation. It feels like a release.

'I Been Around' (McConnell)

Trey delivers his usual pre-song line to Page, 'Hey, Page, how you feeling over there? How you feeling after 13 nights?' Page responds, 'I don't know about you guys, but I'm feeling kinda glazed tonight.' Trey works his way back to the customary 'where you been' and Page finds his way into 'I Been Around'. This underplayed *Joy* track shows that Page's lounge-singing skills are not exhausted by Night 4's monster 'Lawn Boy'. Part of its charm is that it's the least-played song from *Joy* (half as many performances as the second-least-played 'Time Turns Elastic'!). Prior to *The Baker's Dozen*, the last time 'I Been Around' had been performed was almost three years earlier at the Merriweather Post Pavilion. Watching this 27 July 2014 performance on YouTube is something I return to whenever I need cheering up. Apart from the performance itself, the way the band initially walk off the stage, with Fishman and Trey both acting like an extra-louche Randall Graves, is fantastic and always makes me smile.

'Izabella' (Hendrix)

After a slight pause, Trey and the band launch into their final Hendrix song of *The Baker's Dozen*. 'Izabella' was the B-side to the last single Jimi Hendrix released in his lifetime, 'Stepping Stone'. Phish's version sounds more like how 'Izabella' might have sounded if Hendrix had recorded it with the Experience instead of their successors, Band of Gypsys. For all the talk of Phish and the Grateful Dead (or, really, any band), Phish are always the most successful when the foundational element of the tune being covered is a chunky riff. Writing again for *Relix*, Raffaela Kenny-Cincotta included 'Izabella' in a listicle of 13 'forgotten covers' that Phish might play at *The Baker's Dozen*. The fact that the other 12 entries went unplayed is a testament to how vast the band's 'forgotten' history is. Regardless, the opening set of Night 13 ends just as strong as the opening song from Night 1, and there were still classics left to be played in the final set.

Set 2

'Simple' (Gordon) **> 'Rise/Come Together'** (Anastasio/Greenberg/Nicholson) **> 'Starman'** (Bowie)

The final set of *The Baker's Dozen* starts off with an almost 40-minute sequence. It begins with a fiery 'Simple' that recalls the version played in Chicago earlier that summer (and, although the Windy City was not privileged enough to hear Page and his theremin, they did hear some peak Trey and they've nothing to complain about). Written for possible inclusion on *Hoist*, 'Simple' would have to wait for *A Live One* to receive a proper release. As great as the two summer 2017 versions (and the 10 December 1994 version included on *A Live One*) are, the 6 December performance included on the *Vegas '96* live album was the one to beat for years. Then, on 27 July 2024, the band started up a muscular 'Sigma Oasis' that turned into an epic 'Simple'. Playing at the same venue where they delivered a 39-minute 'Ruby Waves' (later released as *Live Phish On Long Play 01*), the band delivered a 41-minute 'Simple' with enough variation to keep everyone happy. With its numerous sections that take the listener on a unique, once-in-a-lifetime trip, the longest 'Simple' to date is anything but simple. It is a massive jam that never loses momentum or focus, a standout example of how well the band's current style fits together. Rather than hinging on any single moment, its strength lies in the full journey – branching out in all directions and landing nearly every one. With all that being said, given the number of times the song has appeared in the setlist and the number of exemplary versions executed over the years, 'Simple' is one of the band's most popular songs. As well as the opening set's 'Most Events Aren't Planned', this track was included on the band's *Baker's Dozen* compilation, being the concluding track of that nearly three-and-a-half-hour compilation.

After 'Simple', the band move into their second-ever performance of 'Rise/Come Together'. Teased at the band's 15 July show in Chicago and fully performed at the subsequent Pittsburgh, Pennsylvania concert, 'Rise/Come Together' would continue to make periodic appearances in subsequent shows and function as the centerpiece of the third side of *Burn It Down*. Starting off melancholic but building to a rhapsodic peak, 'Rise/Come Together' is a great transition from the sequence-opening 'Simple' into the sequence-closing 'Starman'. This *Ziggy Stardust* classic, first performed the previous Halloween and (seemingly) retired after this second performance, includes one of Mike's best vocal performances of the entire *Baker's Dozen* run. Maybe it is because he has been singing along to this song for most of his life, but Mike is on point for this one. Musically, this fourth and final Bowie cover of the run is not perfectly played, but it is perfectly placed, providing just enough of a delay to let the children boogie.

'You Enjoy Myself' (Anastasio)
Once the opening runs are unleashed, the crowd realise they have been rewarded with what they have been waiting for throughout the run. With over 600 performances before *The Baker's Dozen* had even begun, the question was always 'when' the band would get to *Junta*'s 'You Enjoy Myself', not 'if'. Delivered with the energy of a band just kicking off a 13-night run, this 'You Enjoy Myself' stays true to tradition while weaving in uniquely *Baker's Dozen* touches; these include a tease of the first set's 'Izabella' and vocals that reference 'White Winter Hymnal' (Night 5), 'Everything In Its Right Place' (Night 11) and 'The Lizards' (Night 12).

'Loving Cup' (Jagger/Richards)
The band conclude their final full set of *The Baker's Dozen* with their oft-played version of The Rolling Stones' 'Loving Cup'. Originally written and recorded during the sessions for *Let It Bleed* (which means there's a timeline where Rod Stewart recorded a raggedly beautiful 'Loving Cup' instead of the atrociously awful 'Street Fighting Man' for *An Old Raincoat Won't Ever Let You Down*), the Stones held onto it until they got around to re-arranging and re-recording it for *Exile On Main St*. This is the arrangement that Phish would perform close to 50 times before The Rolling Stones would make a half-hearted attempt to reclaim it. The closest the Stones have managed to come is in Martin Scorsese's *Shine A Light* (and they had to recruit Jack White to give themselves a street fighting chance). Although not as rambunctious as the version included on *Live Phish Volume 18, 5.7.94*, this version of 'Loving Cup' is more celebratory – and deservedly so. Like the closing lines say, 'Oh, what a beautiful buzz, what a beautiful buzz'.

Intermission
After giving the audience time to get some of their applause out of their system, the band and MSG staff raise a banner commemorating *The Baker's Dozen* up into the rafters of Madison Square Garden.

Encore
'On The Road Again' (Nelson) **> 'Lawn Boy Reprise'** (Anastasio/Marshall) **> 'Bass Solo'** (Gordon) **> 'Tweezer Reprise'** (Anastasio/Fishman/Gordon/McConnell)
For their final encore, the band take turns singing Willie Nelson's 'On The Road Again'. Delivered with the perfect mixture of humor and accomplishment, 'On The Road Again' could have been the perfect conclusion to *The Baker's Dozen*, but the band still had some unfinished business. First

up, Page needs to inform the audience that they are still working their way through 'Lawn Boy' (Night 4) and Mike is owed a bass solo (from Night 10's 'Weekapaug Groove'). Finally, the band need to wrap up 'Tweezer' (Night 1). Once they settle those debts, they put a pin in their latest bespoke experience. The band had earned the right to go their separate ways ... for a few weeks, at least.

Epilogue (Labor Day Weekend In Denver/NYE Run At MSG)

Upon completion of *The Baker's Dozen*, the members of Phish spent a few weeks focused on other activities: a sit-in with the Mallett Brothers Band for Fishman and a set by Mike and his band at The Peach Music Festival in Scranton, Pennsylvania.

Less than four weeks after the final MSG show, Phish were back on stage together for another Labor Day run at Dick's in Denver. This three-night stand was as well-received as *The Baker's Dozen* run. Perhaps because it was a regularly scheduled tradition, it is often overlooked in discussions of 2017's musical high points. Familiarity breeds underappreciation.

The band closed out 2017 right where they started it: with a four-night New Year's Eve run at Madison Square Garden. The third and final set of the last night of that run featured yet another debut, 'Soul Planet'. Sounding like a rewrite of 'Soul Deep' (made famous by Alex Chilton while with The Box Tops), 'Soul Planet' gave the band a reason to transform their concert stage into a pirate ship (and to ring in the new year while performing water-referencing songs ('Free', 'A Song I Heard The Ocean Sing', 'The Moma Dance', 'Prince Caspian' and 'Wading In The Velvet Sea'). Even after having given Madison Square Garden 21 memorable shows in a single year, the band were still pulling out new and exciting moments. Their determination to never coast and to never repeat themselves ensures they do not atrophy into another nostalgia act.

Aftermath

Counting the 31 December 2016 show that rolled into 2017, the band ended the year with 30 concerts under their belts – every single note of which was made available to audiences at home wishing to groove to one of the most respected live bands of their generation. *The Baker's Dozen* is not mentioned in the same way as the Grateful Dead's tour of Europe in 1972 or the Allman Brothers Band's run at the Fillmore East in 1971. I do not buy that it is because 'not enough time has passed'. Both *Europe '72* and *At Fillmore East* were in record shops and receiving critical praise within months of those concerts concluding. I suspect that Phish are the victims of their own success; it is easy to imagine phans saying, 'Of course, Phish delivered an excellent run ... that's what they always do.'

The band would include versions of five of *The Baker's Dozen* songs on their next studio album, 2020's *Sigma Oasis*. These songs ('Everything's Right', 'Leaves', 'Mercury', 'Steam' and 'Thread') would comprise the bulk of that relatively well-received nine-track album. Before that album, though, the band performed a special 'musical costume' during their 2018 Halloween show. The second set, titled (and later released as) 'Kasvot Växt's *i Rokk*', featured all new songs. Kasvot Växt was later revealed to be a fictional band, complete with a fake backstory and false information on select websites created by Phish. These ten original Phish songs would become concert favorites in the shows leading up to (and after) the Covid lockdown.

Appendix A: Songwriting Credits (Organized By FTP)

Phish performed 237 songs during *The Baker's Dozen*, and in trying to determine the best way to sequence them for accreditation, it was decided to organize them by first time played (FTP). Hopefully, a new phan scrolling through the list below will notice a trend that is unique to their preferences. If someone notices that several of their favorite songs debuted during a certain window or era, they will have a jumping-off point for which shows they should seek out next. For example, if your three favorite Phish songs are '46 Days', 'All Of These Dreams' and 'Mr. Completely', you're likely to find shows you like during the shows held during the spring or summer of 2003.

Note: The 'Studio Version' field only displays content if the song was officially released on a Phish-related studio album. Cover songs are not featured on their original album, nor is there an album listed for the (many) Phish songs that have not had an official studio release. Unless otherwise noted, the 'Studio Version' should be attributed to Phish (and not to one of their outside projects).

Phish 1.0 (1980s To 10/7/00)

'Makisupa Policeman' (Anastasio/Marshall) [The White Tape]
FTP: 23 October 1984 (TBD: 25 July, Set II, 'Jam-Filled')

'Camel Walk' (Holdsworth) [Unreleased]
FTP: 3 November 1984 (TBD: 6 August, Set I, 'Glazed')

'Slave To The Traffic Light' (Abrahams/Anastasio/Pollak) [The White Tape]
FTP: 12 January 1984 (TBD: 21 July, Set II, 'Coconut')

'Cities' (Byrne) [Unreleased]
FTP: 12 January 1984 (TBD: 22 July, Encore, 'Strawberry')

'Fluffhead' (Anastasio/Pollak) [Junta]
FTP: 12 January 1984 (TBD: 4 August, Set II, 'Lemon')

'Fire' (Hendrix) [Unreleased]
FTP: 12 January 1984 (TBD: 5 August, Set I, 'Boston Cream')

'Sneakin' Sally Through The Alley' (Toussaint) [Unreleased]
FTP: 8 March 1985 (TBD: 2 August, Set II, 'Holes')

'Alumni Blues' (Anastasio) [The White Tape]
FTP: 16 March 1985 (TBD: 29 July, Set II, 'Cinnamon')

'Mike's Song' (Gordon) [Unreleased]
FTP: 16 March 1985 (TBD: 2 August, Set II, 'Holes')

'Letter To Jimmy Page' (Anastasio) [The White Tape]
FTP: 6 April 1985 (TBD: 29 July, Set II, 'Cinnamon')

'McGrupp And The Watchful Hosemasters' (Anastasio/Marshall) [Unreleased]
FTP: 4/6/85 (TBD: 1 August, Set I, 'Maple')

'Run Like An Antelope' (Anastasio/Pollak) [Lawn Boy]
FTP: 6 April 1985 (TBD: 2 August, Set I, 'Holes')

'Quinn The Eskimo (The Mighty Quinn)' (Dylan) [Unreleased]
FTP: 6 April 1985 (TBD: 5 August, Set II, 'Boston Cream')

'Possum' (Holdsworth) [Unreleased]
FTP: 27 September 1985 (TBD: 1 August, Set II, 'Maple')

'Harry Hood' (Anastasio/Fishman/Gordon/Long/McConnell) [Unreleased]
FTP: 30 October 1985 (TBD: 29 July, Set II, 'Cinnamon')

'You Enjoy Myself' (Anastasio) [Junta]
FTP: 3 February 1986 (TBD: 6 August, Set II, 'Glazed')

'AC/DC Bag' (Anastasio) [The White Tape]
FTP: 1 April 1986 (TBD: 23 July, Set II, 'Red Velvet')

'Have Mercy' (Ferguson/Hoo-Kim/Shaw/Simpson) [Unreleased]
FTP: 1 April 1986 (TBD: 28 July, Set II, 'Double Chocolate')

'Halley's Comet' (Wright) [Unreleased]
FTP: 17 May 1986 (TBD: 22 July, Set I, 'Strawberry')

'Wilson' (Anastasio/Marshall/Woolf) [Unreleased]
FTP: 12 October 1986 (TBD: 29 July, Set I, 'Cinnamon')

'Golgi Apparatus' (Anastasio/Marshall/Szuter/Woolf) [Junta]
FTP: 12 October 1986 (TBD: 30 July, Set II, 'Jimmies')

'Peaches En Regalia' (Zappa) [Unreleased]
FTP: 15 October 1986 (TBD: 22 July, Encore, 'Strawberry')

'Sanity' (Anastasio/Fishman/Gordon/McConnell/Pollak) [Unreleased]
FTP: 15 October 1986 (TBD: 6 August, Set I, 'Glazed')

'David Bowie' (Anastasio) [Junta]
FTP: 31 October 1986 (TBD: 30 July, Set I, 'Jimmies')

'Good Times Bad Times' (Bonham/Jones/Page/Plant) [Unreleased]
FTP: 6 December 1986 (TBD: 21 July, Encore, 'Coconut')

'Funky Bitch' (Seals) [Unreleased]
FTP: 6 December 1986 (TBD: 22 July, Set I, 'Strawberry')

'Suzy Greenberg' (Pollak) [Unreleased]
FTP: 13 February 1987 (TBD: 21 July, Set II, 'Coconut')

'Boogie On Reggae Woman' (Wonder) [Unreleased]
FTP: 21 February 1987 (TBD: 23 July, Set II, 'Red Velvet')

'Ya Mar' (Ferguson) [Unreleased]
FTP: 21 February 1987 (TBD: 29 July, Set I, 'Cinnamon')

'Timber (Jerry The Mule)' (Gary/White) [Unreleased]
FTP: 29 April 1987 (TBD: 21 July, Set I, 'Coconut')

'Fuck Your Face' (Gordon) [The White Tape]
FTP: 29 April 1987 (TBD: 5 August, Set I, 'Boston Cream')

'Divided Sky' (Anastasio) [Junta]
FTP: 11 May 1987 (TBD: 28 July, Set I, 'Double Chocolate')

'Harpua' (Anastasio/Fishman) [Unreleased]
FTP: 11 May 1987 (TBD: 30 July, Set II, 'Jimmies')

'Fee' (Anastasio) [Junta]
FTP: 9 August 1987 (TBD: 28 July, Encore, 'Double Chocolate')

'The Curtain With' (Anastasio/Daubert) [Unreleased]
FTP: 9 August 1987 (TBD: 30 July, Set I, 'Jimmies')

'The Sloth' (Anastasio) [Unreleased]
FTP: 9 August 1987 (TBD: 5 August, Set I, 'Boston Cream')

'Big Black Furry Creature From Mars' (Gordon) [Unreleased]
FTP: 21 August 1987 (TBD: 4 August, Set I, 'Lemon')

'Rocky Top' (Bryant/Bryant) [Unreleased]
FTP: 21 August 1987 (TBD: 5 August, Set II, 'Boston Cream')

'I Didn't Know' (Wright) [Unreleased]
FTP: 18 November 1987 (TBD: 2 August, Set I, 'Holes')

'Dinner And A Movie' (Anastasio/Pollak) [Junta]
FTP: 19 November 1987 (TBD: 4 August, Set I, 'Lemon')

'The Lizards' (Anastasio) [Unreleased]
FTP: 27 January 1988 (TBD: 5 August, Set II, 'Boston Cream')

'Fly Famous Mockingbird' (Anastasio) [Unreleased]
FTP: 7 February 1988 (TBD: 30 July, Set I, 'Jimmies')

'Tela' (Anastasio) [Unreleased]
FTP: 12 March 1988 (TBD: 29 July, Set I, 'Cinnamon')

'Colonel Forbin's Ascent' (Anastasio) [Unreleased]
FTP: 12 March 1988 (TBD: 30 July, Set I, 'Jimmies')

'Bold As Love' (Hendrix) [Unreleased]
FTP: 7 July 1988 (TBD: 4 August, Set I, 'Lemon')

'Walk Away' (Walsh) [Unreleased]
FTP: 23 July 1988 (TBD: 1 August, Set I, 'Maple')

'Weekapaug Groove' (Anastasio/Fishman/Gordon/McConnell) [Unreleased]
FTP: 23 July 1988 (TBD: 2 August, Set II, 'Holes')

'Poor Heart' (Gordon) [A Picture Of Nectar]
FTP: 4 August 1988 (TBD: 4 August, Set I, 'Lemon')

'Esther' (Anastasio) [Junta]
FTP: 12 September 1988 (TBD: 30 July, Set I, 'Jimmies')

'Foam' (Anastasio) [Junta]
FTP: 29 October 1988 (TBD: 22 July, Set I, 'Strawberry')

'Split Open And Melt' (Anastasio) [Lawn Boy]
FTP: 17 February 1989 (TBD: 22 July, Set II, 'Strawberry')

'Cinnamon Girl' (Young) [Unreleased]
FTP: 1 March 1989 (TBD: 29 July, Encore, 'Cinnamon')

'The Mango Song' (Anastasio) [A Picture Of Nectar]
FTP: 30 March 1989 (TBD: 21 July, Encore, 'Coconut')

'Bathtub Gin' (Anastasio/Goodman) [Lawn Boy]
FTP: 26 May 1989 (TBD: 25 July, Set I, 'Jam-Filled')

'The Oh Kee Pa Ceremony' (Anastasio) [Lawn Boy]
FTP: 12 August 1989 (TBD: 28 July, Set I, 'Double Chocolate')

'Punch You In The Eye' (Anastasio) [Unreleased]
FTP: 17 August 1989 (TBD: 4 August, Set I, 'Lemon')

'My Sweet One' (Fishman) [Lawn Boy]
FTP: 9 September 1989 (TBD: 22 July, Encore, 'Strawberry')

'Reba' (Anastasio) [Lawn Boy]
FTP: 1 October 1989 (TBD: 21 July, Set I, 'Coconut')

'Frankenstein' (Winter) [Unreleased]
FTP: 11 November 1989 (TBD: 4 August, Encore, 'Lemon')

'Lawn Boy' (Anastasio/Marshall) [Lawn Boy]
FTP: 30 November 1989 (TBD: 25 July, Set I, 'Jam-Filled')

'The Squirming Coil' (Anastasio/Herman/Marshall) [Lawn Boy]
FTP: 20 January 1990 (TBD: 22 July, Set I, 'Strawberry')

'Bouncing Around The Room' (Anastasio/Marshall) [Lawn Boy]
FTP: 20 January 1990 (TBD: 6 August, Set I, 'Glazed')

'Rift' (Anastasio/Marshall) [Rift]
FTP: 25 February 1990 (TBD: 6 August, Set I, 'Glazed')

'Tweezer' (Anastasio/Fishman/Gordon/McConnell) [A Picture Of Nectar]
FTP: 28 March 1990 (TBD: 21 July, Set II, 'Coconut')

'Cavern' (Anastasio/Herman/Marshall) [A Picture Of Nectar]
FTP: 28 March 1990 (TBD: 25 July, Set II, 'Jam-Filled')

'Runaway Jim' (Abrahams/Anastasio) [Unreleased]
FTP: 28 March 1990 (TBD: 30 July, Set I, 'Jimmies')

'Uncle Pen' (Monroe) [Unreleased]
FTP: 28 March 1990 (TBD: 5 August, Set I, 'Boston Cream')

'Horn' (Anastasio/Marshall) [Rift]
FTP: 24 May 1990 (TBD: 29 July, Set I, 'Cinnamon')

'Stash' (Anastasio/Marshall) [A Picture Of Nectar]
FTP: 13 September 1990 (TBD: 25 July, Set I, 'Jam-Filled')

'Tube' (Anastasio/Fishman) [Unreleased]
FTP: 13 September 1990 (TBD: 26 July, Set I, 'Powdered')

'Buried Alive' (Anastasio) [Unreleased]
FTP: 13 September 1990 (TBD: 2 August, Set I, 'Holes')

'Destiny Unbound' (Gordon) [Unreleased]
FTP: 14 September 1990 (TBD: 28 July, Set I, 'Double Chocolate')

'Gumbo' (Anastasio/Fishman) [Unreleased]
FTP: 28 September 1990 (TBD: 26 July, Set I, 'Powdered')

'Llama' (Anastasio) [A Picture Of Nectar]
FTP: 27 October 1990 (TBD: 29 July, Set I, 'Cinnamon')

'Tweezer Reprise' (Anastasio/Fishman/Gordon/McConnell) [A Picture Of Nectar]
FTP: 1 February 1991 (TBD: 6 August, Encore, 'Glazed')

'Chalk Dust Torture' (Anastasio/Marshall) [A Picture Of Nectar]
FTP: 1 February 1991 (TBD: 28 July, Set II, 'Double Chocolate')

'Guelah Papyrus' (Anastasio/Marshall) [A Picture Of Nectar]
FTP: 1 February 1991 (TBD: 1 August, Set I, 'Maple')

'Sparkle' (Anastasio/Marshall) [Rift]
FTP: 25 September 1991 (TBD: 21 July, Set II, 'Coconut')

'It's Ice' (Anastasio/Marshall) [Rift]
FTP: 25 September 1991 (TBD: 23 July, Set I, 'Red Velvet')

'Glide' (Anastasio/Fishman/Gordon/Marshall/McConnell) [A Picture Of Nectar]
FTP: 27 September 1991 (TBD: 23 July, Set I, 'Red Velvet')

'Mound' (Gordon) [Rift]
FTP: 6 March 1992 (TBD: 22 July, Set I, 'Strawberry')

'My Friend, My Friend' (Anastasio/Marshall) [Rift]
FTP: 6 March 1992 (TBD: 25 July, Set I, 'Jam-Filled')

'NICU' (Anastasio/Marshall) [Unreleased]
FTP: 6 March 1992 (TBD: 2 August, Set I, 'Holes')

'Maze' (Anastasio/Marshall) [Rift]
FTP: 6 March 1992 (TBD: 2 August, Set I, 'Holes')

'Weigh' (Gordon) [Rift]
FTP: 7 March 1992 (TBD: 28 July, Set I, 'Double Chocolate')

'The Horse' (Anastasio/Marshall) [Rift]
FTP: 7 March 1992 (TBD: 5 August, Set II, 'Boston Cream')

'Silent In The Morning' (Anastasio/Marshall) [Rift]
FTP: 7 March 1992 (TBD: 5 August, Set II, 'Boston Cream')

'Axilla I' (Anastasio/Herman/Marshall) [Hoist]
FTP: 19 November 1992 (TBD: 23 July, Set I, 'Red Velvet')

'Loving Cup' (Jagger/Richards) [Unreleased]
FTP: 3 February 1993 (TBD: 6 August, Set II, 'Glazed')

'The Wedge' (Anastasio/Marshall) [Rift]
FTP: 3 February 1993 (TBD: 1 August, Set I, 'Maple')

'Sample In A Jar' (Anastasio/Marshall) [Hoist]

FTP: 4 February 1993 (TBD: 25 July, Set I, 'Jam-Filled')

'Nellie Kane' (O'Brien) [Unreleased]
FTP: 23 February 1993 (TBD: 30 July, Set I, 'Jimmies')

'Daniel Saw The Stone' (Traditional) [Unreleased]
FTP: 15 July 1993 (TBD: 1 August, Set I, 'Maple')

'2001' (Deodato) [Unreleased]
FTP: 16 July 1993 (TBD: 30 July, Set II, 'Jimmies')

'Ginseng Sullivan' (Blake) [Unreleased]
FTP: 11 August 1993 (TBD: 2 August, Set I, 'Holes')

'Down With Disease' (Anastasio/Marshall) [Hoist]
FTP: 31 December 1993 (TBD: 22 July, Set II, 'Strawberry')

'Wolfman's Brother' (Anastasio/Fishman/Gordon/Marshall/McConnell) [Hoist]
FTP: 4 April 1994 (TBD: 23 July, Set II, 'Red Velvet')

'Julius' (Anastasio/Marshall) [Hoist]
FTP: 4 April 1994 (TBD: 25 July, Encore, 'Jam-Filled')

'Scent Of A Mule' (Gordon) [Hoist]
FTP: 4 April 1994 (TBD: 5 August, Set I, 'Boston Cream')

'Simple' (Gordon) [Unreleased]
FTP: 27 May 1994 (TBD: 6 August, Set II, 'Glazed')

'Guyute' (Anastasio/Marshall) [The Story Of The Ghost]
FTP: 7 October 1994 (TBD: 2 August, Set I, 'Holes')

'Theme From The Bottom' (Anastasio/Fishman/Gordon/Marshall/McConnell) [Billy Breathes]
FTP: 16 May 1995 (TBD: 23 July, Set I, 'Red Velvet')

'Ha Ha Ha' (Fishman) [Unreleased]
FTP: 16 May 1995 (TBD: 6 August, Set I, 'Glazed')

'Free' (Anastasio/Marshall) [Billy Breathes]
FTP: 16 May 1995 (TBD: 28 July, Set I, 'Double Chocolate')

'Taste' (Anastasio/Fishman/Gordon/Marshall/McConnell) [Billy Breathes]
FTP: 7 June 1995 (TBD: 2 August, Set II, 'Holes')

'Prince Caspian' (Anastasio/Marshall) [Billy Breathes]
FTP: 8 June 1995 (TBD: 4 August, Set II, 'Lemon')

'A Day In The Life' (Lennon/McCartney) [Unreleased]
FTP: 10 June 1995 (TBD: 2 August, Encore, 'Holes')

'Billy Breathes' (Anastasio) [Billy Breathes]
FTP: 27 September 1995 (TBD: 21 July, Set II, 'Coconut')

'Cars Trucks Buses' (McConnell) [Billy Breathes]
FTP: 27 September 1995 (TBD: 26 July, Set I, 'Powdered')

'Drowned' (Townshend) [Unreleased]
FTP: 31 October 1995 (TBD: 30 July, Set II, 'Jimmies')

'Character Zero' (Anastasio/Marshall) [Billy Breathes]
FTP: 6 June 1996 (TBD: 26 July, Set II, 'Powdered')

'Train Song' (Gordon/Linitz) [Billy Breathes]
FTP: 21 July 1996 (TBD: 29 July, Set I, 'Cinnamon')

'Swept Away' (Anastasio/Marshall) [Billy Breathes]
FTP: 16 October 1996 (TBD: 1 August, Set II, 'Maple')

'Steep' (Anastasio/Fishman/Gordon/Marshall/McConnell) [Billy Breathes]
FTP: 16 October 1996 (TBD: 1 August, Set II, 'Maple')

'Crosseyed And Painless' (Byrne/Eno/Frantz/Harrison/Weymouth) [Unreleased]
FTP: 31 October 1996 (TBD: 25 July, Set II, 'Jam-Filled')

'My Soul' (Chenier) [Unreleased]
FTP: 13 February 1997 (TBD: 26 July, Set I, 'Powdered')

'When The Circus Comes' (Hidalgo/Perez) [Unreleased]
FTP: 13 February 1997 (TBD: 1 August, Set I, 'Maple')

'Carini' (Anastasio/Fishman/Gordon/McConnell) [Unreleased]
FTP: 17 February 1997 (TBD: 26 July, Set II, 'Powdered')

'Soul Shakedown Party' (Marley) [Unreleased]
FTP: 17 February 1997 (TBD: 5 August, Set I, 'Boston Cream')

'Wading In The Velvet Sea' (Anastasio/Marshall) [The Story Of The Ghost]
FTP: 13 June 1997 (TBD: 23 July, Set II, 'Red Velvet')

'Dogs Stole Things' (Anastasio/Marshall) [Unreleased]
FTP: 13 June 1997 (TBD: 6 August, Set I, 'Glazed')

'Izabella' (Hendrix) [Unreleased]
FTP: 13 June 1997 (TBD: 6 August, Set I, 'Glazed')

'Water In The Sky' (Anastasio/Marshall) [The Story Of The Ghost]
FTP: 13 June 1997 (TBD: 29 July, Set I, 'Cinnamon')

'Vultures' (Anastasio/Herman/Marshall) [Unreleased]
FTP: 13 June 1997 (TBD: 29 July, Set I, 'Cinnamon')

'Limb By Limb' (Anastasio/Herman/Marshall) [The Story Of The Ghost]
FTP: 13 June 1997 (TBD: 1 August, Set I, 'Maple')

'Ghost' (Anastasio/Marshall) [The Story Of The Ghost]
FTP: 13 June 1997 (TBD: 5 August, Set II, 'Boston Cream')

'Twist' (Anastasio/Marshall) [Farmhouse]
FTP: 14 June 1997 (TBD: 23 July, Set II, 'Red Velvet')

'Saw It Again' (Anastasio/Marshall) [Unreleased]
FTP: 14 June 1997 (TBD: 6 August, Set I, 'Glazed')

'Dirt' (Anastasio/Herman/Marshall) [Farmhouse]
FTP: 14 June 1997 (TBD: 29 July, Set II, 'Cinnamon')

'Piper' (Anastasio/Marshall) [Farmhouse]

FTP: 14 June 1997 (TBD: 1 August, Set II, 'Maple')

'Meatstick' (Anastasio/Fishman/Gordon/Herman/Marshall/McConnell) [Unreleased]
FTP: 25 June 1997 (TBD: 29 July, Set II, 'Cinnamon')

'Farmhouse' (Anastasio/Marshall) [Farmhouse]
FTP: 16 November 1997 (TBD: 26 July, Set I, 'Powdered')

'Roses Are Free' (Freeman/Melchiondo) [Unreleased]
FTP: 11 December 1997 (TBD: 26 July, Set I, 'Powdered')

'Birds Of A Feather' (Anastasio/Fishman/Gordon/Marshall/McConnell) [The Story Of The Ghost]
FTP: 2 April 1998 (TBD: 22 July, Set II, 'Strawberry')

'The Moma Dance' (Anastasio/Fishman/Gordon/Marshall/McConnell) [The Story Of The Ghost]
FTP: 30 June 1998 (TBD: 22 July, Set I, 'Strawberry')

'Roggae' (Anastasio/Fishman/Gordon/Marshall/McConnell) [The Story Of The Ghost]
FTP: 30 June 1998 (TBD: 22 July, Set I, 'Strawberry')

'Brian And Robert' (Anastasio/Marshall) [The Story Of The Ghost]
FTP: 30 June 1998 (TBD: 30 July, Set I, 'Jimmies')

'Meat' (Anastasio/Fishman/Gordon/Marshall/McConnell) [The Story Of The Ghost]
FTP: 2 July 1998 (TBD: 2 August, Set I, 'Holes')

'Sweet Jane' (Reed) [Unreleased]
FTP: 8 August 1998 (TBD: 23 July, Encore, 'Red Velvet')

'Rock And Roll' (Reed) [Unreleased]
FTP: 31 October 1998 (TBD: 28 July, Set II, 'Double Chocolate')

'1999' (Nelson) [Unreleased]
FTP: 31 December 1998 (TBD: 26 July, Set II, 'Powdered')

'Back On The Train' (Anastasio/Marshall) [Farmhouse]
FTP: 30 June 1999 (TBD: 23 July, Set I, 'Red Velvet')

'Bug' (Anastasio/Marshall) [Farmhouse]
FTP: 30 June 1999 (TBD: 6 August, Set I, 'Glazed')

'What's The Use?' (Anastasio/Fishman/Gordon/McConnell) [The Siket Disc]
FTP: 4 July 1999 (TBD: 4 August, Set II, 'Lemon')

'First Tube' (Anastasio/Lawton/Markellis) [Farmhouse]
FTP: 9 September 1999 (TBD: 4 August, Set I, 'Lemon')

'Gotta Jibboo' (Anastasio/Lawton/Markellis) [Farmhouse]
FTP: 10 September 1999 (TBD: 5 August, Set I, 'Boston Cream')

'Sand' (Anastasio/Lawton/Markellis/Marshall) [Farmhouse]
FTP: 11 September 1999 (TBD: 28 July, Set I, 'Double Chocolate')

'Heavy Things' (Anastasio/Herman/Marshall) [Farmhouse]
FTP: 11 September 1999 (TBD: 2 August, Set I, 'Holes')

Phish 2.0 (12/31/02 To 8/15/04)

'Walls Of The Cave' (Anastasio/Marshall) [Round Room]
FTP: 31 December 2002 (TBD: 21 July, Set I, 'Coconut')

'Seven Below' (Anastasio/Marshall) [Round Room]
FTP: 31 December 2002 (TBD: 21 July, Set II, 'Coconut')

'Waves' (Anastasio/Herman/Marshall) [Round Room]
FTP: 31 December 2002 (TBD: 23 July, Set II, 'Red Velvet')

'46 Days' (Anastasio/Marshall) [Round Room]
FTP: 2 January 2003 (TBD: August 1, Set II, 'Maple')

'All Of These Dreams' (Anastasio/Herman/Marshall) [Round Room]
FTP: 3 January 2003 (TBD: 22 July, Set II, 'Strawberry')

'Pebbles And Marbles' (Anastasio/Marshall) [Round Room]
FTP: 3 January 2003 (TBD: 26 July, Set I, 'Powdered')

'Scents And Subtle Sounds' (Anastasio/Herman/Marshall) [Undermind]
FTP: 7 July 2003 (TBD: 4 August, Set II, 'Lemon')

'Army Of One' (McConnell) [Undermind]
FTP: 12 July 2003 (TBD: 1 August, Set I, 'Maple')

'Mr. Completely' (Anastasio) [One Man's Trash]
FTP: 15 July 2003 (TBD: 26 July, Set II, 'Powdered')

'Crowd Control' (Anastasio/Marshall) [Undermind]
FTP: 28 November 2003 (TBD: 1 August, Set I, 'Maple')

'A Song I Heard The Ocean Sing' (Anastasio/Herman/Marshall) [Undermind]
FTP: 17 June 2004 (TBD: 30 July, Set II, 'Jimmies')

Phish 3.0 (3/6/09 To ???)

'Backwards Down The Number Line' (Anastasio/Marshall) [Joy]
FTP: 6 March 2009 (TBD: 28 July, Set II, 'Double Chocolate')

'Undermind' (Anastasio/Herman/Marshall) [Undermind]
FTP: 8 March 2009 (TBD: 28 July, Set I, 'Double Chocolate')

'Ocelot' (Anastasio/Marshall) [Joy]
FTP: 31 May 2009 (TBD: 4 August, Set I, 'Lemon')

'Light' (Anastasio/Marshall) [Joy]
FTP: 31 May 2009 (TBD: 5 August, Set II, 'Boston Cream')

'Stealing Time From The Faulty Plan' (Anastasio/Herman/Marshall) [Joy]
FTP: 2 June 2009 (TBD: 29 July, Set I, 'Cinnamon')

'Kill Devil Falls' (Anastasio/Marshall) [Joy]
FTP: 2 June 2009 (TBD: 2 August, Set I, 'Holes')

'Twenty Years Later' (Anastasio/Marshall) [Joy]
FTP: 5 June 2009 (TBD: 29 July, Set II, 'Cinnamon')

'Joy' (Anastasio/Marshall) [Joy]
FTP: 7 June 2009 (TBD: 5 August, Encore, 'Boston Cream')

'Sugar Shack' (Gordon) [Joy]
FTP: 7 June 2009 (TBD: 1 August, Set I, 'Maple')

'Alaska' (Anastasio/Marshall) [Party Time]
FTP: 9 June 2009 (TBD: 5 August, Set I, 'Boston Cream')

'Party Time' (Fishman) [Party Time]
FTP: 15 August 2009 (TBD: 4 August, Set I, 'Lemon')

'I Been Around' (McConnell) [Joy]
FTP: 16 August 2009 (TBD: 6 August, Set I, 'Glazed')

'Shine A Light' (Jagger/Richards) [Unreleased]
FTP: 31 October 2009 (TBD: 22 July, Set II, 'Strawberry')

'Golden Age' (Adebimpe/Bunton/Malone/Sitek/Smith) [Unreleased]
FTP: 27 November 2009 (TBD: 1 August, Set II, 'Maple')

'Halfway To The Moon' (McConnell) [Fuego]
FTP: 19 June 2010 (TBD: 21 July, Set I, 'Coconut')

'I Am The Walrus' (Lennon/McCartney) [Unreleased]
FTP: 29 June 2010 (TBD: 29 July, Set I, 'Cinnamon')

'Pigtail' (Anastasio/Marshall) [Traveler]
FTP: 28 December 2010 (TBD: 21 July, Set I, 'Coconut')

'No Quarter' (Jones/Page/Plant) [Unreleased]
FTP: 1 June 2011 (TBD: 26 July, Set II, 'Powdered')

'Steam' (Anastasio/Marshall) [Sigma Oasis]
FTP: 4 June 2011 (TBD: 26 July, Set II, 'Powdered')

'Yarmouth Road' (Gordon/Murawski) [Overstep]
FTP: 5 July 2013 (TBD: 26 July, Set I, 'Powdered')

'Frost' (Anastasio/Marshall) [Traveler]
FTP: 17 July 2013 (TBD: 5 August, Set I, 'Boston Cream')

'On The Road Again' (Nelson) [Unreleased]
FTP: 31 August 2013 (TBD: 6 August, Encore, 'Glazed')

'555' (Gordon/Murawski) [Fuego]
FTP: 31 October 2013 (TBD: 21 July, Set I, 'Coconut')

'Fuego' (Anastasio/Fishman/Gordon/McConnell) [Fuego]
FTP: 31 October 2013 (TBD: 25 July, Set II, 'Jam-Filled')

'The Line' (Anastasio/Fishman/Gordon/McConnell) [Fuego]
FTP: 31 October 2013 (TBD: 29 July, Set I, 'Cinnamon')

'Waiting All Night' (Anastasio/Fishman/Gordon/McConnell) [Fuego]
FTP: 31 October 2013 (TBD: 2 August, Set I, 'Holes')

'Wingsuit' (Anastasio/Fishman/Gordon/McConnell) [Fuego]
FTP: 31 October 2013 (TBD: 2 August, Set II, 'Holes')

'Winterqueen' (Anastasio/Marshall) [Fuego]
FTP: 31 October 2013 (TBD: 4 August, Set I, 'Lemon')

'Plasma' (Anastasio/Herman/Marshall) [Unreleased]
FTP: 17 October 2014 (TBD: 5 August, Set I, 'Boston Cream')

'Martian Monster' (Anastasio/Fishman/Gordon/McConnell) [Unreleased]
FTP: 31 October 2014 (TBD: 21 July, Set I, 'Coconut')

'Your Pet Cat' (Anastasio/Fishman/Gordon/McConnell) [Unreleased]
FTP: 31 October 2014 (TBD: 23 July, Set I, 'Red Velvet')

'The Very Long Fuse' (Anastasio/Fishman/Gordon/McConnell) [Unreleased]
FTP: 31 October 2014 (TBD: 26 July, Set I, 'Powdered')

'The Dogs' (Anastasio/Fishman/Gordon/McConnell) [Unreleased]
FTP: 31 October 2014 (TBD: 28 July, Set I, 'Double Chocolate')

'The Birds' (Anastasio/Fishman/Gordon/McConnell) [Unreleased]
FTP: 31 October 2014 (TBD: 29 July, Set I, 'Cinnamon')

'Dem Bones' (Traditional) [Unreleased]
FTP: 31 December 2014 (TBD: 4 August, Set II, 'Lemon')

'Blaze On' (Anastasio/Marshall) [Big Boat]
FTP: 21 July 2015 (TBD: July 29, Set II, 'Cinnamon')

'No Men In No Man's Land' (Anastasio/Marshall) [Big Boat]
FTP: 21 July 2015 (TBD: 4 August, Set II, 'Lemon')

'How Many People Are You' (Gordon/Murawski) [Noon]
FTP: 22 July 2015 (TBD: 23 July, Set I, 'Red Velvet')

'Mercury' (Anastasio/Marshall) [Sigma Oasis]
FTP: 22 July 2015 (TBD: 28 July, Set II, 'Double Chocolate')

'Miss You' (Anastasio) [Big Boat]
FTP: 24 June 2016 (TBD: 23 July, Set II, 'Red Velvet')

'Space Oddity' (Bowie) [Unreleased]
FTP: 24 June 2016 (TBD: 28 July, Encore, 'Double Chocolate')

'Breath And Burning' (Anastasio) [Big Boat]
FTP: 26 June 2016 (TBD: 22 July, Set I, 'Strawberry')

'Things People Do' (McConnell) [Big Boat]
FTP: 28 June 2016 (TBD: 28 July, Set I, 'Double Chocolate')

'Waking Up Dead' (Gordon/Murawski) [Big Boat]
FTP: 29 June 2016 (TBD: 30 July, Set I, 'Jimmies')

'Ass Handed' (Fishman) [Unreleased]
FTP: 15 July 2016 (TBD: 28 July, Set I, 'Double Chocolate')

'More' (Anastasio) [Big Boat]
FTP: 14 October 2016 (TBD: 23 July, Set I, 'Red Velvet')

'Home' (McConnell) [Big Boat]
FTP: 14 October 2016 (TBD: 30 July, Set I, 'Jimmies')

'Petrichor' (Anastasio) [Big Boat]
FTP: 14 October 2016 (TBD: 5 August, Set II, 'Boston Cream')

'I Always Wanted It This Way' (McConnell) [Big Boat]
FTP: 15 October 2016 (TBD: 22 July, Set II, 'Strawberry')

'Moonage Daydream' (Bowie) [Unreleased]
FTP: 31 October 2016 (TBD: 21 July, Set I, 'Coconut')

'Starman' (Bowie) [Unreleased]
FTP: 31 October 2016 (TBD: 6 August, Set II, 'Glazed')

'Rock 'N' Roll Suicide' (Bowie) [Unreleased]
FTP: 31 October 2016 (TBD: 1 August, Encore, 'Maple')

'Everything's Right' (Anastasio/Marshall) [Sigma Oasis]
FTP: 14 July 2017 (TBD: 21 July, Set II, 'Coconut')

'In The Good Old Summer Time' (Evans/Liles/Shields) [Unreleased]
FTP: 14 July 2017 (TBD: 30 July, Set II, 'Jimmies')

'Leaves' (Anastasio/Marshall) [Sigma Oasis]
FTP: 14 July 2017 (TBD: 1 August, Set II, 'Maple')

'Thread' (Anastasio/Marshall) [Sigma Oasis]
FTP: 16 July 2017 (TBD: 25 July, Set II, 'Jam-Filled')

'Tuesday' (Anastasio/O'Brien) [Shine]
FTP: 18 July 2017 (TBD: 25 July, Set II, 'Jam-Filled')

'Crazy Sometimes' (Gordon/Murawski) [OGOGO]
FTP: 18 July 2017 (TBD: 6 August, Set I, 'Glazed')

'Rise/Come Together' (Anastasio/Greenberg/Nicholson) [Unreleased]
FTP: 19 July 2017 (TBD: 6 August, Set II, 'Glazed')

'Shake Your Coconuts' (Laursen/Mortensen/Troelsen) [Unreleased]
FTP: 21 July 2017 (TBD: 21 July, Set I, 'Coconut')

'Coconut' (Liles/Nilsson) [Unreleased]
FTP: 21 July 2017 (TBD: 21 July, Set II, 'Coconut')

'Strawberry Fields Forever' (Lennon/McCartney) [Unreleased]
FTP: 22 July 2017 (TBD: 22 July, Set I, 'Strawberry')

'Strawberry Letter 23' (Otis) [Unreleased]
FTP: 22 July 2017 (TBD: 22 July, Set II, 'Strawberry')

'Sunday Morning' (Cale/Reed) [Unreleased]
FTP: 23 July 2017 (TBD: 23 July, Set I, 'Red Velvet')

'End Of Session' (Anastasio/Fishman/Gordon/Marshall/McConnell) [The Story Of The Ghost]
FTP: 25 July 2017 (TBD: 25 July, Set II, 'Jam-Filled')

'Powderfinger' (Young) [Unreleased]
FTP: 26 July 2017 (TBD: 26 July, Encore, 'Powdered')

'White Winter Hymnal' (Pecknold) [Unreleased]

FTP: 26 July 2017 (TBD: 26 July, Set I, 'Powdered')

'MSG Jam' (Anastasio/Fishman/Gordon/McConnell) [Unreleased]
FTP: 26 July 2017 (TBD: 26 July, Set II, 'Powdered')

'Chocolate Rain' (Bahner) [Unreleased]
FTP: 28 July 2017 (TBD: 28 July, Set I, 'Double Chocolate')

'You Sexy Thing' (Ainsworth/Brown) [Unreleased]
FTP: 28 July 2017 (TBD: 28 July, Set II, 'Double Chocolate')

'The Wind Cries Mary' (Hendrix) [Unreleased]
FTP: 30 July 2017 (TBD: 30 July, Encore, 'Jimmies')

'O Canada' (Lavallee) [Unreleased]
FTP: 1 August 2017 (TBD: 1 August, Set I, 'Maple')

'Maple Leaf Rag' (Joplin) [Unreleased]
FTP: 1 August 2017 (TBD: 1 August, Set I, 'Maple')

'Way Down In The Hole' (Waits) [Unreleased]
FTP: 2 August 2017 (TBD: 2 August, Set I, 'Holes')

'O Holy Night' (Adam/Clappeau) [Unreleased]
FTP: 2 August 2017 (TBD: 2 August, Set II, 'Holes')

'See That My Grave Is Kept Clean' (Jefferson) [Unreleased]
FTP: 4 August 2017 (TBD: 4 August, Set I, 'Lemon')

'Everything In Its Right Place' (Greenwood/Greenwood/O'Brien/Selway/Yorke) [Unreleased]
FTP: 4 August 2017 (TBD: 4 August, Set II, 'Lemon')

'Sunshine Of Your Feeling' (To Be Determined) [Unreleased]
FTP: 5 August 2017 (TBD: 5 August, Set I, 'Boston Cream')

'Bass Solo' (Gordon) [Unreleased]
FTP: 6 August 2017 (TBD: 6 August, Encore, 'Glazed')

'Most Events Aren't Planned' (Batiste/Burbridge/Dillof/McConnell) [Vida Blue]
FTP: 6 August 2017 (TBD: 6 August, Set I, 'Glazed')

Appendix B: Album Representation

The section below discusses how Phish's studio albums and their foundational live albums were represented during *The Baker's Dozen*. For those songs included on one of those releases but not played during *The Baker's Dozen* for some reason, a brief description is provided. Coupling the following appendix with the previous sections provides an overview of Phish's discography through 2017.

The White Tape (1986)

Saying *The White Tape* is where it all began is like saying The Beatles began when Tony Sheridan released 'My Bonnie'. There is some truth to it, but it does not feel accurate for some reason. Compiled by Trey Anastasio in the late 1980s, *The White Tape* is a compilation of early demos and recorded experiments. Sold by the band at early shows and then going out of print for several years, *The White Tape* circulated amongst fans before receiving a wide release in 1998. The album features only five tracks by the band (four of those – 'Alumni Blues', 'You Enjoy Myself', 'AC/DC Bag' and 'Letter To Jimmy Page' – were played at *The Baker's Dozen*). The fifth, 'Dog Gone Dog', was only infrequently played in the 1980s and 1990s before being retired in 2003 (except for a bust-out in 2012 and an appearance at a Mexican soundcheck in 2022). Outside of the recordings, which include the four of them, *The White Tape* also features recordings by Trey (playing all instruments) as well as recordings with Anastasio's high school friends and future Phish collaborator Tom Marshall. Another noteworthy aspect of *The White Tape* is the inclusion of Mike's Zappa-esque 'Fuck Your Face' (which made an appearance on 'Boston Cream' night). Though amateurish at times, *The White Tape* offers a charming glimpse into early Phish and hints at the band's future complexity.

Junta (1988)

Phish's 1988 release, *Junta*, is where the band's studio output really began. (Note: Fans of the band's more prog-influenced performances during *The Baker's Dozen* should definitely start here.) The original cassette release (from 1988) featured 11 tracks. All but one of those, Mike's fun yet inessential 'Contact', appeared in *The Baker's Dozen*.

Independently recorded at Sound & Vision Media (when it was still known as Euphoria Sound Studio), the *Junta* cassette was originally available at the band's merch table and, starting in 1989, began officially appearing in stores. When the original cassette-only title was re-released by Elektra Records in 1992, additional music was needed to fill out the second disc. This was accomplished with a 25-minute studio version of the band's never-performed-live 'Union Federal' and two live tracks from 1988, 'Icculus' and 'Sanity' (the latter of which was also performed during the 13th night of *The Baker's Dozen*).

Recorded when the band members were in their early to mid-20s (Fish and Mike were 23, Trey was 24 and Page was 25), *Junta* may not have made waves commercially, but it stands as a very musically adventurous debut. In his four-star review for *AllMusic*, Steven McDonald wrote, 'With great sound and better playing, Phish's debut, *Junta*, is highly recommended whether you are starting to discover Phish or are backing up to the beginning. It may be a bit long-winded and unfocused, yet it establishes their dedication to musical exploration effectively, not to mention the typical wild and wooly Phish humor spilling out all over the lengthy tracks.' Packed with inventive melodies and unexpected turns, *Junta* has a variety that recalls The Beatles' 1968 self-titled album. And like that then-20-year-old album, Junta rewards patient listeners who are in it for the full ride.

Lawn Boy (1990)

Originally released in the fall of 1990 and reissued by Elektra Records in 1992, Phish's second proper studio album is another masterclass in progressive rock, fusion, bluegrass, jazz and barbershop quartet. Recorded and mixed at Vermont's Archer Studios, Phish won their initial studio time by winning a Rock Rumble in 1989. Local musicians helped out during the recording; some of these, while working under the name 'The Giant Country Horns', would later join up with Phish for a series of concerts.

All nine of *Lawn Boy*'s tracks would be featured during *The Baker's Dozen*. Outside of anniversary tours, where an album is played front-to-back, not many bands are still including every song from an album in their setlists more than a quarter of a century after its release. Although the band's origin story ends with *Lawn Boy* getting them signed to Elektra Records, it is not an album that (upon first listen) seems designed to woo a major label.

In a review that reads better than its three-star rating would indicate, Jim Smith referred to Lawn Boy as 'relaxed, friendly and a lot of fun.' He referred to it as 'their true statement of purpose' that captures 'Trey Anastasio's unique visions in their rawest form.' Mr. Smith concludes this *AllMusic* review with 'Anastasio may have played with greater force and potency later on, but his creative spark was rarely brighter than here, and he proves himself to be not only a student but a master of many divergent styles.' In a 2015 celebration of 1990 albums, *Classic Rock Review* complimented Phish's 'unique fusion rock sound' and said their 'sophomore effort, *Lawn Boy*, is chock full of diverse ditties and extended jams.'

A Picture Of Nectar (1992)

To put this album into perspective: Elektra Records released an hour-long blending of psychedelia, jazz-pop, bluegrass and prog rock just one month after Nirvana's *Nevermind* reached number one on the *Billboard* 200. It was a chaotic moment for rock; on the same day *A Picture Of Nectar* dropped, Reprise released the *Wayne's World* soundtrack (fueled by Queen's 'Bohemian Rhapsody') and Vince Neil officially parted ways with Mötley Crüe to pursue a career in auto racing. But, in their own wonderfully weird way, Phish were well-positioned to carve out a lane no one else was driving in.

Sue Drew, the A&R rep who 'discovered' the band and first signed them to Elektra Records, offered a great account of that experience in a post on Phishbase – a fan-run blog site – a few months after *The Baker's Dozen*. 'I went to the record store and I bought the record [*Lawn Boy*] and I checked it out and I listened to it and thought this is probably the strangest album I have ever heard. But there's something about it.' She went on to state that 'in all honesty, the deal was not difficult to conclude because they weren't greedy … So, we gave them some sort of advance, which I don't remember what it is now and that indeed was true: From the minute the record shipped, they started making money for us.'

With Elektra's backing, the band recorded the album (with co-producer Kevin Halpin) at Burlington's White Crow Studios. In his four-and-a-half star review for *AllMusic*, Timothy Monger stated the album featured 'plenty of excellent songs built for the stage' and he went on to praise 'Tweezer', 'Guelah Papyrus' and 'Chalkdust Torture' in particular. Mr. Monger was on the right side of history, and combined, those three have been played over 1,100 times to date. *People Magazine*, which has never been known as a musical tastemaker, called the album 'insufferable' and a 'neo-hippie, techno-nerd fusion', but Phillip J. Reed (writing for noiselesschatter.com) has the better take: 'When the band has fun, we have fun, and *A Picture Of Nectar* is absolutely a portrait of a band having fun.'

A Picture Of Nectar provided the band with two singles, 'Chalk Dust Torture' and 'Cavern', and they would both be played (along with eight other songs from the album) at *The Baker's Dozen*. With ten of its 16 tracks being represented during the run, *A Picture Of Nectar* fans were undoubtedly happy. In fact, of the six tracks not played ('Eliza', 'Manteca', 'Magilla', 'The Landlady', 'Faht' and 'Catapult'), four were instrumentals and the other two hovered around the 30-second mark.

Rift (1993)

The band's fourth album was also their first commercially released concept album. Whereas the *Gamehendge* songs were about a Long Islander, his friends and their battle against the evil Wilson, *Rift* was built around a sleeping man and his dreams about his girlfriend and their relationship. That is not to say the album was not fantastical; as Tom Volk wrote for *Spectrum Culture*, '*Rift* is a remarkably dark album. Nightmarish imagery abounds throughout its length, with lyrical references to falling through a sheet of ice, being trapped in a maze, decapitation, hidden knives, betrayals and laughing into a nervous breakdown.'

Recorded in their hometown of Burlington and also in Nashville, *Rift* featured production work from the legendary Barry Beckett (Muscle Shoals Rhythm Section and (briefly) Traffic, plus production work on Bob Seger's best albums and Bob Dylan's worst albums). Writers have claimed that Becket's background in rhythm & blues, soul, rock and folk contrasted with Phish's jam-focused style, but those writers are overlooking the foundational elements of the songs themselves. Phish chose to once again record in Burlington and to use their preferred engineer, Kevin Halpin. Reflecting on the experience in Parke Puterbaugh's biography, the band admitted they did not give Beckett enough creative control. Mike is quoted as saying, 'We worked with a great producer but didn't let him do anything because we had preconceptions about all the arrangements and sounds.'

All but three of *Rift*'s songs were played at *The Baker's Dozen*. The excluded songs included the initial single ('Fast Enough For You'), Fishman's lullaby ('Lengthwise') and the *NPR* homage ('All Things Reconsidered'). All three songs are solid contributions to an oft-underappreciated album.

Hoist (1994)

Although the band did play over half of *Hoist*, sacrifices needed to be made. The biggest is (arguably) their best ballad, 'If I Could'. One of their all-time best studio recordings (aided in large part by the vocals of National Medal of Arts winner Alison Krauss), 'If I Could' is a fitting example of how Trey can describe what is in the heart he wears on his sleeve. Although not played during *The Baker's Dozen*, a fantastic version was played in New Jersey on 28 June 2000. It is currently available on YouTube, but hopefully, it will be added to the LivePhish app at some point).

Another song not played during *The Baker's Dozen* was 'Riker's Mailbox'. The studio version (which is all we have since it has never been performed live) is 30 seconds of trombone bursts, backwards yelling and manic banjo. The song's origins trace back to a version of 'Buffalo Bill' recorded during the *Hoist* sessions (but left off the album due to its contrasting tone). The trombone on 'Riker's Mailbox' is played by Star Trek's Commander Riker, actor Jonathan Frakes.

'Lifeboy' is another *Hoist* ballad left out of *The Baker's Dozen*. The studio version, like 'If I Could', features outstanding contributions by outside musicians (in this case, Béla Fleck on banjo and Morgan Fichter on violin). That is where the similarities end because 'If I Could' is optimistic, whereas 'Lifeboy' is Trey at his most pessimistic. Sung in the first-person (a somewhat rare occurrence in their discography), 'Lifeboy' carries the tone of a solemn, reflective ballad, not unlike the kind of songs you might hear in a traditional church setting. Its most repeated lyric, 'God never listens to what I say', could be an expression of doubt or frustration with faith. However, because the listener does not know what is being asked of God (or his plans), the prayers could have been rightfully ignored. The ambiguity leaves space for interpretation, which is part of what makes the song so haunting.

The third (and final) Hoist ballad that was not played was 'Dog Faced Boy'. If the first two were reductively referred to as 'optimistic' and 'pessimistic',

'Dog Faced Boy' can be called 'apologetic'. The lyrics about the guilt the protagonist feels for lying and cheating, coupled with the vocal delivery, imply that he seeks forgiveness. Just as 'Lifeboy' did not feature answered prayers, we've no idea if the recipient accepted the singer's apology. But the fact that he tried might just be enough.

The closing track to *Hoist*, 'Demand', is one of the band's most intense songs (and one they have only attempted twice this century). The song ends with lyrics about yelling in a parking lot, throwing beer cans downstairs and driving home. It then features the sound of a radio dial being tuned and a Phish cassette being popped into the player (the 'Split Open And Melt' from 21 April 1993). The jam portion of this Columbus, Ohio, concert is the driver's soundtrack until the sounds of a police chase and a car crash bring everything to a close (but not the end). *Hoist* then concludes with Phish performing 'Yerushalayim Shel Zahav', an Israeli song of exile and longing. (Note: What was intended by Phish at the time of the recording, and if their intentions would be the same if they were recording it today, is outside the scope of this book. For more/better information on Judaism and Phish, *This Is Your Song Too: Phish And Contemporary Jewish Identity* by Oren Kroll-Zeldin and Ariella Werden-Greenfield is highly recommended.)

A Live One (1995)

In his introductory paragraph about the band's next studio release, *Billy Breathes*, Richard Gehr wrote:

> Phish's last album, the double CD *A Live One*, distilled a decade's worth of dedicated road work by a group that have reinvented improvised rock for a new generation. If Phish have an identity, it is one characterized by endless change and musical risk, a yesterday-today-and-tomorrow sound that draws liberally from rock history and jazz innovation. Combine that with a rich, interactive mythology binding the band and its audience into the coziest symbiosis since you know who and you've got a cultural force to be reckoned with. An exhaustive – and nearly exhausting – consolidation of Phish's tightly wound tunes and electrifying jams, *A Live One*, which went gold, finally gave the rock mainstream a chance to see what all the fuss was about.

Later, in that same review, he offered that '*A Live One* was Phish's variation on the Grateful Dead's *Live/Dead*...'

The band's first widely available concert experience, *A Live One* was released in 1995 by Elektra Records. It became one of their best-selling records (and was the first to be certified Platinum by the RIAA). Inspired by fans frequently asking, 'When are you gonna put out a live one?', the band's first live release featured tracks recorded at assorted US concerts (primarily from the Autumn tour of 1994, but the included 'Stash' was from that same year's summer tour). Because of difficulties in securing rights from the various venues, the band credited all tracks as being from 'The Clifford Ball'. The following year, they would actually hold a *Clifford Ball* at the Plattsburgh Air Force Base in New York.

After reviewing tapes from their 1994 autumn tour, the band started with a list of 560 potential performances to include on their debut live album. With help from users of the then-burgeoning rec.music.phish Usenet newsgroup, the band were able to narrow the track list down to 12 songs that best represented what the band were capable of during this era.

The only song listed on *A Live One* that is not also listed in *The Baker's Dozen* setlist is 'Montana', the reason being the song does not really exist. 'Montana' is a two-minute excerpt from a glorious 45-minute version of 'Tweezer' the band played in Bozeman, Montana. Readers are encouraged to check out the entirety of that 28 November 1994 show via the LivePhish app.

Billy Breathes (1996)

The band followed *A Live One* with a polished, radio-friendly effort, *Billy Breathes*. Working for the first time with the once-and-future Dave Matthews Band producer Steve Lillywhite, the band recorded *Billy Breathes* at the famed Bearsville Studios in Woodstock, New York. Recording occurred between February and June 1996, and during that time, the band stayed off the road. They did have a solitary set at the New Orleans Jazz & Heritage Festival on 26 April 1996 and a surprise, unannounced show on 6 June 1996 at Joyous Lake in Woodstock, New York.

The band performed ten of the 13 songs on *Billy Breathes* during *The Baker's Dozen*. Of the three songs skipped, 'Waste' would be played during the band's Labor Day run at Dick's a few weeks later, the instrumental 'Bliss' would be performed at Madison Square Garden the following year and 'Talk' would (eventually) be revived in Chicago in 2023.

The reviews for *Billy Breathes* were mixed but, for the most part, positive. Stephen Thomas Erlewine gave the album four stars for *AllMusic* and wrote that the band 'finally delivered a concise pop album.' He praised the choice of Steve Lillywhite, who, he said, 'had the band cut away their jams and accentuate their songwriting, resulting in a series of tightly written, melodic folk-rock and psychedelic pop songs.' *Rolling Stone* was also complimentary towards the album when (future band biographer) Richard Gehr provided a four-star review on 9 December 1996 that stated, 'As rustic as the New England countryside, *Billy Breathes* is a warm declaration of optimism packaged in concise, radio-attractive songs.' He also wrote that *Billy Breathes* was 'part Workingman's Dead and part Abbey Road, focused on musical essences often obscured by rock-concert spectacle.' Although the Grateful Dead comparisons were already getting old, the Beatles comparisons were not quite as cliche in 1996.

Slip Stitch And Pass (1997)
The band's second live album in two years is sometimes overlooked by its more famous predecessor and its (arguably) more fun successor. That being said, it's an excellent album and (at 78 minutes) easier to consume than the two-disc *A Live One*. Writing for *AllMusic*, Stephen Thomas Erlewine went as far as to say, 'The group's second live record surpasses its predecessor in many ways, drawing a more complete picture of the Phish concert experience.' Writing for *The Village Voice*, Robert Christgau wrote that *Slip Stitch And Pass* 'Kinda restores your faith in humanity for these guys know the difference between intelligent and pretentious.' His rating of a B+ is even higher praise when you consider it is only a half-step away from the A- he gave Bob Dylan's *Time Out Of Mind* that same day.

All but two of the songs included on *Slip Stitch And Pass* were played during *The Baker's Dozen*. The two excluded songs were 'Hello My Baby' and 'Jesus Just Left Chicago'. On *Slip Stitch And Pass*, the band performed the barbershop quartet version of 'Hello My Baby' (presumably to put to rest rumors they were influenced by Michigan J. Frog's more ragtime version). The band also performed a burning version of ZZ Tops 'Jesus Just Left Chicago'. Still performed on an occasional basis (unlike the largely forgotten 'Hello My Baby'), 'Jesus Just Left Chicago' allows the band to demonstrate their (third-generation interpretation) of the blues. Original co-writer Billy Gibbons has stated, 'We took what could have been an easy 12-bar blues and made it more interesting by adding those odd extra measures. It's the same chords as 'La Grange' with the Robert Johnson lick, but weirder.'

The Story Of The Ghost (1998)/**The Siket Disc** (1999)
Phish's seventh studio album, produced by Andy Wallace (Slayer, Nirvana and Jeff Buckley) and released by Elektra Records in 1998, is the best studio representation of the 'cow-funk' style the band had recently been exploring in concerts. This 'cow-funk' era of Phish is ideal for people who think 'I Heard It Through The Grapevine' is Creedence Clearwater Revival's best 11 minutes. The phrase 'cow-funk' had been developed by Trey in order to appease purists who knew that 'real funk is not played by four white guys from Vermont.' Much of its content came from large-scale improvisation sessions, with the band selecting their favorite moments and developing those into songs (with longtime lyricist Tom Marshall then providing lyrics).

Although I love this era of Phish just as much as I do every other era, others disagree. *Spin* went as far as to reference the Grateful Dead's 1970 masterpiece in their disparaging aside: 'Confusing *American Beauty* with American booty never works for Phish.' *AllMusic* referred to *The Story Of The Ghost* as the band's 'most commercially accessible offering to date, a slinky (and slightly funky) trip through a slim conceptual piece about a life-affirming spiritual quest – or something like that; it all gets pretty confusing midway through.'

In his review for *Rolling Stone*, Greg Kot stated that *The Story Of The Ghost* was a turning point for the band:

> The strained cleverness of the quartet's previous five studio releases gave way to a relaxed, bucolic groove in which melody reigned. *The Story Of The Ghost* picks up that simpler, song-oriented thread in a most appealing fashion; it's a jam-band album for people who hate jam bands.

He later writes that ...

> ... some may be tempted to dismiss *Ghost* as a song cycle for bong huggers. But once the buzz wears off, Phish still sound fresh. Among the disc's abundant charms, the loveliness of the melodies, the intricate but understated interaction of the instruments and the life-affirming glow of the lyrics, Phish continue their relentless attack on post-grunge self-pity.

His review is not entirely positive, but what is interesting is that he directs his criticisms towards two of the three songs the band did not perform at *The Baker's Dozen*:

> Not everything works. In trying to make a kind of pop music that is tuneful, graceful and reassuring without actually resorting to verse/chorus pop structure, Phish sometimes fall short. 'Fikus' and 'Shafty' are more like fragments than actual songs, experiments that never quite coalesce. Mike Gordon sings 'Fikus' in a high, soft voice that evokes the elfin mumble of British prog rocker Robert Wyatt, while percussion left over from a Tom Waits record clatters in the background; 'Shafty' sounds like a low-key outtake from a blaxploitation-movie soundtrack.

The third song notably absent from the MSG run is 'Frankie Says'. This meandering, hook-free exercise in atmosphere divides the fanbase like few others. Ethereal and sparse, it often feels less like a song and more like a mood the band decide to inhabit for a few minutes. When it works, it casts a spell. When it doesn't, it risks snapping the set's momentum like a twig. The 16 October 2021 performance in San Francisco is a great example of 'Frankie' used to full effect: placed mid-set, it acted as a breath of strange, quiet air between more kinetic material, allowing the crowd to drift before being pulled back into the flow. But context is everything. Take, for instance, the 24 June 2000 show in Atlanta. There, 'Frankie Says' felt like an ill-timed diversion, unmoored and slightly deflating after the energy that preceded it. It's easy to imagine why the band left it off the *Baker's Dozen* setlists. With so much attention on pacing, novelty and crowd engagement across 13 nights, a song as delicate and potentially divisive as 'Frankie Says' might have been more risk than reward. Still, in the right hands and the right slot, it's a curious little gem, just one that requires more setup than most to shine.

Recorded concurrently with *The Story Of The Ghost*, the largely instrumental *Siket Disc* is considered to be the band's eighth studio album. It was originally released through the band's website in June 1999; it was released almost 18 months later via traditional channels by Elektra Records to tide fans over while Phish were on their self-imposed hiatus. *The Siket Disc* consists of unique segments that Page sequenced together from larger jams performed during the sessions for *The Story Of The Ghost*. Its ambient sound recalls the Grateful Dead's 1991 release, *Infrared Roses*.

Although 'What's The Use?' was played on 4 August (as the introductory song in the final sequence of 'Lemon' night's second set), the rest of *The Siket Disc* was skipped during *The Baker's Dozen*. This is not surprising since 'What's The Use?' has been played over 60 times since its 1999 debut and the album's remaining tracks have (combined) been played less than ten times.

Phish have since officially dropped several comparable releases (including *Glen Falls Soundcheck Jam*, *Headphones Jam*, *Flatbed Jam*, *Tower Jam* and (the best of the bunch) *Mondegreen Ambient Jam*), but the spiritual sequel to *The Siket Disc* is *The Victor Disc* – it remains officially unreleased. With the former being recorded just prior to the band's indefinite hiatus and the latter being recorded immediately after their reformation, *The Victor Disc* (and its more song-based approach to jamming) deserves a spot in the discography.

Hampton Comes Alive (1999)

The last of the band's live albums to be discussed here, *Hampton Comes Alive* was the band's first attempt at releasing a concert experience in its entirety. In fact, they released two concerts in their entirety. From their Fall Tour of 1998, the band's November 20th and 21st performances were included in their entirety. Of the 45 songs performed those two nights, 20 (primarily covers) had not previously appeared on a Phish album. Some of those (such as Bob Dylan's 'Quinn the Eskimo (The Mighty Quinn)' and Ween's 'Roses Are Free') were played during *The Baker's Dozen*. Unfortunately, others (like The Beastie Boys' 'Sabotage' and Chumbawamba's 'Tubthumping') were not. After *Hampton Comes Alive*, the band transitioned to their Live Phish series before then returning to a more traditional release methodology with *New Year's Eve 1995*.

Farmhouse (2000)

The band's ninth studio album, *Farmhouse*, was released by Elektra Records a few months before the band began their first hiatus in October 2000. It is an oversimplification to call *Farmhouse* their *Workingman's Dead/American Beauty,* but with all three albums being tagged as 'earnest', 'organic' and 'reflective', it is not without warrant.

Farmhouse was the group's first album to be largely recorded at Anastasio's studio, The Barn, in Vermont. *The Los Angeles Times* played up the location in their review of *Farmhouse* (while also acknowledging that the Grateful Dead comparisons are not going anywhere). Their two-and-a-half-star review opens with:

> Nobody's going to stop thinking of Phish as a latter-day Grateful Dead after hearing this album, but the Vermont quartet's model this time out seems to be The Band's *Music From Big Pink*. As *Big Pink* came to life in The Band's home studio in upstate New York, Phish's 11th album ... was born in guitarist Trey Anastasio's restored, 150-year-old barn studio in Vermont. Musically, there's a feeling of timeless Americana in both, but Phish simply can't manage the kind of incisive look inside the fabric of American society and culture that was The Band's signature. Phish's lyrics generally just add sonic texture rather than provoke mental stimulation.

The album was very much dominated by Trey's songwriting. In fact, he is the only member of the band to receive songwriting credits. The playing is exceptional from start to finish, so it is unfair to call the rest of the band 'hired hands' during the recording (especially considering how much their backing vocals bring to the songs).

There were two numbers originally included on *Farmhouse* that did not make an appearance during *The Baker's Dozen*. The first, 'Sleep', is an acoustic lullaby that could have found a home on *Rift* (had it been written a few years earlier). It was performed periodically before the band's 2000 hiatus and then a handful of times afterwards, but was essentially retired by the time *The Baker's Dozen* came to town. The second track not performed, Trey's acoustic 'The Inlaw Josie Wales', is one of two instrumentals included on *Farmhouse*. It was performed a dozen times by the band in 2000 and was then retired at their second to last concert of the 1.0 era. (As an aside, the *Farmhouse* instrumental that was played during *The Baker's Dozen*, 'First Tube', was nominated for the Best Rock Instrumental Performance Grammy. It lost to Michael Kamen, Metallica and the San Francisco Symphony Orchestra's performance of 'The Call Of Ktulu'. This was the same year Steely Dan's *Two Against Nature* 'stole' the Album of the Year award from (take your pick) Beck, Eminem, Radiohead or Paul Simon. So, it is important not to assume 'First Tube' was inferior to 'The Call Of Ktulu'.)

Two bonus tracks, 'Driver' and 'Mist', were included on the Japanese version of the album (and later vinyl pressings). Neither track was played during *The Baker's Dozen*, which is unfortunate, considering how popular both are. Their omission was likely based on how they are better delivered in an acoustic format. 'Mist' (now better known as 'Mountains In The Mist') was performed at the Dayton, Ohio, concert just prior to *The Baker's Dozen*. 'Driver' had not been played for over a year when *The Baker's Dozen* started but has made a handful of appearances since the run concluded.

Round Room (2002)

Round Room, the first of two albums released during the 2.0 era, was recorded in four days in October and then released by Elektra Records in December 2002. The band had intentions of recording the album during their first reunion concert (31 December 2002), but upon playing back the rehearsal recordings, they decided they had a keeper.

The *PopMatters* staff were glad to see Phish return, writing: 'A large part of the improvement comes from Anastasio, whose voice has progressed from a pinched nasal yelp to a rich timbre as sticky sweet as real Vermont syrup. While McConnell earns MVP awards for his keyboard playing, standing out on all 12 tracks.' Their unsigned write-up concluded with, 'In a world where musical ability often comes second to marketability, *Round Room* serves as a testament to what a band can do when they are allowed to grow on their own.'

Rolling Stone opened their largely positive three-star review by stating, 'The first two minutes of *Round Room* lift the curtain on what sounds like a brand-new Phish.' The review continues to say that 'There are five extended adventures on *Round Room*, and while they're each unique compositionally, all of them are compelling for the same reason: these guys are actually listening and responding to one another. Gone is the cruise-control comportment of their occasional bad gigs, their overreliance on a riveting groove. In its place is the collective pursuit of upheaval.'

The band played half of *Round Room*'s 12 tracks during *The Baker's Doze*n and the unplayed half was largely retired by the time the band hit MSG. Trey's 'Anything But Me', a highlight of *Round Room*, is difficult for the band to perform in a live environment. The song is just too intimate. 'Mexican Cousin' is not only the best of the *Round Room* songs to be skipped at *The Baker's Dozen* but also the best song ever written about tequila (no disrespect intended to either The Champs or Jimmy Buffet). Straddling the line between jokiness and self-awareness, 'Mexican Cousin' manages to be a party song and a confession. YouTube features the band performing 'Mexican Cousin' during the encore of their 19 June 2012 concert in Portsmouth, Virginia. It is an impressive performance, and even though they donned comically large sombreros for the occasion, the band's awareness of the ridiculousness of the situation gives them a pass on any criticism.

Another song the band largely avoids during live concerts, 'Friday', is a somewhat underappreciated ballad. The song features a melody reminiscent of The Beatles' 'Let It Be', but unlike that classic, 'Friday' never fully takes off. Considering *Round Room* started as a rehearsal session, that restraint is understandable. Mike's vocal contributions to the chorus also deserve praise. The lyrics 'Why can't the burden we carry go away/And why isn't it Friday today?' are amongst the band's most universal.

'Thunderhead' is (in my opinion) the weakest song on *Round Room*, but a song that is still capable of greatness on occasion. The studio version is searching for a hook, but in the right context, it can overcome this deficiency. The second disc of the band's *Live Phish 07.29.03* album opens with a 34-minute sequence that ends with an all-time 'Thunderhead'. (Full disclosure: the fact that this jam started with 'Crosseyed And Painless' does not hurt.)

The two remaining songs not played during *The Baker's Dozen* were also Mike's two songwriting contributions to the album. 'Mock Song' is the most underplayed song from *Round Room* (only three performances to date). It is a great song and one that could easily fit into most setlists; it is unfortunate the band never found a home for it whenever the audience needed a breather. The title track is the second of Mike's songs not to be played during *The Baker's Dozen*. 'Round Room' is a fan favorite and an example of the ebullience that Mike can bring to his melodies, a great 'deep cut' for fans of the band's studio output to cite when they advocate for the strength of *Round Room*.

Undermind (2004)

The band's second – and final – album of the 2.0 era was announced as their last. In May 2004, they revealed that both the upcoming June album and summer tour would mark the end of Phish. Unlike their 2000 'hiatus', this was presented as a permanent breakup. Fortunately, *Undermind* ended up merely being their last album for a major label; the Elektra Records release would conclude their obligations and subsequent albums would be released through their own JEMP Records imprint.

The sole single from *Undermind*, 'The Connection', is criminally underrepresented in Phish setlists. Not played at all during the band's summer 2004 tour, the song had to wait until the 3.0 era to receive its half-dozen performances. Arguably the most Byrds-esque song in their catalog, 'The Connection' is a tightly constructed pop song that works because it doesn't deviate from the course the melody lays out. Not every song needs to be explored; some are strongest in their original form, and 'The Connection' is a perfect example of that. On the bright side, 'The Connection' did make its way into a setlist during the writing of this book; hopefully, this means it has (finally) found its way into a regular rotation.

'Maggie's Revenge', the one song from *Undermind* never performed live, is the name given to the brief instrumental break between 'Crowd Control' and 'Nothing'. Culled from the much-larger 'Headphones Jam' (which would be given a standalone release a few years later), 'Maggie's Revenge' features a cacophony of sounds and one of Fishman's all-time best John Bonham impressions. The remainder of the eventually released 'Headphones Jam' does not always rock as hard as 'Maggie's Revenge', but it is definitely worth checking out (especially the portion titled 'Tiny' (around the 6:48 mark) that was included as a bonus track for online versions of *Undermind*).

Sounding as if the listener is joining the song mid-performance, 'Nothing' is a fun track that, like 'The Connection', deserves dusting off more frequently.

Played a half-dozen times and then brought out in January 2017 for the band's Mexican run, 'Nothing' would have been a fantastic addition to *The Baker's Dozen*. Played only once more since that 2017 performance, this driving song includes one of Phish's most memorable choruses (and an instrumental bridge that includes some of Page's sprightliest playing).

'Two Versions Of Me' is another strong song that, in another time, could have found an occasional home on an album-oriented radio station. It is not a song that demands to be played in concert and it is not as egregious of a missed opportunity as 'The Connection' or 'Nothing'. 'Two Versions Of Me' is likely someone's favorite Phish song and I would have a hard time telling them they are wrong.

Trey's 'Secret Smile' is a song that lives and dies by its melody. Perhaps too twee for a segment of Phandom, it was likely never destined for regular rotation in Phish's setlists. With that being said, 'Secret Smile' was performed during Phish's 'first full-length acoustic set'. This noontime performance on the third day of *Festival 8* shows included complimentary coffee, festival-themed donuts and a muscular version of 'Secret Smile' to conclude the encore.

The *Undermind* album was another Trey-heavy release. Besides the group-composed instrumental ('Maggie's Revenge'), each of the other members only received a single songwriting contribution. Page had the *Baker's Dozen*-performed 'Army Of One' while Mike and Fishman had 'Access Me' and 'Tomorrow's Song', respectively. Lyrically, 'Tomorrow's Song' can be compared to Fishman's (also skipped during *The Baker's Dozen*) 'Lengthwise'. Lyrically, 'Tomorrow's Song' shares DNA with Fishman's equally brief (and also skipped) 'Lengthwise'. Each of these songs contains just two lines, though 'Tomorrow's Song' takes more liberties with repetition and phrasing. Unfortunately, while 'Lengthwise' has a memorable melody, 'Tomorrow's Song' sounds like something Paul Simon might have given up on during the demo sessions for *Rhythm Of The Saints*. Mike's 'Access Me', on the other hand, is a keeper. The propulsive 'Access Me' allows Mike to channel something that would not sound out of place on They Might Be Giants' *Flood*. Although not a joke song, it is easy to be amused by the lyrics. 'Access Me' has only been performed six times by Phish, but considering that is six times as many performances as 'Tomorrow's Song', that is a win for Mike.

The final song (on what was thought to be the band's final album) is 'Grind'. This less-than-a-minute a cappella number has been compared to The Beatles' *Abbey Road*-closing 'Her Majesty'. There is something to that, but considering it was originally written during the *Billy Breathes* era and then dusted off for *Undermind*, it always reminds me of 'One After 909' (from *Let It Be*, whose album cover is not dissimilar to *Undermind*'s). Regardless, it is a fun chance to hear the four of them harmonizing one last time, and if it would have been 'the end', at least they would have gone out with a smile.

Joy (2009)/**Party Time** (2009)

For their first studio album of the 3.0 era and the first on their newly formed JEMP Records label, the band reunited with *Billy Breathes* producer Steve Lillywhite. Instead of returning to Bearsville Studios in Woodstock, New York, the band and Lillywhite stayed within NYC and recorded at Chung King Studios, 'the Abbey Road of Hip Hop' (where The Beastie Boys and Public Enemy recorded *License To Ill* and *It Takes A Nation Of Millions To Hold Us Back*, respectively). Sessions occurred during April and May 2009 and the album was released in September 2009. During that interim period between recording and release, all ten of *Joy*'s tracks were performed during the band's summer 2009 tour.

In his four-star review for *Rolling Stone*, Will Hermes praised the album. He said the opening track, 'Backwards Down The Number Line', is 'the epitome of a Phish song, complete with bouncy country-rock groove, merrily cryptic chorus and immaculately ecstatic guitar solo. And it leads off an unlikely gift: a genuinely great album from a touring phenomenon not known for great albums ... If you can't enjoy *Joy*, you will probably never enjoy Phish.'

Although the band had previously played all of the album at various points, not all of the tracks made the cut for *The Baker's Dozen*. The album's first single, 'Time Turns Elastic', which *Rolling Stone* referred to as 'Phish's own 'Terrapin Station'', was unplayed. The studio version of this over-13-minute-long song reportedly took the band 278 takes to perfect and Thom Jurek called it 'easily the best thing here, it is far more a constructed prog rock opus than jam journey.' A dozen performances occurred in 2009 and a handful occurred in 2010 before the song was temporarily shelved. The band did bring it back during the opening set of their audience-free NYE show in Lititz, Pennsylvania, on 31 December 2021.

Included with the deluxe edition of the album and later made available digitally, the band also marked their return with the companion album, *Party Time*. Featuring songs recorded during the *Joy* sessions and previously unreleased material stretching back over a decade, Party Time was their version of *Physical Graffiti*. Only two of the *Party Time* tracks made it to *The Baker's Dozen* (the title track and 'Alaska'), but other tracks have appeared periodically (and in the individual member's solo shows). The most noteworthy of these is 'Let Me Lie', a beautiful tune that could not possibly be more representative of Trey and his songwriting talents. Performed by Phish only ten times (including that Festival 8 performance mentioned in the Night 2 chapter), 'Let Me Lie' has been included on not just *Party Time* but also Trey's *Bar 17* and *Traveler* albums. Despite the heavy push and much to Trey's confusion, 'Let Me Lie' has never taken off with the Phish community. 'Let Me Lie' did have a stretch where it was heavily played during Trey's solo concerts, but it was essentially retired on 14 November 2015. There was a fantastic bust-out of the song on 3 December 2018, but the best post-retirement version of 'Let Me Lie' was the full Trey Anastasio Band performance included as part of the *Beacon Jams* series of shows Trey did during the band's Covid hiatus.

This 20 November 2020 performance of 'Let Me Lie' was sandwiched between the debut performances of 'Heather McDougal Song' and 'Heather McDougal Song Reprise'. For eight consecutive Fridays, Trey (and occasional guests) performed live streams from the Beacon Theatre in New York City. During the seventh Friday show, Trey read a comment from Heather McDougal, a 15-year surgical nurse, who wrote: 'Thank you, this has gotten me through these weeks, you people keep killing it and I'll keep saving it.' The band and Trey applauded Heather's efforts and then improvised the 'Heather McDougal Song'. After wrapping up their tribute, the band delivered a breathtaking 'Let Me Lie' (which was then followed by the equally improvised and equally amusing 'Heather McDougal Song Reprise'). Post-*Beacon Jams*, Heather McDougal enjoyed a moment of fame within the Phish community and was able to draw attention to her various charitable endeavors.

Fuego (2014)

As mentioned previously, the band's Halloween performance in 2013 included a full run-through of their yet-to-be-released album *Wingsuit*. When the band and producer Bob Ezrin finished with it, the title changed to *Fuego*, the track list was slightly altered and the performances felt different enough to almost classify it as a 'reimagining'. Fred Thomas, writing for *AllMusic*, praised the attributes missing from most of the band's on-stage performances: 'Horns, synthesizers, background singers and other various sprinklings of production pop up throughout the album, keeping the already sharp tunes sonically interesting on top of solid interplay between the core band members.' *NPR*, like *Rolling Stone* with their previous album (*Joy*), said it was their best album since *Billy Breathes*.

Of the ten songs included on *Fuego*'s final track list, seven were performed at *The Baker's Dozen*. Of the three songs not performed, 'Wombat' was played in Dayton, Ohio, a few days prior to the start of *The Baker's Dozen,* while 'Devotion To A Dream' and 'Sing Monica' were seemingly 'retired' in 2016 (although future bust-outs are a definite possibility).

Big Boat (2016)

Two years after *Fuego*, the band reteamed with producer Bob Ezrin. Because of how good the album is, it is unfair to say the band are treading water with *Big Boat* (but reviews tended to compare it favorably to their previous effort). Timothy Monger of *AllMusic* praised *Big Boat* for continuing the studio success of their previous release, *Fuego*, under the guidance of Bob Ezrin. Like its predecessor, *Big Boat* emphasizes streamlined songwriting and concise lyrics, many of which were refined during live performances. Sean Barry of *Consequence Of Sound* noted a shift in perceptions of Phish, suggesting that their studio albums, including *Big Boat*, offer a way for newcomers to appreciate the band's accessible and communal vibe. *NPR*'s Mike Katzif observed that while *Big Boat* may lack the musical complexity of previous Phish records, its simpler approach provides insight into the band members' perspectives. However, Sam Sodomsky of *Pitchfork* criticized *Big Boat* for being inconsistent and not distinctive enough from previous Phish albums.

Conversely, Chris Ingalls of *PopMatters* commended the album for its diverse range of musical styles and its accessibility, suggesting that it stands strongly on its own while also serving as a fitting follow-up to *Fuego*. His *PopMatters* write-up also took the time to defend the very idea of a Phish studio album: 'It's an unfortunate fact that Phish studio albums are often met with varying degrees of indifference. Obviously, people who don't like the band couldn't care less. And the mega-fans will shrug and tell you that the live albums and – more importantly – the in-concert experience is how you can best experience the music of Vermont's famous sons.' He later writes that the 'misconceptions surrounding Phish do a disservice to the studio albums, which contain plenty of smart composition and easily digestible tracks for non-fans to appreciate.' Finally, he writes that 'the albums are a fairly accurate barometer of the band's headspace and can provide definitive recordings of songs that can't be easily recreated on stage.' While I am not entirely willing to co-sign that last sentiment, I appreciate him attempting the point.

The band tackled ten of *Big Boat*'s 13 songs during *The Baker's Dozen*. Of the three not performed, 'Running Out Of Time' has the longest history. Starting off as an outtake of 2002's *Round Room*, the song was revived for *Big Boat* and then only played twice by the band in the weeks following the album's release. 'Tide Turns', a song *NPR* described as a 'stirring gospel blues', made half a dozen appearances in 2016 (and a single appearance in 2018) before being put away. The final *Big Boat* track not included in *The Baker's Dozen* is the opening number, 'Friends'. Only played twice by the band, the song is big, dumb and not dissimilar to what Bob Ezrin might have produced with Pink Floyd if Syd Barrett had still been with the band.

Sigma Oasis (2020)

Their (eventual) studio follow-up to *The Baker's Dozen*, *Sigma Oasis* was recorded during a single week in November 2019. Featuring nine songs in total, with five of those being debuted at *The Baker's Dozen*, *Sigma Oasis* is (in the words of *PopMatters*) a 'vibrant and uplifting album for the fanbase in their hour of collective spiritual need.' In a more positive review than previously afforded *Big Boat*, *Pitchfork* said the 'performances are lived-in and confident, at turns adventurous and refined.' The title track has been around (in a solo acoustic form) since 2018 and was first played by Phish in 2019. 'Shade', a *Big Boat* outtake, debuted during the summer of 2015. 'Evening Song' opened the band's 2019 New Year's run at MSG. 'A Life Beyond The Dream' was originally part of Trey's *Ghosts Of The Forest* project during the spring of 2019 before making its Phish debut the subsequent summer.

Appendix C: Additional Resources

The following online resources were invaluable in drafting this book.

https://archive.org/search?query=Phish
https://attendancebias.buzzsprout.com/
https://www.audacy.com/podcast/long-may-they-run-883fb
https://groovesafe.org/
https://mbird.org/
https://phish.com/tour-archives/
https://phish.in/
https://phish.in/1984-12-01
https://phish.in/2017
https://phish.net/
https://soundcloud.com/555-filk/tube-mashup
https://www.dividedskyfoundation.com/
https://www.livephish.com/
https://www.myfaithucc.org/
https://www.nyctaper.com/
https://www.nugs.net/phish
https://www.phansforracialequity.org/
https://www.phantasytour.com/bands/phish/stats
https://www.youtube.com/@phish

Anyone looking to build a library of Phish-related books should consider the following titles:

Gehr, R. and Phish, *The Phish Book* (Villard, 20 October 1998).
Holland, W., *A Live One* (Bloomsbury Academic, 22 October 2015).
Kroll-Zeldin, O. and Werden-Greenfield, A. (ed.), *This Is Your Song Too: Phish And Contemporary Jewish Identity* (Penn State University Press, 5 September 2023).
Puterbaugh, P., *Phish: The Biography* (Da Capo Press, 24 November 2009)
Steinberg, D., *This Has All Been Wonderful: A Travel Monologue From Summer 1994: The Year Phish Became Phish* (CreateSpace Independent Publishing Platform, 18 April 2014)
Walsh, M. and Zerbo, P. (ed.), *The Phish Companion, 3rd Edition* (The Mockingbird Foundation, 22 June 2016).

Would you like to write for Sonicbond Publishing?

We are mainly a music publisher, but we also occasionally publish in other genres including film and television. At Sonicbond Publishing we are always on the look-out for authors, particularly for
our two main series, On Track and Decades.

Mixing fact with in depth analysis, the On Track series examines the entire recorded work of a particular musical artist or group. All genres are considered from easy listening and jazz to 60s soul to 90s pop, via rock and metal.

The Decades series singles out a particular decade in an artist or group's history and focuses on that decade in more detail than may be allowed in the On Track series.

While professional writing experience would, of course, be an advantage, the most important qualification is to have real enthusiasm and knowledge of your subject. First-time authors are welcomed, but the ability to write well in English is essential.

Sonicbond Publishing has distribution throughout Europe and North America, and all our books are also published in E-book form. Authors will be paid a royalty based on sales of their book.
Further details about our books are available from www.sonicbondpublishing.com. To contact us, complete the contact form there or email info@sonicbondpublishing.co.uk